SECURING THE NARROW SEA

By the same author

The Scapegoat: the life and tragedy of a fighting admiral and Churchill's role in his death

The Coward? The rise and fall of the Silver King

Formidable: a true story of disaster and courage

Blockade: cruiser warfare and the starvation of Germany in World War One

www.steverdunn.com

SECURING THE NARROW SEA

THE DOVER PATROL
1914–1918

STEVE R DUNN

Seaforth
PUBLISHING

Dedication

For Joseph
Because we can only understand if we know

Copyright © Steve R Dunn 2017

First published in Great Britain in 2017 by
Seaforth Publishing,
An imprint of Pen & Sword Books Ltd,
47 Church Street, Barnsley S70 2AS

www.seaforthpublishing.com

British Library Cataloguing in Publication Data
A catalogue record for this book is available from the British Library

ISBN 978 1 84832 249 3 (HARDBACK)
ISBN 978 1 84832 251 6 (EPUB)
ISBN 978 1 84832 250 9 (KINDLE)

Typeset and designed by Mousemat Design
Printed and bound in Great Britain by CPI Group (UK) Ltd,
Croydon, CR0 4YY

CONTENTS

Plate section located between pages 96 and 97

PREFACE

When Britain declared war on Germany on 4 August 1914, the Royal Navy had not fought a major sea engagement for more than a hundred years. Secure in the knowledge of its victories over the French, and also in Nelson's tactical dictums, the navy had allowed much of its thinking to remain ossified in the early part of the nineteenth century. Until 1911 it had planned, in the event of war, for close blockade of the enemies' ports, engagement and destruction of its battlefleet at close quarters, and the sweeping from the seas of the foe's commerce raiders; and, of course, for much of the time the anticipated enemy was France (when it was not the United States of America).

Only in the years immediately before the Great War did tactical doctrine begin to shift, under the twin pressures of advances in materiel, and the industrial, political and naval growth of Germany. As a result, the British navy which entered the war was one whose commanders, especially the senior ones, had grown up in a world that was suddenly out of date. Their learning was irrelevant to the situation. As the American sociologist Eric Hoffer put it, 'in times of change learners inherit the earth, while the learned find themselves beautifully equipped to deal with a world that no longer exists.' Unfortunately, learners were in short supply in a navy which prided itself on tradition, iron discipline, the omniscience of rank, and the advantages of superior breeding and courage over brains.

War came and with it a new set of challenges: mines, torpedoes, the submarine, and economic warfare. Long-distance blockade, a defensive posture, the protection of commerce and capital ships – all became more important than broadside-to-broadside engagements among battleships. Furthermore, the demand for men to crew the vessels of war far outstripped the limited manpower resources that the navy possessed. Similarly to the British army, the navy's professional core was soon stretched thin and volunteers from home and the empire became an important component of the service.

Creative and lateral thought were necessary to address the many problems now faced, and such thinking was not always welcomed, or a core competence of the Admiralty body. New ideas, tactics and organisations grudgingly came into being.

One such was the Dover Patrol, which was called into existence only in October 1914. Comprised of an assortment of vessels ranging from the modern to the antique, inventing tactical doctrine as it went along, commanded by a series of radical and polarising personalities and increasingly manned by citizen volunteers, the Patrol shut down one end of the German egress from the North Sea: preventing trade going in, and submarines, commerce raiders and warships going out. They were, as a contemporary writer described them, 'the Keepers of the Gate'.[1]

This book is the story of the Dover Patrol and its leaders, men, successes and failures. Together with its northern counterpart, the 10th Cruiser Squadron (the Northern Patrol), the men from Dover ensured that Germany's attempt to destroy British freedom of the Channel, commerce and trade (and hence the British will to continue the fight) was eventually unsuccessful – and that it was Germany itself that was slowly starved into submission.

Few people today have heard of the Dover Patrol, and if they have, it is usually only in the context of the Zeebrugge and Ostend raids of 1918. And yet theirs was the longest continuous naval operation of the war and without it there could not have been a British army in Europe. As the author Paul Unwin put it '[for] troops on their way to the front and coming back across the Channel in their leave ships and hospital ships ... the Dover Patrol kept them safe, securing the Channel against a German invasion threat that would have cut the British army off from home'.[2] Historian William Philpott noted that 'the [Allied] navies held and kept the seas against German submarines throughout the war, enforcing an ever tighter blockade that starved enemy populations and by 1918 had severally degraded the Central Powers' ability to manufacture war materials'.[3]

It was essentially an amateur show: hundreds of fishermen and fishing boats; yachtsmen; merchant seamen; volunteers from all walks of life and all parts of the empire. These were the brave souls who made up the backbone of the Dover Patrol and whose stories I have tried to tell.

This is not a meticulous record of every day and action in the life of the Patrol. Nor does it cover in detail the war in the air. It is a narrative which focuses on the men – heroes and villains – and the challenges that they faced in the waters of the Narrow Sea. It examines, from a British perspective, the highs and the lows of the four years that the Patrol played a vital part in the war and the character of those who led and served in it.

The part played by the men of the Dover Patrol in the Allied victory is often overlooked. This book sets out to correct that omission.

A note on the structure of the book

Securing the Narrow Sea is divided into five sections. Part One gives the background and context to the operations of the Dover Patrol. It is primarily concerned with change: change in politics and naval strategy in the years leading up to 1914 and the change in materiel that followed the outbreak of hostilities. The developments at, and changes to, the naval base at Dover before the war are also considered in this section. It concludes with the opening naval initiatives of the war and the ultimately unsuccessful attempt to defend the critical Belgian ports of Antwerp, and subsequently Zeebrugge and Ostend, from German occupation.

Parts Two, Three and Four tell the story of the men and the actions of the Dover Patrol under the leadership of its three contrasting admirals – Horace Hood, Reginald Bacon and Roger Keyes – in roughly chronological order. Finally, Part Five considers the activities of the Downs Boarding Flotilla, examines the impact of the war on the Patrol's key ports of Dover and Ramsgate, and describes the conditions under which the men of the Patrol had to serve, before analysing and contrasting the relative merits and successes of the operation and its three leaders. The story concludes with an examination of how the Dover Patrol was, and is, remembered, then and now.

For consistency, the 24-hour clock is used throughout the book.

How can I live among this gentle
obsolescent breed of heroes and not weep?
Unicorns, almost
for they are fading into two legends
in which their stupidity and chivalry
are celebrated. Each, fool and hero, will be an immortal.

Keith Douglas; *Complete Poems*, ed Desmond Graham,
OUP (London) 1978, p139.

'An unsuccessful naval war of the duration of even only one year
would destroy Germany's sea trade and thereby bring about the
most disastrous conditions, first in her economic and then, as an
inevitable consequence of that, in her social life.'

Memorandum to the German Naval Act 1900,
quoted in the *Daily Telegraph*, 3 August 1915.

Others may use the ocean as their road
Only the English make it their abode.

Edmund Waller (1606–1687), *Of a war with Spain and a fight at sea.*

PART ONE

A Changing World

It must be considered that there is nothing more difficult to carry out, nor more doubtful of success, nor more dangerous to handle, than to initiate a new order of things; for the reformer has enemies in all those who profit by the old order, and only lukewarm defenders in all those who would profit by the new order.

Niccolò Machiavelli, *The Prince* (1532).

1

A Change of Plan

'I do not say they cannot come; I only say they cannot come by sea.'
Thus spoke First Lord of the Admiralty John Jervis, Earl St Vincent,
at the height of the Napoleonic invasion scare in the early years of
the nineteenth century. It was no idle boast: the combination of a
powerful British navy and a narrow stretch of water proved too
much for the French revolutionary forces, just as it had for the
Spanish and royalist Frenchmen in times past.

The English Channel is an insubstantial stretch of water, 30,000
square miles in area, only 350 miles long and just 21 miles wide at
its narrowest point (South Foreland to Cap Gris-Nez). Its diminutive
nature is shown by its nicknames: the Ditch, the Trench, the Narrow
Sea. Shakespeare has John of Gaunt call it a 'moat defensive'.[1] The
name 'Channel' itself comes from the Dutch word *canal*, a small
waterway. To the French, it is known as La Manche – the sleeve,
owing to its shape – from at least the seventeenth century.

For northern Europeans, it is, and was, the gateway to the world.
But it was also a route to new conquests. First Saxons, Jutes and
Vikings all sailed down the Channel to settle England's pleasant
shores. Then Normans crossed it to create a new dominion. But
from that time on, with the single exception of the invited landing
of William of Orange, England's shores remained safe from foreign
intrusion. Mastery of the Channel gave security from invasion and
control of passing trade. The Cinque Ports of Hastings, New
Romney, Hythe, Dover, Sandwich (and later Rye) were established
to provide ships for naval defence and promote trade. Prevailing
winds and strong currents, together with an aggressively handled
navy, saw off the Spanish Armada in 1588. Repeated Spanish and
French attempts to subjugate England fell to the same combinations.

Trade wars with the Dutch ended in an uneasy peace, the Channel having proved too difficult a fortress to master. And Napoleon was never able to launch his projected invasion. Control of the English Channel and the Strait of Dover rendered England inviolate. Ptolemy's *Oceanus Britannicus* proved just as sure a shield as did the Royal Navy.*

Britain's defences pointed at France, the traditional enemy. Portsmouth and Plymouth grew in size and stature. Germany was still a collection of statelets, bar Prussia, and Prussia was not a naval power. But then something happened which changed the way both Britain and France viewed the world and each other.

Germany and France

The seeds of the First World War were sown in 1870. By then, under the leadership of Prussia and her chancellor, Bismarck, the previously myriad small German states had coalesced into a north German confederation, which would eventually lead to a united Germany under Prussian leadership. France had been considered by most to be the major military power on the continent of Europe, both in the nineteenth century and previously, and had been Britain's traditional enemy. Now she was concerned by the growing pan-German strength and, latterly, by the candidacy for the Spanish throne of a Hohenzollern prince, related to the Prussian royal house. Led by the unpopular Napoleon III, France declared war on Prussia in July 1870; what followed was a shambles. The French army was beaten and humiliated by a well-organised German confederation force led by the Prussian general staff, under General Helmuth von Moltke (whose nephew would command the German armies in 1914).

The French defeat had far-reaching consequences. It established both the German empire and the French Third Republic. The Germans' crushing victory over France in the war consolidated pan-German faith in Prussian militarism, which became an almost religious force in German society until 1945. And Germany's annexation of Alsace–Lorraine aroused a deep longing for revenge

---

* Such belief in invulnerability was of course misplaced. In July 1909 the Frenchman Blériot completed the first cross-channel powered aircraft flight. The British journalist Harold F Wyatt wrote an article in which he speculated as to how many of the crowd assembled at Dover to welcome Blériot realised that they were 'assisting at the first stage of the funeral of the sea power of England.'[2]

in the French people. France would never again be considered a world power, its self-belief was shaken and its desire for revenge and retaliation would grow and grow. But for Germany it was proof of the strength of the new nation, which fuelled the desire for a seat at the world's table of power, for an empire, and for Germany to be able to fulfil its perceived manifest destiny. German ambition, both imperial and commercial, and French fear and wish to retaliate would be the mainsprings which helped drive the world to war in 1914. For the French, it propelled them into a search for new allies; Britain became one, France and Britain coming together for mutual safety, although with different aims in mind.

In 1870 Germany was just starting to look for an empire, but Britain had one already. The British Empire, under Queen Victoria, was approaching its apogee in 1870. She had been on the throne for thirty-three years and would continue her rule for another thirty-one. In six years' time she would take the additional title of Empress of India in recognition of her huge domains in Asia. The empire was the largest in the world, encompassing Canada, Australia, about 40 per cent of Africa, all of India, the Caribbean, and some Pacific Islands. The empire was built on, and for, trade, and to protect that trade, keep the seaways free for British and imperial commerce, and enforce Britain's rights where necessary, Britain needed a strong navy. By tradition and by need, the Royal Navy, the largest navy in the world, was the senior service, Britain's saviour at Trafalgar and elsewhere. Admirals such as Hood, Rodney, Jervis and Nelson were names familiar to every Victorian child and adult. To be a Royal Navy man had a cachet; to be a naval officer was to be in the front rank of empire.

The Germany of 1870 had no navy to speak of, but this lack began to foment a jealousy of Britain's ability to project force across the world through her navy, which would eventually lead to the development of a modern and powerful fleet, a fleet which became another proximate cause of war in 1914.

Britain's naval strategy changes
Britain's nineteenth-century navy had largely been configured on the principle that France would be the enemy. The major naval bases were Portsmouth and Plymouth, facing the enemy across the English Channel. There was little in the way of defence facing Germany across the North Sea.

Furthermore, Britain's naval strategy, right up until 1911, had been to follow the Nelsonian doctrine of 'close blockade'. The fleet would be deployed close up to the enemy's ports, preventing exit of its fleet or forcing it to seek battle, and stopping the inflow of war materials. Close blockade had some advantages, the best perhaps being that it was legal under the Hague Convention. This was effectively the strategy adumbrated by First Sea Lord Sir Arthur Wilson VC when called to present to the Committee of Imperial Defence after the Agadir crisis in 1911. This, together with his presentation of a plan for using the army to capture objectives on the German littoral through amphibious operations, led to his subsequent departure and Winston Churchill's arrival at the Admiralty as First Lord and its political master.

But, in fact, change in materiel, begun under Wilson's predecessor, the remarkable Jacky Fisher, had undermined this strategy completely. The torpedo and the submarine had changed the rules. Fisher was one of the few Royal Navy leaders who clearly saw that the advent of submarines had revolutionised naval warfare.

Jacky Fisher, First Sea Lord 1904–1910, and the man who created *Dreadnought*, was an iconoclast and forward thinker who had driven the development of submarines in the British navy, and when out of office continually badgered First Lord Winston Churchill to increase the numbers being built. More than anyone, Fisher recognised that the advent of the torpedo-armed submarine meant that the narrow waters of the North Sea and English Channel became a very high-risk environment for large and expensive capital ships. Rather than chance battleships in such a situation, it was better, he argued, to police those waters through 'flotilla defence', using large numbers of torpedo boats (surface vessels carrying on-deck torpedoes), submarines and torpedo-boat destroyers (more usually abbreviated to 'destroyers') to render the waters uninhabitable for enemy battleships, potential invasion fleets and the like. Fisher's was something of a lone voice in the wilderness, however, for much of the early part of the twentieth century.

For example, his successor as First Sea Lord, Arthur Wilson (see above) was resolutely unimpressed by the claims of submarine warfare. He shared the view, held by most senior officers in the navy, that submarines were a relatively new and much reviled and distrusted class of ship. Many sailors believed them to be a dishonourable and underhand weapon, suitable only for weaker nations, and only then for coastal defence. Wilson thought that enemy submarine crews should be hanged as pirates if captured and whilst in office did much to retard the development of the weapon for the British navy, in part because he did not want to set an example which would be followed by weaker, foreign navies. In 1911 the Inspecting Captain of Submarines (the man in charge of the navy's submarine development and training) was Captain Sydney Hall. He was a man of firm opinions, and at odds with Wilson on tactical matters, particularly the pace of building new submarines (he wanted more), and the type of boat which should be built (oceangoing, not coastal defence) and by whom. When it appeared to Wilson that Hall was getting too close to the engineering companies building the navy's submarines, Wilson took the opportunity to fire him from his post and assigned him to an old and useless third-class cruiser, *Diana*, 2,500 miles away. Wilson appointed the more congenial Roger Keyes instead.[*]

Keyes's best friend in the navy was Rear Admiral Sir Christopher 'Kit' Cradock. His view, expressed in a letter to Keyes after his appointment, was typical of the views of the admiral breed: 'it would be far more satisfactory to these "playthings" to know whether they were observed or made hits or misses ... I am sure you will know what to do'.[3] 'Playthings' was the common view; retired Admiral Lord Charles Beresford MP called submarines 'Fisher's playthings'; Wilson's successor Bridgeman hated them; Rear Admiral Horace Hood wrote 'really these submarines are the Devil; it is a great misfortune they were ever invented'.[4]

Nonetheless, Churchill, under Fisher's constant prodding, drove the Admiralty to examine the potential of the submarine and, more so, Fisher's ideas for the North Sea, which had now coalesced around the strategy of distant blockade – the shutting off of the whole of the North Sea at its northern and southern exits. Under this plan, the British fleet would be held beyond the northern blockade, to enter the disputed seas only when the enemy battlefleet itself ventured out. Otherwise small ships would patrol and keep free the North Sea and English Channel and prevent German trade and ships entering or leaving.

---

[*] As an interesting corollary to Hall's dismissal, when Fisher once more became First Sea Lord in 1914 he tried to have Hall reinstated at Keyes's expense. This was blocked by Churchill (who was trying at the time to pack the Admiralty with men loyal to him) and instead Fisher made Hall his 'additional private assistant' in his private office, ostensibly to accelerate submarine construction.

Fisher's theory of 'flotilla defence' appealed to Churchill primarily for its economy, given the political need to stabilise the naval estimates. With this in mind, in early 1912 he asked new Naval Chief of Staff, Rear Admiral Ernest Troubridge, to work on a plan for the North Sea deployment that would adopt the idea of 'intermediate blockade' by light forces. This plan was ready to issue to the Commander-in-Chief (CinC) Home Fleet by May, but a last-minute intervention by Churchill, demanding that it be tested in manoeuvres, both stopped its issuance and infuriated Troubridge. When tested in the summer, the fleet manoeuvres showed the scheme to be seriously flawed. Troubridge's war plan proposed a cordon of three hundred miles from Norway to the Dutch coast – an intermediate blockade of German access to the North Sea, as opposed to the close blockade planned for in 1911 and for many years beforehand. This was shown to be unworkable, for the navy did not have enough cruisers or destroyers to support it. Churchill was forced to make an embarrassing climb-down in front of the Committee for Imperial Defence.

Nonetheless, in practice, distant blockade became the strategy, as fear of the submarine and mine menace in the closed waters of the North Sea grew amongst the naval planners. At the outbreak of war, Britain had nowhere near enough small craft to pursue such a policy and, instead, settled for patrols by ancient cruisers to the north, and destroyers in the south, assisted by old pre-dreadnought battleships from Sheerness and Portland. Distant blockade also had the slight disadvantage of being illegal in international law.

Commercial imperatives

As an island nation, Britain has always been vulnerable to interdiction of its export and import trades. More than four hundred years ago this universal truth was recognised by Sir Walter Raleigh when he wrote 'there are two ways in which England may be afflicted. The one is by invasion ... the other by impeachment of our trades.' Growing industrialisation, the repeal of the Corn Laws (1846), allowing cheaper wheat to enter the country and reducing the incentives for home-grown grain, and the drift of population from the countryside to the cities caused a dependence on seaborne trade for both earnings through export, and feeding the population through imports.

Britain had, in fact, become highly dependent on imported food supplies. During the five years between 1909–1913, imports accounted for 78.7 per cent of wheat and flour consumed, and 56.2 per cent of cereals and pulses overall. British agriculture had responded to the Corn Laws' repeal by specialising in meat and dairy produce, but even here imports still accounted for 35.7 per cent of meat, 43.4 per cent of butter and 74.2 per cent of cheese consumption. By 1913, Britain imported 18.1 million tons of foodstuffs and 64 per cent of the calories consumed came by sea.

Germany, too, was a net importer of food as a consequence of her rush to catch up with Britain in industrial production. Her industrialisation, forced through with Teutonic vigour, had neglected agricultural productivity as an essential tool to drive a denuded countryside to increasing levels of agricultural output. By 1914, for example, the German population was reliant on imports for a substantial proportion of all the calories it consumed. Over 40 per cent of protein utilised and 42 per cent of fats came from abroad. Additionally, Germany had, unlike Britain, followed a protectionist agricultural policy which sheltered its farmers from market forces and gave them little incentive to improve either efficiency or output.

These trends had not gone unnoticed by Britain's traditional enemy across the channel. For most of the nineteenth century, the British considered that their most likely opponent at sea would be the French, and vice versa. However, the French also observed that they were deficient in heavy ships (battleships) and unlikely to make up the deficit for reasons of cost and resources.

Out of this strategic conundrum they developed a new concept known as the *Jeune École* (Young School). This posited a two-pronged strategy: first, the use of small, powerfully equipped units to combat a larger battleship fleet, and secondly, commerce raiders capable of ending the trade of the rival nation. Without overtly saying so, the plan was clearly aimed at Britain, the largest navy in the world at the time, and heavily reliant on trade for economic prosperity and survival.

The French developed and commissioned a new class of vessels specifically designed as raiding ships, typified by *Dupuy de Lôme*, for this role. Laid down in 1888 but not commissioned until 1895, by which time her originality had been lost, she was fast, capable of 23 knots, and intended to raid enemy commerce ships during extended cruises. Such strategic thinking exerted a considerable influence on the development of smaller navies during the century, particularly as they tried to compensate for weaknesses in battleships. And when the torpedo-armed submarine became a reality for most navies, its use in the role originally envisaged for the fast raiding cruiser was apparent to all. Such developments particularly resonated with German naval planners, especially the use of the submarine weapon in the war on trade.

In Britain, Jacky Fisher, as so often, grasped the point before others did. He clearly understood that in wartime the navy's task would not just be to protect the homeland, but also to exert a choke on the economy of other enemy nations through the Royal Navy's ability to impose a stranglehold on the oceanic trade routes. This belief was encapsulated in his statement that the Royal Navy held all five keys to lock up the world: Dover, Gibraltar, Suez, the Cape of Good Hope and Singapore.

So it was that both Britain and Germany approached the conflict with this strategic intent of a war on commerce in mind. For Britain, the navy had not just to bottle up the North Sea, but also to both prosecute actions against German worldwide trade and protect British merchant shipping from interdiction by enemy raiders. Neither country was self-sufficient in food or vital war materials, and both countries assumed that the other could be severely incapacitated by a successful campaign against trade.

That the submarine would be a major weapon of war was a concept which gained little acceptance in the higher echelons of Royal Navy thinking, as we have seen above. In Germany, the new weapon was embraced rather more enthusiastically as part of a general 'anti-commerce' strategy which included naval cruisers, armed merchant cruisers (AMCs), minelaying ships and U-boats.

In Britain, the navy was unprepared for the submarine and its 'underhand' methods. Little attempt had been made to find an effective counter, and detection methods relied on visual methods. Cruiser squadrons could be sent to all major sea routes to clear the seas of surface raiders, but no-one really expected that the submarine could make the seas around the British coast unsafe for trade. Soon they would find out.

2

Dover Harbour and the Dover Strait

The sudden advent of France as an ally, and Germany as a potential enemy, caused a re-evaluation of the worth of the naval harbour at Dover.

There had been a harbour at Dover from time immemorial, but it was only in the mid nineteenth century that it was decided that a haven of refuge for the Royal Navy and merchant shipping should be built in Dover Bay. Construction of the Admiralty Pier, which was envisaged as the western arm of this proposed haven, commenced in 1847.

Overlooked by the castle directly above it, the harbour when completed had on its western side the Admiralty Pier. On the pier was a railway station, opened in 1864 and closed to civilian traffic as soon as war broke out. The station delivered passengers to the Channel packets, but was owned by the Admiralty, and the railway companies had to pay rent to use it. Slightly to the east of Admiralty Pier was Prince of Wales Pier, constructed from 1893. This was designed to meet the increasing demand for the Channel trade.

In 1897 the harbour works were furthered by the building of the eastern arm, the southern breakwater (of 1898) and an extension to the Admiralty Pier. This work, which was considered to be one of the greatest feats of port construction in its time, was completed in 1909. The walls and piers were built of large blocks of concrete faced with granite and weighing from 30–40 tons. Associated with the Admiralty Pier were a tidal harbour and the Granville and Wellington docks. There was also a coaling station.

Access to the harbour was through two gaps in the southern breakwater, called the eastern and western entrances, but captains were explicitly warned that the tides at the entrances were very strong, and ingress and egress could be difficult. In total, the Admiralty section of the harbour enclosed 610 acres and the commercial section 68 acres. It was the largest manmade harbour in the world.

But it was no sooner complete than outmoded. Shell and ships were now such that no thought could be entertained of basing large ships at Dover and it became a coastal defence facility until the beginning of the war. Prior to the test mobilisation in July 1914, the Admiralty 'pink lists' appear to show no vessel permanently based there.*

In any case, Dover was not an obvious place to build a major naval port, owing to its strong Channel currents and exposure to southwesterlies. Indeed, it was rejected as a base for the Eastern Destroyer Flotilla by their commander, Commodore Lewis Bayly, in 1907. He was required by the Admiralty to take his destroyers to Harwich and to Dover, and report on which was more suitable to use as the destroyers' headquarters. As Bayly later put it 'at Dover we rolled and knocked about while at anchor; at Harwich we were in still water, and far away from the perilous attractions of a big town'.[1]

And most sailors thought it a harbour only in name. The tidal streams were powerful, good shelter difficult to find, and coaling and oiling difficult. Lieutenant John Brooke once spent two and a half hours trying to get his destroyer fast to a buoy, lost a man overboard in the attempt, rescued him and then gave it up and ran for the Downs for a safe anchorage. And the future First Sea Lord Andrew Cunningham thought that 'in any sort of weather Dover harbour is one of the worst in the world'.[2]

A member of the Dover Patrol was moved to express his dissatisfaction with the harbour in verse:

There is a lovely place
Called Dover Bay,
Where it snows and rains and blows
Almost every day.
Oh! It's bliss without alloy.
Oh! It is our greatest joy
To roll our guts out at the buoy
In Dover Bay.[3]

* The 6th Destroyer Flotilla was sent from Portsmouth to Dover as part of the mobilisation.

The source of such problems lies in the original formation of the Dover Strait, which is thought to have been created by the erosion of a land bridge that linked the Weald in Great Britain to the Boulonnais in the Pas de Calais. This formed a funnel, which reaches its narrowest point near Dover itself. Into this funnel blow the prevailing winds from out of the broad Atlantic Ocean. At their worst they can reach hurricane intensity. Tides too increase in their power passing through the Strait, scouring the coastline and driving their way through the many sandbanks and half-submerged islands that lie in wait for the unwary sailor. The Goodwins, Sandettie, the Varne – names to worry many a mariner (see map in picture section).

But the outbreak of war brought this uncomfortable harbour and its tricky waters to new strategic importance. First, with France an ally and with fighting taking place on French soil, the proximity of Dover to the major French ports of Calais and Dunkirk meant that Dover became an important hub for both the transportation of soldiers and equipment to the Western Front and for their protection from German naval attack. Secondly, trade entering into Britain's largest port, London (through which over one-third of Britain's overseas trade passed), would largely have to traverse the Dover Strait; such trade had to be protected and at the same time any vessels carrying supplies for the enemy had to be interdicted. And thirdly, the Strait was the obvious route for German commerce raiders, primarily U-boats, to reach the strategically vital Western Approaches.

Named by the academic geographer Sir Halford John Mackinder as 'the marine antechamber of Britain', the Western Approaches were vital for the continuance of British supplies and the maintenance of the supply chain into Britain and, indeed, into France.

Ships bound for the key ports of Liverpool, Bristol, London, Portsmouth, Plymouth and Southampton had to transit through this area, passing Kinsale Head and the Fastnet Rock as they navigated towards the St George's Channel or the Irish Sea. Meat and wheat and other cereals flowed in from the USA, Canada and South America; other foodstuffs came from the sons of empire in the Caribbean. In addition, Australian, New Zealand and South African produce all came through the area. On top of these requirements, with the onset of war Britain would suddenly need to receive large quantities of guns and ammunition from manufacturers in the Americas, ores and raw materials from South America, and fighting men from Canada, Newfoundland, India and other far-flung parts of the westerly and southerly possessions. All of this traffic would have to transit the Western Approaches.

For German U-boats based at their harbours in the North Sea, such as Heligoland, or with the fleet at Wilhelmshaven, the Dover Strait and English Channel route was the most efficient and shortest way to get there. And if they were able to gain bases on the Belgian or French coast, the transit to the Western Approaches became even easier. If U-boats gained unfettered access to this vital area by this route, it could lead to a major disruption in supply of essentials and men, and cost the Allies the war.

For all these reasons, in August 1914 Dover assumed a strategic importance unimaginable when work started on Admiralty Pier in 1847.

3

New Technology, New Tactics

At the outbreak of hostilities, the Royal Navy found itself having to fight a war for which it was largely unprepared. There had been a continuous armament revolution throughout much of the latter part of the nineteenth century, which the Royal Navy had struggled to completely understand or master. It was only a decade since new weapons, if only in their most primitive form, had been tested out in the Russo-Japanese War of 1904: heavy, fast-firing guns, contact mines, long-range torpedoes. Submarines capable of more than coastal defence were completely new, aircraft in their infancy. Additionally, the much anticipated fleet-to-fleet battle which would wipe the German navy from the seas did not materialise. Instead, the war became one of attrition, focused in the main on small ship actions, anti-U-boat measures, protection of trade and interdiction of enemy commerce.

These tasks increasingly became the lot of the Dover Patrol. Officers and men alike had to learn new techniques and tactics whilst 'on the job'.

This chapter examines the development of new technologies which, for better or worse, impacted on the story of the Dover Patrol. It encompasses the subjects of mines and minesweeping, the concept of anti-submarine deterrence, both passive and active and the development of new types of vessel, all both in general terms and with specific relevance to the four-year struggle of the Patrol.

Mines

In the early twentieth century, and at the beginning of the war, there was a strong body of opinion at the Admiralty that the widespread deployment of mines was poor strategy. Mines were a defensive weapon and the navy prided itself on being an offensive force, seeking the next Trafalgar to destroy the German High Seas Fleet in battle. Mining near enemy coasts would deter the foe from coming out into open seas for that much wished-for culmination of climacteric battle. First Lord of the Admiralty Winston Churchill himself articulated this policy, in opposition to Fisher and Jellicoe.

As a result, although much technical innovation had taken place at HMS *Vernon*, the navy's torpedo and mine school, the navy had not focused over-much on the development of the mine as a serious weapon of war.

Nevertheless, the Royal Navy had perfected reliable automatic contact mines during the 1890s. Captain Charles Ottley RN was responsible for the invention of the automatic 'Ottley' sinker for mines, which allowed them to be dropped from a suitable vessel whereupon they would moor themselves at a preselected depth. But, 'since 1894 Admiralty policy had been to suppress the system and suspend further experimentation ... in the hope that rival powers perhaps would not realise its full potential'[1] and adopt them too. The Russo-Japanese War renewed Royal Navy interest in mines, however, and in 1906 the navy spherical mine was developed (see below). Nonetheless, at the Hague conference of 1907 Britain had proposed restrictions on the localities where mines could be sown, but had been voted down by thirty-seven of forty-four states attending, including the USA and Germany.

There were effectively three types of mine, all detonated by electrical, chemical, direct or mechanical methods. Moored harbour-defence mines could be fired from a shore installation by triggering an electric current when an enemy vessel was deemed to be close enough to the mine or mines to be damaged. Contact mines had one or more horns (the Hertz horn) which required contact by a vessel to cause an explosion. These horns (actually hollow lead protuberances) studded the upper half of the mine, each containing a glass vial filled with sulphuric acid. When a ship's hull crushed the metal horn, it cracked the vial inside it, allowing the acid to run down a tube and into a lead-acid battery which until then had contained no acid electrolyte. This caused an electrical current to flow from the battery, which detonated the explosive. This was the type of mine with which the Germans started the war.

Mechanical mines used an arm-operated firing mechanism which moved differentially to the body of the mine when the mine was disturbed by a vessel hitting it. It was this type – the navy spherical mine Mk I and Mk II (a moored mine using an automatic anchor and an arm-operated firing mechanism with a charge of about 250lbs of gun cotton) which was the British navy's main mine weapon at the start of the war. Production had started in late 1906 with about a thousand on hand by 1907, but only 4,000 were available by August 1914, again highlighting the lack of emphasis placed on the weapon. In the words of one historian, 'after 1911 mining effectively fell off the back of the truck.'[2] Indeed, mine stocks were so sparse at the start of the war that in November 1914 Britain acquired 1,000 Russian mines left at Port Arthur at the end of the Russo-Japanese War. These were Hertz horn triggered devices.

Worse still, in practice British mines proved to be woefully inadequate, with problems concerning mooring wires, sinkers and firing pistols, and which lent weight to those voices in the Admiralty who opposed mining on principle. As experience grew, however, wiser counsels prevailed, especially those of Jacky Fisher, and further, better types were developed by the simple expedient of copying German mines, which were seen to work all too well. Information about the German mines had, in fact, been obtained by the intelligence service pre-1914, yet 'in spite of this information we ourselves clung to an obsolete and ineffectual type of mine for nearly two years after the outbreak of war'.[3] It was not until February 1916 that the first British Hertz horn mines were manufactured and they proved very successful. Further technical developments brought acoustic and magnetic triggered mines in 1917 and 1918.

The initial lack of interest in mines meant a concomitant lack of provision of minelayers. In 1914 the Royal Navy had only seven minelaying vessels, all converted cruisers of the *Apollo* class, *Latona, Apollo, Intrepid, Iphigenia, Andromache, Naiad* and *Thetis*. These were old ships, built around 1892–94, converted in 1907 and capable of carrying 150 mines each. As the war progressed, they were supplemented by modified merchant ships, trawlers and, from 1916 onwards, destroyers (thirteen were so equipped during the war and formed, from time to time, the 20th Minelaying Flotilla).

The German navy had taken a different view of the mine. The naval writer Peter Smith has noted that 'Germany was fully committed to the offensive use of these weapons [mines] and had few scruples how and where they could be used'.[4] At the outbreak of war, the German navy had immediately laid mines in defence of its harbours and in minefields across major trade routes. It had also laid drifting mines, unmoored, to roam the seas on tide and wind, seeking an unlucky victim. In both of these latter two activities they were in defiance of international law as then defined, and as adumbrated at, among others, the Hague conferences and the Declaration of London.

Churchill, who it will be recalled was against the use of mines, found himself coming under increasing pressure in Cabinet to 'institute a policy of mining in the narrow seas thus making the area between the Strait of Dover and line Galloper–Hook of Holland a *mare clausum*'.[5] He wrote to Jellicoe on 1 October 1914 asking his opinion. Admiral Jellicoe responded the next day. He endorsed laying mines from Dover towards the Ruytingen light vessel as being the best approach, and the removal of buoys to the east of the light ship, as this would render the use of mines between it and the shore unnecessary. And he pleaded that contact, not mechanical, mines be used (his plea was largely ignored). And so the die was cast. Minelaying was immediately undertaken, and in early October four minelayers laid 1,064 mines between the Goodwin Sands and the Sandettie Bank. The Admiralty also declared a danger area in the Northern Approaches on 2 October 1914, which effectively closed all but safe channels off the British coast. Captain Philip Wylie Dumas RN, Assistant Director of Torpedoes at the Admiralty, was amazed: 'as our mine sinkers and mooring ropes are all worthless the results must be a failure,' he confided to his diary.[6] He was proved correct; no sooner laid than they became a liability to all sides, as they broke free of their moorings very easily and became drifters, carried randomly by the tides. Indeed, on 23 November Rear Admiral Hood reported that the Patrol had that day destroyed no fewer than seventeen drifting British mines.[7] As the quondam intelligence agent and journalist Hector Bywater noted, 'our elaborate minelaying operations were to a great extent wasted energy'.[8]

Nonetheless, by the end of the war a weapon which the navy had inherently distrusted had inflicted very considerable damage. During World War One, the Allies laid an estimated 160,000–190,000 mines in the North Sea and English Channel, accounting for some thirty-five U-boats. Worldwide, British mines are reckoned to have sunk a total of 1,047 enemy vessels and damaged a further 541. The Germans laid around 45,000 mines worldwide, including 1,360 minefields containing 25,000 mines in British waters. Mines are believed to have sunk forty-four Royal Navy warships, 260 merchant ships and sixty-three fishing vessels, and damaged a further eighty-four merchant vessels.[9]

Minesweeping

The advent of widespread mining called for the remedy of minesweeping. Perhaps not surprisingly, as the navy had not embraced the use of mines, it had not thought very much about the use of minesweepers either.

Britain entered the war with a small fleet of minesweepers which were actually old torpedo boats, dating from the nineteenth century, and which had been converted to fit the minesweeping needs as then perceived. They were only ten in number and were fitted with the Actaeon, or 'A', sweep (see below) in and around 1908. The need for them, and more, was perhaps demonstrated on the second day of the war when the new 3,500-ton light cruiser *Amphion* was sunk by a mine laid in the Thames Estuary by the German auxiliary minelayer *Königin Luise.*

The indiscriminate use of mines was clearly a threat not just to British naval vessels, but to Britain's trade and supply chain too. At the urging of, amongst others, Admirals Sir Arthur Wilson and Lord Charles Beresford, a trawler section of the Royal Navy Reserve had been established in 1910. Trawlermen were used to the sea, working trawls and nets, lines, otter boards and snags. They had the expertise to operate as minesweepers, if not always the desire. This RNR section, supplied with mine gear, rifles and uniforms, became the front-line minesweepers, nowhere more so than with the Dover Patrol.

Early British minesweeping was limited to the towing of a ground chain from two spars set across the stern of a vessel. Clearly, this resulted in an extremely narrow swept path and the chain was easily snagged by seabed obstructions. The next development was a serrated wire sweep towed between two ships. Otter boards, used by fishermen to keep open the mouths of their nets, were employed to increase the width of wire in contact with the seabed. But again, this design frequently became snagged on rocks and wreck. Finally, HMS *Vernon*'s technical experts got round this problem through the introduction of redesigned otter boards known as 'kite otters'. These were also able to maintain a specified depth. This development was the basis for the British Actaeon sweep used for most Royal Navy minesweeping operations during the war, effective for depths down to 50 fathoms.

Given the lack of purpose-built minesweepers, trawlers became the vessel of choice for the task. They were sturdily built and because of their peacetime role of trawling the world's ocean dragging their nets behind them, they tended to have engines powerful enough to tow anti-mine equipment.

Trawler minesweeping was usually carried out in pairs, towing the sweep between them. The wire cut the mine mooring rope and the weapon floated to the surface where it was destroyed. On occasion, the serrated sweep wire would fail to do its job and the mine, mooring rope and sinker would become entangled in the sweep. To cope with this crisis there were three potential methods used. First, the sweep wire could be slipped immediately – both ends of the sweep were cast off from the trawlers, so that the mine would sink and the position was marked by laying buoys. Secondly, the mine might be towed into shallow water away from the shipping lanes before slipping took place. And thirdly, the mine could be towed to a designated dumping ground before being slipped. Generally, before attempting any of these approaches, the trawlers would steam towards each other, heaving in the sweep until they could be clear that it was a mine they had captured and not some other piece of jetsam.

The necessary trawlers were swiftly deployed. By 8 August 1914, a grand total of ninety-four fishing trawlers had been mobilised and converted for minesweeping. A further 100 trawlers were hired and fitted out by 22 August. These trawlers, increasingly supplemented by paddle steamer minesweepers (whose shallow draught suited them to the role), many of which had been coastal ferries in their previous life and generally with their original crews now sailing as RNR men, were the backbone of the minesweeping efforts of the Dover Patrol.

By the end of the war the auxiliary minesweeping forces comprised 412 trawlers, 142 drifters and fifty-two paddle steamers. Most were hired by the navy, but some were simply commandeered and purchased off their builder's slips. Ships and crews came wholesale and, with the addition of a small signalling staff, the trawlers largely remained under their own skippers – who became warrant-ranked skippers RNR. The towns of Tynemouth and South

Shields alone contributed sixty-nine trawler minesweepers, of which twenty-nine were sunk.[*] In all, 214 British minesweepers and small patrol craft were lost to mines (all but nine of them in home waters), while sweeping over 30,000 mines.

The poet Rudyard Kipling had visited Dover and seen the Patrol's trawler minesweepers. In 1915 he wrote a poem about them, which starts:

Dawn off the Foreland – the young flood making
Jumbled and short and steep –
Black in the hollows and bright where it's breaking –
Awkward water to sweep.
'Mines reported in the fairway,
'Warn all traffic and detain.
'Sent up *Unity, Claribel, Assyrian, Stormcock*, and *Golden Gain*.'[10]

During 1916 the average number of mines swept by the Patrol was 178 per month. By 1917 this had risen to 355, with April seeing the sweepers destroy a record 515.

But sometimes another, simpler, method was used – shooting randomly encountered mines with a rifle from the deck of a ship to make them explode at sea. Signalman G E Haigh, serving in the destroyer *Swift*, kept a log of mines sunk by his ship using this primitive method during patrols in the summer of 1917: 29 July, six; 7 August, seven; 8 August, four; 11 August, two; 11 September, two; 12 September, two; 15 September, two.[11]

Anti-submarine measures: explosive sweeps

Sweeps were an anti-submarine device in which an 80lb charge was towed between two ships on a plain wire sweep. When a submarine got caught in the wire, the idea was that it would be forced into the bight of the sweep and explode the charge.

An improved sweep – called a 'modified sweep' – was an early wartime improvement in which a long row of nine such charges was deployed from a single ship. The towing wire was forced by a

---

[*] In all, 1,450 fishing trawlers were hired/requisitioned by the Admiralty during the war. Of these, half had been built since 1910, but some dated back to the 1880s. In total, 266 were sunk, of which 142 were lost to mines. There were additionally the so-called 'Admiralty trawlers', which were built to the Admiralty's commission and design or were purchased by the Royal Navy while building.

minesweeping kite to run at depth. The wire was paid out over the stern of the vessel and trailed around preparatory to being exploded from the ship over the presumed position of the enemy submarine; the charges were fired electronically from the towing vessel.

Both systems were only really suitable for low-speed patrol work. Lieutenant John Brooke RN described the modified sweep in 1915. 'Its row of cigar shaped floats of charges lay in a long discharge tray on the upper deck like some dormant Loch Ness monster. It was difficult to handle and operate and, in my opinion, an ineffective contrivance.'[12]

Anti-submarine measures: nets

In the First World War, the Royal Navy had an unreasoning conviction in the benefit of anti-submarine nets. Because salmon could be caught in nets stretched across river estuaries it was believed that U-boats (just a bigger fish after all) could be caught in bigger nets stretched across larger waters.

Nets originally took two forms, moveable and fixed. At the war's beginning, fishing drifters, such as herring drifters, were taken up into the navy alongside the trawlers. Drifters were smaller and less powerful than trawlers, but were able to shoot and tow wire-mesh nets which they slowly pulled to and fro across the designated waterway, hoping to entangle a U-boat in them and force it to surface to clear the obstruction. Entanglement of the U-boat's screws would additionally compromise its ability to escape. In the unlikely event of the submarine being so entrapped, drifters could call for assistance from larger units and were also often armed with small guns, rifles or lance bombs.

The next iteration of this tactic was the development of indicator nets. These were wire-mesh nets supported by flotation devices, and laid and maintained by drifters. They were fitted with buoys which were released by the violent motion of the submarine manoeuvring against the net, or by a hydrostatic trigger when the buoy was dragged under. When fouled, the buoy released a calcium carbide flare which allowed the drifter to track the victim's progress. The British vessel could then summon help or slip its equipment and give chase; given the drifter's slow speed, this latter tactic was unlikely to meet with success. Some later types of indicator net were also fitted with small mines which were powered from batteries carried on the drifters or, in the case of the ECII net mine, armed hydrostatically and fired when one of its eight contacts was pressed, thus exploding against a U-boat's flanks.

Bad weather often caused the little drifters to have to ditch their gear and run for shelter, and so the maintenance of a permanent deterrent was problematical, compounded by the fact that there were often gaps between the nets laid by one vessel and another, even in calm waters.

Thus came the final attempt to make net barriers effective – the permanent net. These were moored to the seabed, fitted with net mines, backed up by minefields and patrolled by drifters to maintain them, together with other units to provide protection and offensive capability in the event of a U-boat being forced to the surface.

All three types of net barriers were operated at various times by the Dover Patrol and they are detailed chronologically in Part Two of this book. The fixed barrage, in particular, caused the Patrol much grief.

Other anti-submarine measures

At the beginning of the war there were no means of detecting a submerged submarine, except perhaps by sight in very clear water, and no really effective method of attacking it whilst it was submerged.

As it became clear that the submarine would not be conquered by traditional means, encouragement was increasingly given to those who were experimenting with new technology to attack the U-boat menace. Jacky Fisher had been recalled from retirement in 1915 to head the government's Board of Invention and Research, a position he held until 1917. This board recruited a number of scientists who worked in six science and technology divisions which assessed and evaluated invention proposals from the public, the objective being to apply them to naval technology and/or tactics. During its operation from 1915 to 1918, the board received over 41,000 submissions. Additionally, various Admiralty bodies considered the issue from a technological standpoint, including the Dover Barrage Committee, which was convened towards the end of 1917 under the chairmanship of Rear Admiral Roger Keyes.

Some of Britain's greatest scientists were recruited to bring science to bear on the U-boat problem, not least the remarkable father and son combination of Professor Sir William Henry Bragg and his son William Lawrence, both of whom had been jointly awarded the 1915 Nobel Prize for Physics in connection with their work on crystal structure using X-ray spectrometry. William Lawrence did much work for the army during the war on sound-ranging methods for locating enemy guns. The father, William Henry, worked on methods of submarine detection, initially at Aberdour (see below), then at Harwich and finally at the Admiralty itself.

One of Bragg senior's inventions was the indicator loop (or Bragg loop). This consisted of a length of cable looped around a line of mines. When a steel-hulled vessel passed over the cable, a shore-based galvanometer indicated its presence. If identified as a U-boat, the shore-based operator electrically fired the mines. The first recorded use of indicator loops was at Dumpton Gap, Broadstairs, and they were in use from 27 April 1918 to the end of the war. They were intended to be accompanied by mines which would be automatically detonated by sound waves, or by the magnetic lines of force generated when an iron ship passed over them, and Bragg was latterly engaged in this research too.

Bragg was also involved in the invention of the hydrophone, a device for detecting underwater sound and thus pinpointing the location of a submarine. Sir Ernest Rutherford (a Nobel laureate for chemistry in 1908 and the man who first postulated the existence of a charged nucleus in an atom) had originally produced a paper suggesting that underwater microphones offered the best potential for experimentation and Bragg, working for the Board of Invention and Research, co-operated with the navy's own Hawkcraig experimental research station at Aberdour, HMS *Tarlair*, under the control of Commander (later Captain) Cyril Ryan RN and a staff of RNVR officers.

Here 1,000–2,000 men were employed, a mixture of scientists and sailors. Starting with shore-based listening systems, and then the non-directional 'portable general service' model, the end result was the Mk II hydrophone, large numbers of which were ordered in 1917. By the war's end, 1,500 vessels had been so equipped, which included the drifters, trawlers and motor launches of the Dover Patrol. Jellicoe noted in his memoirs that:

MLs were organised into submarine hunting flotillas during 1917 … equipped with the directional hydrophone as soon as its utility was established and were supplied with depth charges. In the summer of 1917, four such hunting flotillas were busy in the Channel and they certainly contributed towards making the Channel an uneasy place for submarine operations.[13]

By the end of 1917, over five thousand phones had been deployed. And in 1918, 199 'Fish' outboard phones, towed behind a submarine-hunting vessel, were added to the armoury. Asdic (not named after the Anti-Submarine Detection Investigation Committee, as popular myth would have it, but a way of making A/S Division into a catchy word)* too had been developed by June 1917, but was not used until after the end of the war.

Jellicoe was the instigator of another anti-submarine weapon, the depth charge. Primitive depth charges had existed for some time before the war, comprising aircraft bombs attached to lanyards which would trigger their charges; a similar idea was a 16lb gun-cotton charge in a lanyard-rigged can – two of these lashed together became known as the depth charge Type A. Problems with the lanyards tangling and failing to function led to the development of a chemical pellet trigger, known as the Type B. These were effective at a depth of around 20ft.

At Jellicoe's request, another type of depth charge was developed, based on the standard Mk II mine which was fitted with a hydrostatic pistol (ie, actuated by water pressure) preset to fire at 45ft and launched from a stern platform. Weighing 1,150lbs, this so called 'cruiser mine' was, in fact, a potential hazard to both the dropping ship and the putative enemy. But further development was swift. By January 1916, the first really effective depth charge, the Type D, became available. These were barrel-like casings containing a high explosive, TNT or amatol. There were initially two sizes – Type D, with a 300lb charge for fast ships, and Type D*, with a 120lb charge for ships too slow to clear the danger area of the more powerful charge. A hydrostatic pistol set to a preselected depth detonated the charge and they were supplied with two depth settings of 40ft or 80ft.

Production could not keep up with demand, and anti-submarine vessels initially carried only two depth charges, to be released from a chute at the stern of the ship. The new weapon's first success was the sinking of *U-68* off Kerry on 22 March 1916, by the Q-ship *Farnborough*.

* According to Norman Friedman.

By 1917, a new water-pressure-activated pistol could fire the depth charges at 100–200ft, allowing use of Type D on most ships, but production was slow in 1917, only 140 per week in July, rising to 800 per week in December. July 1917 also saw the introduction of a ship mounted anti-submarine howitzer (or bomb-thrower) for the backs and sides of vessels in various calibres ranging from 3.5in to 11in. These were designed as a short-range weapon to be fired at a nearby periscope. Only 377 such howitzers were delivered in 1917, but by the end of the war some merchant ships were being fitted with them too.

However, the depth charge did not necessarily live up to its promise. U-boat hulls proved to be very strong, and the charge had to be exploded within 14ft to crack a hull, and within 28ft or so to cause damage to hull plating, thus making great demands on the accuracy of the delivery. Nonetheless, by the war's end, 74,441 depth charges had been issued to Royal Navy ships, and 16,451 fired, scoring thirty-eight claimed kills and 140 alleged 'assists'.

Ships
From its inception as a homogeneous force of destroyers and submarines, the Dover Patrol quickly expanded to encompass a wide range of new types of vessel. They included, among others, monitors, slow, shallow draft bombardment vessels originally intended for foreign navies or for Jacky Fisher's pet Baltic coast landing scheme; motor launches (MLs), maids of all work, initially meant for U-boat hunting; P-boats (aka coastal sloops), designed primarily for anti-submarine and minesweeping work; and coastal motor boats, fast torpedo-armed anti-ship boats able to skim over the top of minefields. Pleasure yachts acted as escorts and sub-hunters, and paddle steamers became minesweepers; as did, of course, the ubiquitous trawlers and drifters. All these were new to the Royal Navy and new to the officers and men of the Dover Patrol, the majority of whom were themselves new to the Royal Navy; and these novel types of vessel had to be understood, mastered and the tactical uses of them developed. All of these weapons of war will be considered and described in more detail in the narrative that follows, or in the appendices.

By the middle of the war, the array of vessels comprising the Dover Patrol was kaleidoscopic in its variety, and each one required dedicated sailors working hard duties and long hours to manage them. This is their story.

4

War: August to October 1914

On 28 June 1914, at around 1030, a nineteen-year-old Bosnian Serb named Gavrilo Princip fired the shot which started the First World War. His assassination of Archduke Franz Ferdinand of Austria, heir presumptive to the throne of Austria–Hungary, and his pregnant wife Sophia, lit the fuse which would eventually blow Europe apart. Austria–Hungary was spoiling for a fight with Serbia to reassert its dominance in its own backyard. This was the *casus belli* she wanted. Despite Serbia giving in to most of the reparations demanded of her, Austria–Hungary began to mobilise. That led the Russians to mobilise to protect Serbia, Germany to protect Austria–Hungary, France to protect herself and finally England, ostensibly to protect Belgium. That is the accepted history. In fact, the German general staff and some members of the Kaiser's government badly wanted a war with Russia there and then, before the sleeping giant to their backs modernised and became too big a threat to their eastern borders. The Germans gave a blank cheque to Austria–Hungary to deal with Serbia as they wanted, and government officials constantly egged on their Austrian counter-parts. Germany drove the world to war.

And once Belgium was invaded, with the risk that Germany would gain access to her major North Sea and Channel ports and hence threaten Britain's coast and trade, Britain could not stay out. Not for a 'piece of paper' (the 1839 Treaty of London), but for imperial self-defence, Britain went to war.

Monday, 3 August 1914 was a bank holiday. Not everybody noticed the outbreak of war. It was a beautiful summer's day, hot and cloudless. Many people were away from home; many politicians were out of touch, expecting a long break. First Lord of the Admiralty Winston Churchill was on holiday in Norfolk. He and his family had travelled to the East Anglian coast, which had become a fashionable holiday destination. In the 1890s Cromer and nearby Sheringham and Overstrand had been developed as bracing resorts attractive to the middle and upper classes. Overstrand, however, was built by the architect Edwin Lutyens for the brewer Cyril Flower (later Lord Battersea) as an exclusive resort for the rich and famous. Churchill stayed at Overstrand.

Edward Elgar, the composer, and his wife were on holiday in Gairloch, Scotland. They only realised something was amiss when they could not get transport home and everywhere they saw marching bands of soldiers. It took them a week to get back to London.

In fact, the bank holiday turned into a four-day break as the banks remained closed to prevent a run on gold. The Stock Exchange closed too (on Friday, 31 July) and was not open again until 4 January 1915.

Up until a few days prior to the sudden war crisis, Britain had been more concerned that there would be a civil war over the issue of home rule for Ireland. The Curragh mutiny of March, when the majority of British officers ordered to Belfast to quell resistance to home rule threatened to disobey orders and resign their commissions, had called into question the ability of the government to resist civil disobedience and paralysed parliamentary decision-making. On the declaration of war, John Redmond, the Nationalist Irish leader, offered his full support to the government and said that they could 'withdraw every one of their troops from Ireland without fear of trouble'. Britain went to war and the navy went to work.

Initial dispositions
With the declaration of war, the Admiralty put its plans for distant blockade into action. The Grand Fleet sped to the north to take station at Scapa Flow in the Orkneys. The 10th Cruiser Squadron took its patrol position at the top of the North Sea. Old battleships and cruisers guarded the Kent and Channel coasts from invasion.

The protection of the British coast from invasion was considered a key task for the navy, and was certainly a preoccupation of Parliament and the British public at large. In 1908 the Committee of Imperial Defence had appointed an invasion inquiry before which former prime minister A J Balfour, amongst others, testified. The conclusion was that a successful invasion could not be mounted, but the public were not aware of this and the 'idea of invasion became almost a psychosis.'[1] In reality, the Germans had no such plans and had never had such plans – it was a complete red herring. The protective duty fell upon the so-called Admiral of Patrols, Commodore (Rear Admiral from 27 August) George Ballard, who had control of all the destroyer flotillas, except numbers 1–4 which were attached to the Grand Fleet (with 1–3 based at Harwich), and the 5th which was in the Mediterranean. He also had ultimate responsibility for the sixty-five submarines in home waters. The destroyers were organised into 'patrol' and 'local defence' flotillas. The patrol flotillas were the 6th, 7th, 8th and 9th, with their attached scout cruisers. The local defence flotillas, which consisted of older destroyers and torpedo boats, were attached to the naval ports which they were intended to protect.

As it was believed that the invasion, if it came, would come across the North Sea, the patrol flotillas were distributed along the east coast. The 7th was based on the Humber, the 8th on the Tyne and the 9th on the Forth. Protecting the Strait of Dover was the responsibility of the 6th. Thus Ballard had ultimate control of nearly all the freely available destroyer forces, an onerous responsibility to be sure, and one which led to a degree of administrative complexity.

The 5th, 7th and 8th Battle Squadrons of old battleships had assembled at Portland to escort the British Expeditionary Force across the Channel. But to enforce the blockade and prevent enemy access and egress at the lower end of the North Sea, the Dover choke-point had to be secured. The Dover Strait itself was held by French destroyers and submarines from the Boulogne Flotilla in combination with British 6th Destroyer Flotilla, which, since it had taken up its war station on 3 August, had been examining all British and neutral vessels that passed, searching for goods destined for the enemy. Immediately in advance of this patrol was another line held by Commodore Keyes with *Firedrake* and twelve submarines of the 8th Submarine Flotilla, and tasked with U-boat detection. This ran from the North Goodwins through the Sandettie light-vessel to Ruytingen. Still further north, as an early detection force for enemy submarines, a seaplane and airship patrol was established between the North Foreland and Ostend, and beyond this were the 1st and 3rd Destroyer Flotillas at Harwich (administratively part of the

Grand Fleet), ready to form an advance patrol in the waters off the Dutch coast, known as the Broad Fourteens, and elsewhere as might be directed. They were, in turn, covered by the armoured cruisers of Cruiser Force 'C'.

The western entrance to the Channel was also guarded by an Anglo-French cruiser squadron (the 12th Cruiser Squadron), which was operating a similar blockade to that of the 6th Flotilla and had the additional task of preventing disguised ships laying mines on the army's lines of passage.

Thus were the dispositions made which the planners believed would be sufficient for the purpose of closing the Channel to German-bound trade, submarine transit and protection of the Anglo-French supply lines into France itself.

But war did not start well for the Royal Navy and its political head, Winston Churchill. The first naval shots of the conflict were fired on 5 August when the scout cruiser *Amphion* and the destroyers *Lance* and *Landrail* sank a German minelayer. The following day *Amphion* went back to the exact location of the exchange and sank herself on a mine – the first success turned by carelessness into the first loss. Then, on the 6th and 7th, Admiral Archibald Berkeley Milne and Rear Admiral Ernest Troubridge, commanding the Mediterranean Fleet, conspired together to allow the escape of the German battle-cruiser *Goeben* to Turkey, an act which was contributory to bringing Turkey into the war on the German side and which was thus a proximate cause of the later disaster of Gallipoli.

On 5 September the scout cruiser *Pathfinder* was torpedoed off St Abb's Head with the loss of most of its 270 crew; and on 22 September three old cruisers – known officially as Cruiser Force 'C' but unofficially as the 'live bait squadron' – were patrolling off the Dutch coast when first *Aboukir*, then *Hogue*, then *Cressy* were all torpedoed in the space of forty-five minutes. Sixty-two officers and 1,397 men were lost. A public which had eagerly anticipated some major new Trafalgar and sweeping from the seas of the German fleet was disappointed.

Antwerp

The German advance through Belgium was now threatening the Belgian ports, especially Antwerp, and this posed a clear and present danger to British control of the English Channel and North Sea. Finding himself without success at sea, Churchill decided to seek it on land through the formation of the new Royal Naval Division. At the outbreak of war, the Marine Brigade of four infantry battalions had been formed, from men of the Royal Marine Light Infantry and Royal Marine Artillery, intended as an advanced base force, and meant to allow the Admiralty to take and hold forward bases for the fleet. So far, so sensible. But now hubris took over. The Admiralty had many volunteers at the start of the war in the Royal Naval Volunteer Reserve (RNVR). On 16 August Churchill had decided to create two more naval brigades with these reservists, which he deemed surplus to requirements, by joining them with the Marine Brigade to produce a composite Royal Naval Division. A few petty officers and ratings were transferred from the navy to provide stiffening, and some officers were seconded by the army, but most of the recruits were RNVR men who had volunteered on the outbreak of war. They made eight battalions, which were named after naval commanders, Drake, Benbow, Hawke, Collingwood, Nelson, Howe, Hood and Anson. They had no access to artillery or heavy weapons and were equipped only with older infantry armaments. They were also poorly trained in infantry warfare. They had had no rifle drill (and indeed had no rifles until the end of September) and only a month's training.

As the German steamroller poured through Belgium, driving the opposing Belgian forces before them, the Belgian command ordered a withdrawal of their armies to the national 'strategic redoubt' of Antwerp, a heavily defended city-camp surrounded by forts and for-tifications, which they reached on 20 August. Here they intended to conduct a last stand. As Antwerp was an important Channel port and lay across the line of the German northern flank, the German invasion plan called for its isolation and reduction.

German General von Boseler was given the task of capturing Antwerp. Assigned a force of five divisions of mostly reserve forces and 173 guns, his artillery began a bombardment of the outer south-eastern forts on 28 September. The British Cabinet viewed the Antwerp situation with concern, for they foresaw that its fall would open the way to the Belgian and French channel ports and possibly to the invasion of Britain itself. Churchill was sent by the Cabinet to the city to report on the situation and British troops intended for the Western Front were despatched to assist the Belgians.

Churchill was in his element. He left London on his personal train at 0300 on 3 October, promising Asquith a report as soon as possible. With his naval secretary, Rear Admiral Horace Hood, at his side he spent three nights within the fortifications. On 4 October Churchill reported that Belgian resistance was weakening, with morale low. It was clear that the city was unlikely to last out much longer. It was now that Churchill persuaded his colleagues that he should send his newly formed Naval Division into the breach.

In addition, in an act of more than usual ambition, he telegraphed Prime Minister Asquith on 5 October to say that he wanted to resign his post, take the rank of major general and command the troops in Antwerp himself. It was rash and Asquith could hardly control his mirth in declining the offer. But the Royal Naval Division was nonetheless sent, on 4 and 5 October, with the German troops already amongst the outer forts of the city. Arthur Conan Doyle described the operation thus:

> No troops were available for a rescue for the French and British old formations were already engaged, while the new ones were not yet ready for action. In these circumstances, a resolution was come to by the British leaders which was bold to the verge of rashness and so chivalrous as to be almost quixotic. It was determined to send out at the shortest notice a naval division, one brigade of which consisted of marines, troops who are second to none in the country's service, while the other two brigades were young amateur sailor volunteers, most of whom had only been under arms for a few weeks.[2]

On Churchill, Conan Doyle added, 'Mr Winston Churchill showed his gallantry as a man, and his indiscretion as a high official, whose life was of great value to his country, by accompanying the force from England.'[3]

It was, of course, a disaster. The Naval Brigade went into action, arriving on the outskirts of the city in the small hours of the 6 October. In the early evening of the 8th, orders were given for them to retire from the city. In the confusion of the withdrawal, most of the 1st Brigade, the Hawke, Benbow and Collingwood battalions – 1,500 men in total – crossed the Dutch frontier and were interned at Groningen for the rest of the war; a further 1,000 men were captured by the Germans. Only the Drake Battalion got away, having left the city early. Amongst those who did escape was the poet Rupert Brooke, who had signed up as a naval volunteer only weeks earlier. On 10 October the city surrendered.

Many observers were critical of Churchill for throwing away naval resources and, to a point, of Admiral Hood for not effecting some form of restraint whilst with him in the war zone. Vice Admiral Sir David Beatty, for example, thought that Hood had proved 'unable to control Churchill'. He went on, 'WC must be mad if he thinks he could relieve one of the most modern fortresses by putting 8,000 half trained troops into it'.[4] And Captain Herbert Richmond, assistant director of the Operations Division at the Admiralty, confided:

> the First Lord is sending his army there; I don't mind him sending his untrained two-penny rabble but I do strongly object to 2,000 invaluable Marines being sent to be locked up in a fortress and become prisoners of war if the place is taken ... it is a tragedy that the navy should be in such lunatic hands at this time.[5]

Antwerp damaged Churchill; the action came to be seen as evidence of his lack of judgement and impulsiveness. Asquith, on hearing of it from his son Arthur (who had joined the RNVR), wrote of 'the wicked folly of it all'.[6]

There was another problem created by the formation of the Royal Naval Division: the men were not, as Churchill had claimed, surplus to the requirements of the fleet. The big ships were already finding that every additional man, and especially stokers, was useful. Commanders at sea, and the Admiralty itself, resented the scheme, complaining bitterly about undermanning.

Meanwhile, in late September the German army finally asked the Imperial Navy to disrupt the flow of men and equipment across the Channel to France. *U-18*, under Kapitänleutnant Heinrich von Hennig, was despatched from Heligoland to attack transports. On the morning of 27 September *U-18* was submerged off the Dover harbour entrance, but he could see no transports and was proscribed by cruiser warfare rules from attacking the merchant ships he saw.

At 1100, still submerged, von Hennig turned away from Dover and headed towards Calais looking for a warship to sink. He found HMS *Attentive*, a scout cruiser built in 1904, and she saw him. *Attentive* went into a power turn and nearly ran the submarine down; Hennig's torpedo missed, running alongside the ship. The surprise of being attacked in the Strait convinced the British that the

U-boats were finally going after the cross-channel supply lines. All movements across to France were halted for twelve hours and the Admiralty placed an outright ban on daytime sailings. The Channel was *the* important artery to France and had to be protected. Coupled with the deteriorating military position of the Flanders ports, something had to be done.

That something was twofold: first, to lay an enormous minefield across the entrance to the Dover Strait, between the coast of Belgium and Dover, designed to prevent enemy U-boat transit of the Dover Strait. It was completed by the Royal Navy on the night of 2 October. As part of the field lay in international waters, it was technically illegal, but Germany had already mined international waters and thus no one in the Admiralty much cared. But the effort was betrayed by poor design and poor mine construction. Mines went off as they were being laid, all the firing pistols had to be replaced and the mines immediately dragged their moorings, becoming as much a liability as an asset to the British naval forces (see Chapter 3). Secondly, it was decided to create a specific naval command to cover the Strait.

Horace Hood had found working for Churchill uncongenial. Hood's character – his humility, keen intelligence and 'intense sense of duty' – made a poor foil for the mercurial and unpredictable First Lord. Battenberg, First Sea Lord and both a previous captain over Hood when the latter was his commander and a great fan of his abilities, suggested instead appointing him to command the 4th Battle Squadron in the Grand Fleet. Churchill vetoed the idea, selecting Rear Admiral Alexander Duff (director of the Mobilisation Division) and explaining by letter to Battenberg that Duff had been promised this post when mobilisation was complete. Instead, it was with relief that Hood received the offer on 13 October of a newly created appointment as Rear Admiral Commanding the Dover Patrol and Senior Naval Officer Dover (two days before the loss to torpedo of the old cruiser *Hawke*, killing 524 more men, and two weeks before the loss to a mine of the modern *King George V*-class battleship *Audacious*).

PART TWO

Hood

'one of the best brains in the service, remarkably young in spirit and full of enthusiasm, the perfect leader in any circumstances ... he drew from all of us our love and respect.'

Quoted in Arthur Marder,
From the Dreadnought to Scapa Flow (2014), p44.

5

Horace Hood

Rear Admiral the Honourable Horace Lambert Alexander Hood, known to his friends as Bertie, to the lower deck as 'the 'On 'Orace', and to his wife as Robin, was the second youngest flag officer in the Royal Navy. The second son of a viscount, born in 1870 into a family with long naval associations, he carried a naval bloodline of three admirals and a captain. The first Viscount Hood, Admiral Samuel, who had fought in the American War of Independence and commanded in the Mediterranean during the French Revolutionary Wars, was his great-great-great grandfather.

Horace Hood had come to notice as an extremely clever young officer and had first shown himself to be academically inclined by passing his entrance exam into the navy's training school *Britannia* first in his year. He subsequently demonstrated that this was no flash in the pan. In October 1890 he achieved a first-class pass in his qualifying certificate for the rank of lieutenant with 1,697 marks out of a possible 1,800. In trigonometry and dynamics he scored 100 out of 100. In nautical astronomy he gained 198 out of 200. Only in 'steam engine' did he let himself down with 79 out of 100.[1] He followed this up with first-class passes in torpedo (December), gunnery (March 1891) and pilotage (May 1891) – an almost unheard-of four first-class passes.

His performance earned him no less than three naval prizes. In December 1890 he was awarded the Beaufort Testimonial, which gained Hood a prize of 'instruments or books of a professional character and of practical use to a Naval Officer'. It was given annually to the candidate who passed the best examination in navigation and pilotage for the rank of lieutenant in the Royal Navy. In the same month he also won the Ryder Memorial Fund, which was a prize of books to the sub lieutenant who took the first place at the examination in French at the Royal Naval College, Greenwich. And finally he was awarded the Goodenough Medal for the year of 1890. This was a gold medal conferred on the sub lieutenant who, when qualifying for the rank of lieutenant, passed the best examination of his year in gunnery, provided he had also taken a first-class certificate in seamanship.

These were distinctive achievements, particularly in a navy which, at the time, did not value intellectual achievement – indeed regarded 'brains' with suspicion – preferring officers who would obey orders without question and fit in socially amongst 'gentlemen'. But there is no evidence that Hood was seen as an outsider or a prig. He fitted in well and was liked by his peers. He was able to straddle the bridge between superior intelligence and general acceptance, an achievement not very common in the navy as the careers of, amongst others, Percy Scott, George Ballard and the Dewar brothers would demonstrate: all intelligent men who found frustration in challenging the system.

Promoted to lieutenant in 1891, he gained further notice serving as a gunboat commander on the Nile in Kitchener's Sudan campaign and the taking of Khartoum in 1898, where he was mentioned in despatches by the Sirdar, Kitchener himself. Accelerated promotion to commander followed and then to captain, the second youngest in the Royal Navy, and he served in that rank with great bravery in the Somaliland wars of 1904, winning the Distinguished Service Order (DSO). In this campaign he demonstrated his unusual penchant for delegation and teamwork. One vehicle he chose to assist in this aim was to form an officers' cricket team on his ship, of which he was the captain. One of the officers on the vessel was F W B Wilson, who had represented the Royal Navy at Lords and was a fair all-rounder. This stiffened the side considerably!

Service running Osborne, the navy's cadet school, followed, as did command of a battleship and flag rank, until in 1914 he was appointed naval secretary to First Lord Winston Churchill.

Physically, he was not imposing, standing only 5ft 6in tall, slight of build, with a fair complexion, but he had amazing eyes, each of a different colour. His adopted son George was at Eton, where his housemaster's daughter, Elizabeth Heygate, later recalled that 'this hereditary distinction proved so fascinating that I found it hard not to stare at him and lament my own pair that matched.'[2] Like his great friend and contemporary, David Beatty, he had married (in 1910) a wealthy American heiress and was thus free of money concerns.

An uxorious family man, his second child had been born on 11 March 1914. A brave man, in war and in peace he had demonstrated his courage and energy. Hood was intelligent and had won the glittering prizes, but was also shy, reserved, humble, sometimes a little whimsical, characteristics which endeared him to his crews and made him a natural, effortless leader. Despite his reserve, he was good socially, and relaxed mixing with royalty and society. He was not without ambition and a keen amateur cricketer. An officer serving under him wrote '[Hood] was by nature extremely highly strung, but in a real emergency no one could be quieter, calmer and more collected. The strain on his nerves must have been very great but he never raised his voice or displayed the slightest anxiety'.[3]

His handwriting gives something of him away. Despite his neat and tidy appearance and manner, his writing is almost illegible. Large letters, words all linking together, and only fitting a few lines to the page, it must have provided a real challenge of decryption to his correspondents. It is the writing of a man whose brain is well ahead of his hand, whose thoughts are tumbling out, whose quickness of mind outstrips his ability to record it.

The historian Arthur Marder saw Horace Hood as holding 'all the aces'. This referred to the (post-war) definition by Admiral William James of the three aces that distinguished Nelson and any other 'perfect admiral'. Ace number one was the gift of leadership; the second, a fertile mind and creative brain; and three, an eagerness to delegate and make full use of the brains of junior officers. In Marder's view, only Hood, Beatty, Jellicoe, Tyrwhitt and Duff had these attributes at the outbreak of war.[4] Others considered Hood 'highly competent and renowned for his intellect'.[5]

Fisher, shortly to return to the Admiralty as First Sea Lord at the age of seventy-three, held Hood in high esteem. After the end of the conflagration Fisher wrote:

I was blessed with a succession of Naval Assistants who knew so exactly their limitations as regards Admiralty work and allowed the Admiralty machine to be, as was officially stated, the best, most efficient, and most effective of all the Government Departments of the State. I have a note of this, made by the highest authority in the Civil Service. I would like here to name my Naval Assistants, because they were out and away without precedent the most able men in the Navy: Admirals Sir Reginald Bacon, Sir Charles Madden, Sir Henry Oliver, Sir Horace Hood, Sir Charles de Bartolome, Captain Richmond and Captain Crease – I'll back that set of names against the world.[6]

A colleague of Hood's at the Admiralty at this time, Captain Herbert Richmond, assistant director of operations on the naval staff, described Hood as having 'an intense sense of duty and moral courage of the highest order'.[7]

Hood also stood out for what he wasn't. The navy was still very much a top-down organisation. Admirals' staffs were administrative, not strategic, and admirals took the important decisions alone. Father knew best, knowledge came with rank, juniors were there to obey, not to contribute. As Rear Admiral Sir Christopher 'Kit' Cradock wrote in 1907, 'obedience is the soul of the navy; he that has not learnt to obey is wanting in the first essential of command'.[8]

Hood did not fit this mould. He was consultative, delegated to his junior officers, sought and took advice. He was decisive; he was well aware of his own shortcomings and humble in his demeanour. This made him very different from most of his peers; and fitted him to be a leader in a command where new ideas would be needed and men led in difficult circumstances. This was the man who would now have to create the Dover Patrol and form it into an efficient operating unit.

Shells from the Sea, October 1914

Churchill's expedition to Antwerp had failed and the German forces continued to push along the Belgian coast towards Ostend and Zeebrugge. Their advance posed a direct threat to British communications with France, and the Admiralty was extremely concerned as to the impact on its ability to defend the Channel, and ferry troops and supplies to the front line in France, if the Germans took control of these ports. Such an eventuality would also pose a clear danger to the British coast and shipping too. Thus the Dover Strait was considered important enough to require a separate command, rather than come under the control of the Admiral of Patrols George Ballard, whose duties were at that time seen as coastal defence. In any case, the scope of Ballard's command was proving to be too broad, given the extra pressures bought by the beginning of minelaying and the evacuation of Antwerp.

Consequently, the Dover command was called into being as a separate entity and Hood hoisted his flag on board *Attentive* on 13 October. His remit included the patrols from the naval base at Dover, the naval base itself, and the Downs Boarding Flotilla, with the title Rear Admiral Commanding the Dover Patrol and Senior Naval Officer, Dover.

The initial objectives set for the Dover Patrol were threefold. To maintain a safe passage for men and supplies from England to France; to lay and clear mines from the channel; and to check the cargoes of merchant ships passing through the Dover Strait as part of the blockade of Germany. But the Patrol also had more quotidian duties. As a contemporary writer described it:

> upon [the Dover Patrol] falls all the convoy work for the short cross-channel passages. It is to escort to France the vessels

carting troops there. Officers and men returning to Blighty must rely on its mine sweepers to keep a clear passage for the leave boat and upon its agile destroyers to see that argosy of happy souls safely from shore to shore. Our hospital ships are dependent upon it for protection against murder, hiding ghoulishly beneath the waves.[1]

The forces that fell under Hood's new command consisted of the 6th or Dover Destroyer Flotilla, with its attached scout cruisers *Attentive, Adventure, Foresight* (*Attentive* class, all launched in 1904) and *Sapphire* (*Topaze* class, also launched 1904); the 3rd and 4th Submarine Flotillas (thirteen 'B' and 'C' class), together with the Downs Boarding Flotilla, and all trawlers and auxiliary patrol vessels within his area. As an augury of things to come, Hood also gained the hospital ship *St Petersburg*, previously a steamer for the Great Eastern Railway Company (see also Appendix 1).

Hood's destroyers were a mixed bunch. He had twelve fast destroyers – the Tribal class (also known as the 'F' class) – all launched between 1907 and 1909 and capable of 33 knots. However, they were very uneconomical of fuel, although oil-fired, and had a limited radius of action between refuelling. Five of them had an armament of five 12pdr guns and two torpedo tubes; the remainder had two 4in weapons and also two torpedo tubes. Lieutenant John Brooke (of *Zulu*) described them thus: 'by 1914 they were slightly passé but their high speed and sea-keeping qualities were a recommendation. The *Zulu*'s two 4in guns and two 18in torpedo tubes hardly constituted an armament to boast of but she was as fast as most later destroyers.'[2] In addition there were twelve '30 knotters', small and obsolete torpedo-boat destroyers built as far back as 1896 and in various stages of decay. They were armed with one 12pdr gun, five 6pdrs and two torpedo tubes. They may once have been capable of 30 knots but none of them had achieved that speed in many a long year. All were under the direct control of Hood's Captain (D), Captain Charles Duncan Johnson in *Attentive*.

His submarines too were of doubtful quality. The 'C'-class submarines, the last of the petrol-powered submarines and dating back to 1906, were originally intended for coastal defence work. This meant that they had limited endurance and, owing to only a 10 per cent reserve of buoyancy over their surface displacement, they were poor surface vessels. But their spindle-shaped hull made for good underwater performance compared to their contemporaries. The older 'B' class dated back to 1904. Both types suffered from being petrol driven, which meant that the hull was constantly full of fuel vapour to the detriment of breathing, and which could be easily ignited by the many unsheathed electrical devices carried on board.

Hood was, as has been noted, a man who liked to get a good team around him; and the most important appointment an admiral can make is his flag lieutenant. On taking up his new position Hood turned to Jameson Boyd (Bill) Adams, who had been a lieutenant under him in *Berwick*. Since those days, Adams had been to the Antarctic with Shackleton as second in command, given up the sea, become a key man at the Board of Trade, and at the outbreak of war enlisted in the Territorials. This was no obstacle to Hood, who had Adams enlisted in the RNR and promptly made him his 'Flags'.* Adams was the only RNR flag lieutenant to an admiral in the whole of the war.

The submarine threat to British trade and shipping was at the root of the reorganisation which created the Dover Patrol. It was not anticipated at the time of formation that this force would be involved in coastal operations supporting the army, and the type of vessel involved was unsuited to this purpose, the destroyer's armament being too light for such a task.

However, things were not going at all well for the Allies on land. When Antwerp fell to the Germans on 9 October, the Belgian army was driven out and began a retreat towards the French. The Germans formed a new Fourth Army, made up of three divisions freed from Antwerp and four army corps newly created in Germany, giving a total of twelve divisions. This new army then proceeded southwest toward the channel ports. Standing in their way were the six remaining divisions of the Belgian army and a French division, all of whom had taken up positions along the River Yser. These Allies, exhausted and low on ammunition, stretched from the small port of Nieuwpoort a dozen miles inland to the town of Diksmuide, along the length of the Yser river and canal.

---

* Adams returned to government service for a period of special work at the Ministry of Munitions. He was subsequently posted to Flanders to command a battery of naval siege guns. A bad wound in the head necessitated his return in 1917, and he was awarded the DSO and the Croix de Guerre. After the war, he went to the Ministry of Labour as Controller for the Northeastern Division.

On 15 October the Germans entered Ostend and Zeebrugge. The Belgian government urgently asked for naval gunfire support from seaward as they had little or no artillery of their own. This request was amplified on the 16th by the French CinC, General Joffre. He was concerned that the Belgians would be unable to stem the flood of the German armies and asked that the Allied fleets should act to support the extreme left of his line and engage the German right if that flank was extended to the coastal dunes. Additionally, he expressed a wish that the naval officer in command would concert operations through the governor of Dunkirk with General Foch, who was now in command of the extreme French left wing.

Orders were immediately sent to Hood ('Proceed with all haste to Dunkirk'). However, there was one problem. His destroyers were ill-equipped for bombardment operations. When he had arrived at Dover, Hood had found three monitors lying in the harbour which were not part of his command. They were *Severn*, *Mersey* and *Humber*, ships originally built at Vickers' Barrow yard for the Brazilian navy for service on the River Amazon and armed with two 6in guns and two 4.7in howitzers. In 1913 the Brazilian government told Vickers they could not afford to pay for them and in August 1914 they were purchased by the Royal Navy, who had ordered them to Dover without much thought as how to utilise them. Indeed, on 12 October the Admiralty had used them, slow, ponderous and largely unseaworthy as they were, as escorts for the evacuation by sea of the retreating Belgian army from Ostend to Le Havre, during the course of which the monitors were attacked by *U-8*; in all probability, her torpedoes passed under their shallow draught.

Hood now requested that they be handed over to him. On 15 October he telegraphed the Admiralty, 'suggest they might be useful at Dunkirk to protect coast roads and railways to eastward'. Rather less perceptively, he suggested that the howitzers might be useful against enemy aircraft. He also expressed his confidence that they could sail by day if escorted by destroyers.[3] His lords and masters agreed and Hood was ordered to support the French left by the monitors firing from the sea. Perhaps rather unnecessarily they added, 'submarine attack must be anticipated'.[4]

Despite bad weather, Hood needed no second invitation to get into action and, flying his flag in the light cruiser *Attentive*, he took four scout cruisers and twenty destroyers into battle. The weather delayed the monitors in harbour (being of shallow draught and mainly intended for riverine work, they were unsuited to heavy seas), and operations eventually started using the squadron's scout cruisers. These began their attack on 17 October, using their 4in guns in support of the newly established Belgian line, which ran from Boesinghe (north of Ypres) along the Ypres canal and river until reaching the sea at Nieuwpoort. The monitors joined in when the weather abated.

On the 18th the flotilla was off Nieuwpoort pier, where it had passed the night, and then went up the coast seeking targets to bombard. At 1000 the Belgian military HQ requested Hood's attention be transferred to Lovie, a village in front of the Belgian advanced post at Rattevalle on the Bruges Canal, and to Blokhuis Farm, about half a mile to the north of it, both points being about 1,500yds inland from Westende. *Attentive*, as well as the monitors and *Foresight* with four destroyers, were engaged in bombardment all day. Owing to the height of the sand hills, the effect of the ships' fire was difficult to ascertain but, while the Germans succeeded in establishing themselves in part of the village of Mannekensvere and both Schoore and Keyem were lost, the attack on Lombartzyde entirely failed, a failure to which Hood's guns had contributed.

Spotting for the guns, to give range corrections, was arranged from naval balloons on shore, provided by the RNAS (Royal Naval Air Service) based at Dunkirk, and the damage done was considerable. Batteries were put out of action, a number of Germans killed and, importantly, the German infantry attacks did not succeed in breaking through to the coast. There was substantial return fire from German positions inland, but fortunately the guns were of small calibre and could not always reach the bombarding ships. Nonetheless, damage from shrapnel was sustained, but no fatal injuries. In the afternoon, Albert I, King of the Belgians, sent Hood a special message of thanks for the services he had rendered, which the admiral caused to be read out to all ships' companies.

As soon as the monitors had arrived, Hood had sent a landing party ashore at Nieuwpoort from *Severn*, with several heavy machine guns to lend support to the Belgian forces, commanded by Lieutenant Edward Selby Wise. They were in action all through the night, but were eventually forced to withdraw, at which point Wise was killed. He was mentioned in despatches (MID) by Hood who noted '[he] landed in command of machine guns ... Lt Wise who gallantly led his men into action was killed.'[5] Wise also received a mentioned in despatches from Sir John French. Wise's younger brother, a 22-year-old sub lieutenant, had died less than a month earlier when *Cressy* was torpedoed and sunk.

Finding the cruisers unsuited to the task, owing to their short endurance, Hood sent them back to port and on the 20th, with his flag in *Amazon*, a destroyer, he led a bombarding force of the 6th Flotilla, monitors, and five French destroyers assigned to his command. They attacked batteries near Lombartzyde, just north of Nieuwpoort, but this time the return of fire was fierce. *Amazon* was badly holed by return fire and had to be returned to Dover for repair, whilst on board *Viking* a 4in gun burst and she retired disabled.

The haste with which the deployments had been made is shown by the signal Hood sent to Captain (D) at Dover, by destroyer, on the 20th. 'I have no cypher books except for the ordinary books. Ammunition for the monitors must be hustled to Dover. When will the other Tribals arr [sic] for me to hoist my flag in? I must always have one good Tribal.'[6]

The ships fired off their ammunition until the barrels glowed red; they then retired to Dunkirk and filled up with coal or oil and ammunition to start all over again. Hood and his men slept in their clothes and sleep was at a premium. But after two days' continuous firing, his ships were running low on ammunition and gun barrels were wearing out.

Ammunition was a particular problem. The Admiralty signalled him: 'there is no more special 6in and 4.7in ammunition [for the monitors] for a month. Scouts [cruisers] are to proceed taking place of monitors before ammunition becomes exhausted.'[7]

Nor did he have all the necessary ships to carry out the tasks being asked of him. As the continuation of the bombardment was vital, something had to be done. The Admiralty wanted to send him back his scout cruisers (see above) which he had returned to their bases. They also offered an old battleship. But, not wishing to risk them, the ever ingenious Hood had seen a different and better answer.

His quick mind lighted on new uses for forgotten ships. The old torpedo gunboat *Hazard*, launched in 1894 and now a submarine depot ship mounting two 4.7in guns, would serve better than the cruisers. *Rinaldo* was a sloop launched in 1900 and originally fitted with a full rig of sails. At the outbreak of war she had been serving as a tender to HMS *Vivid* (a naval barracks and training establishment), Devonport RNR; but she mounted six 4in guns. *Bustard* was a very old flatiron gunboat with a 6in and a 4.7in gun, launched in 1871. She had a draught of only 6ft and was thus ideal for Hood's purposes, assuming she could still float. And then there was *Wildfire*, an old (1888) composite sloop which had been slowly rotting since 1906, serving with the gunnery school at Sheerness, and then as a general depot ship.

Any gun platform would suffice if it could carry suitable weapons and had a shallow draught in order to get close inshore. At Portsmouth, the old gunboat *Excellent*, sister ship to *Bustard*, was made ready to be armed with a 9.2in gun.

All these suggestions were immediately adopted, 'and so these discredited old craft came by their own, and under the realities of war were called from the neglect to which a long peace had condemned them'.[8] One of the destroyer captains described these antique gunboats as 'smaller than the Thames penny steamboats and slower than Philadelphia snails they literally crawled about like tortoises ... it was extremely comic.'[9] (See also Appendix 2.)

Starting on the 19th, the naval bombardment was extended along the coast in the Westende–Middlekerke–Slype area, and eventually as far as Ostend; and the coast was swept by heavy fire from up to thirty naval guns for about six miles inshore. Against this the Germans could do little or nothing, as they had no heavy artillery to bring against the ships. They shifted their concentration of attack to the Yser Canal, where desperate fighting took place. Here the Belgians took final drastic measures and cut the banks of the already swollen canal, causing a flood over the surrounding low-lying countryside. The Germans had now to withdraw, leaving many of their troops drowned behind them. The Belgians attempted to advance along the coast, but were beaten back, and the line was finally consolidated by the beginning of November with the Allied left resting on Nieuwpoort, which was protected by Hood's ships at sea.

Eventually, the German forces reacted by withdrawing out of range, which meant that heavier ships and weapons had to be added to Hood's command; he gained an old battleship *Venerable*, and *Brilliant*, an ageing (1893) cruiser, together with more submarines and destroyers which were used to screen his forces from German naval reprisals.

Throughout all this activity Hood was directing his armada, pouring gunfire into the German positions, rotating his ships and thinking of ways to add to his forces. By the 23rd he had flown his flag in six destroyers or cruisers. On one occasion he flew his flag in a French destroyer, *Intrepide*, one of four sent to his command, which was reputed to be the first time a British admiral had flown his flag in a French vessel. Jacky Fisher wrote to Ellen Hood, wife of the admiral, recounting his son-in-law Eric Fullerton's* (who was commanding the monitor *Severn*) view of her husband in action. 'Adm Hood has been really splendid. He has no fear and is always in a destroyer where the shots are falling thickest. I admire him tremendously. I have been to see him several times and he has always been more than pleasant.'[10]

The continuous operations and bombardment were not easy work. As one historian noted, 'Hood and his ships had a hot time'.[11] On 21 October Hood, now with his flag in *Foresight,* reported that she had fired 1,100 shells in the day in support of Belgian troops. That same day, he was warned by the Admiralty that submarine attack was possible. Special arrangements were made for safeguarding the flow of ammunition, while Hood shifted his flag to the destroyer *Crusader* and took charge of a protective screen, and French vessels laid a protective minefield off Ostend.

The 28th was a particularly bad day for the Dover Patrol. At 1230 *Falcon*, a destroyer on anti-submarine watch off Westende, came under heavy, accurate shore fire from a German shore battery. She returned fire and stayed on station but, at 1400 between Nieuwpoort and Ostend, was hit by 8in shell on the port forward 6pdr gun muzzle. Her captain was killed outright and the ship seriously disabled; she was brought home in a sinking condition by Acting Sub Lieutenant Charles John Houssemayne Du Boulay with fully a third of her crew dead or wounded.** There were several heroes that day on board *Falcon*, apart from Du Boulay, who had taken command after his captain was killed. Able Seaman Ernest Dimmock, finding himself the only unwounded man on deck, immediately took the helm. Petty Officer Robert Chappell had both

---

* Fullerton had married Fisher's second daughter, Dorothy Sybil, on 28 December 1908.
** *Falcon* survived and in 1916 was under the command of an RNR Lieutenant Charles H Lightoller, perhaps better known for his role as second officer on RMS *Titanic* when she sank. *Falcon* sank on 1 April 1918 in the North Sea after a collision with an armed trawler.

his legs shattered by the enemy shell and was dying, but continued to try and assist in the tending of the wounded. He died of his wounds shortly afterwards. Petty Officer Frederick William Motteram braved ongoing shellfire to attend to the wounded. And the ship's captain, Lieutenant Hubert Osmand Wauton, had maintained an exposed position under a heavy fire to keep a lookout for submarines and was killed as a result. All, together with Du Boulay, were mentioned in despatches by Admiral Hood.

That same day *Venerable*, an old battleship, *Brilliant*, together with *Wildfire*, *Rinaldo*, *Bustard* and the three monitors, were bombarding targets between Westende and Lombartzyde. The return of fire was fierce and serious damage was only avoided by continual course alterations, although *Wildfire* was badly hit on the waterline and sent home for repairs. That afternoon *Venerable* ran aground, but was helped off on a rising tide by *Brilliant* with no damage. The cruiser lost one man killed and had several wounded, whilst *Rinaldo* suffered eight wounded and one fatality.

On the 29th, the destroyer *Liberty* was torpedoed and sunk. With typical British humour, one Colonel Bridges sent from the shore base 'your help is invaluable. Hope you are enjoying the Aquatic Sports';[12] and the following day the ancient sloop *Vestal* was hit by a German battery at Westende. An 8in shell burst on her forecastle, killing a rating and causing the ship's withdrawal.

And not content with bombarding the enemy from the sea, Hood also deployed land-based artillery. He landed two 6in guns and one 9.2in on a railway mounting to assist in holding in check the Germans on their attempted advance along the coast. These guns, which were commanded by Commander Henry Crosby Halahan and manned by naval ratings, did much counter battery artillery work.

Hood, Churchill and the Admiralty

At the Admiralty, Churchill had long held a reputation for taking executive power into his own hands. He himself acknowledged this, stating that 'I exercised a close supervision over everything that was done or proposed and I claimed an unlimited power of suggestion and initiative'.[13] Now, as was his wont, he overrode the process of command and sent a stream of instructions to Hood, determined to ensure that both he and the navy were recognised as key players in the battles in France. Hood received a 'bombardment' of signals during October 'unquestionably originated by Churchill'.[14] These included, for example, on the 23rd, '[you must] recognise importance of navy dominating Belgium coast. Make the most of your opportunity';[15] and 'have everything ready at Dunkerque for Ostend bombardment. Congratulate you on vigorous bombardment of so much hazard'.[16] One thinks them hardly necessary for a man of Hood's ability and experience.

The taking of the ports of Ostend and Zeebrugge by the Germans were the source of nightmares for Churchill and the Admiralty. If the Germans took them intact they would be perfect as submarine bases, and right astride the vital supply line to the Western Front. On 23 October, Churchill sent Hood a telegram reporting that the Germans had brought submarines to Ostend in sections by train. Hood was ordered to destroy the railway station, lines and rolling stock, together with the quays and docks. But no sooner had he put together his plan to do so than a new telegram arrived the following morning, advising that air reconnaissance of the two ports had been ordered up and that he was not to bombard Ostend railway or docks, but continue to support the left flank of the Belgian army. The same day he received another telegram. This one suggested it would be better to wait a couple of days before destroying the docks, etc, but that he should destroy the railway station. Hood could be forgiven for feeling a little confused, a condition which probably worsened when on the 30th he received another communication from Churchill which asked what his plans were for preventing the use of Ostend and Zeebrugge by the Germans as submarine bases, whilst ordering him to continue to support the Belgian left!

Hood was asked to ease off the bombardment to save on ammunition. Churchill signalled him on 27 Oct at 2337: 'You have done very well ... keep it up. Certainly go on; but husband ammunition till good targets show,'[17] but the admiral declined to follow the order and kept up the firing, his sense of moral purpose to the fore, as he was well aware of the problems that the beleaguered defenders had. He signalled to the Admiralty: 'Belgian authorities beg me to fire more rapidly; deliberate firing will not produce the result as it is all unmarked. I understand that forty-eight hours more clinging on to Nieuwpoort may achieve a more decisive result. If I am to order the firing to be more deliberate, I shall not be able to do what the Belgian army requests.'[18] Such support was, however, easier said than done. The same day as he sent this signal, the monitor *Mersey* reported that her turrets were out of action and she was holed below the waterline; another monitor, *Humber*, was also holed below and her guns were worn out, *Bustard* was out of ammunition, and German submarines were reported in the area.

By the end of the month it became increasingly clear that the position of Hood's ships was untenable and precarious. The threat from submarines was growing while, owing to the guns the Germans had now placed all along the coast, it was increasingly difficult for the vessels to get any result from their fire. The Germans were well dug in, the sand dunes of the coast precluded accurate firing and the German 'counter-battery fire' was now considerable and from heavier weapons than previously. Only by constantly keeping on the move at high speed could the British vessels avoid heavy casualties.

Hood's dispatches highlighted the problems. Submarines, for example, were a constant worry. On 27 October Hood reported that *Mohawk* had sighted a U-boat and as a result he had set his destroyers searching for it and withdrawn the battleship *Venerable* to Dunkirk harbour for safety. She was an old vessel with four 12in guns, which the Admiralty had sent out to Hood rather against his wishes, although he did fly his flag in her between 27 and 29 October. His problem was that she was too tempting a U-boat target and too large for the confined waters he was operating in (and moreover carried 760 valuable crewmen on board). 'I really do not need *Venerable*,' he telegraphed home.[19]

Hood clearly thought that the squadron's gunfire was beneficial: 'I do believe that fire has effected a useful purpose and I can continue this indefinitely,' he wrote. But he was mindful of the danger to his ships. 'I have not allowed ships to take undue risks when guns could not be located. I have always withdrawn ships until information has been obtained and in every case I have been able to return the battery [fire] and overcome its fire.'[20] But his natural modesty and perfectionism drove him on. 'One day I failed to locate some long range guns but next day I was able to return to the same place and apparently overcame the enemy's fire.'[21] In reply, the Admiralty stated their confidence in his decisions: 'You have full discretion to obtain the best results,' they telegraphed. [22]

Frustration, November 1914

As noted in the previous chapter, the battle on land had not been going well. By 24 October, the Germans were attacking along the entire front and the Belgians were running low on ammunition. The only reinforcement they received was a French division to strengthen the garrison at Nieuwpoort. The same day the Germans staged fifteen separate attacks on Diksmuide alone. The situation was clearly impossible and General Ferdinand Foch, commanding the French forces, advised the Belgian king to pull back into France and join the French army in preparing defences. This King Albert refused to do, reluctant to give up the last tiny bit of his country that he held.

The area between Nieuwpoort and Diksmuide was a tract of land reclaimed from the sea using a network of canals, drainage systems and sluice gates, known as a polder. Belgian engineers had dammed the culverts south of Nieuwpoort and now, in their desperation, and taking advantage of the high tides, they began opening the sluices to flood the surrounding countryside and create an impassable barrier.

The main force of Belgians and French had taken up positions along the railroad embankment stretching from Nieuwpoort to Diksmuide behind the Yser on the 26th, but on 29 October Diksmuide fell and on the 30th the Germans launched an all-out attack against the Belgians along the embankment, which petered out in ankle-deep water. The next day, the Germans closed down their offensive because of the impossible battlefield conditions. In future, they would turn their attention to Ypres further south, which took them out of range of all but Hood's biggest guns.

By the 30th, Hood was beginning to have misgivings about the soldiery and their needs. His exasperation is clear from a telegram back to Churchill. 'It was stated on Oct 16 that if the trenches at

Nieuwpoort could be held for forty-eight hours all would be well; at intervals during the last fourteen days ... I have received assurances that if we could only hold on for forty-eight hours ... success is promised.'[1] And his desire for action was being tested by the monotony and (to Hood's mind) futility of their activities. 'I hope ... that I may return with the torpedo boats to my Dover Patrol; there will not be anything to keep me in Dunkirk ... there will really be nothing for me to do compared with the Dover Patrol.'[2]

The publicity his squadron was gaining for its exploits annoyed his natural modesty too. 'I am sorry for all the exaggeration about the flotilla in the newspapers,' he wrote. 'I wish they would keep a sense of proportion.'[3]

On 2 November Hood was ordered to stand down and rest his ships and men. He signalled to the soldiers ashore, 'It seems to me that my guns are not heavy enough to do much good against the guns now mounted ... is it considered that heavy guns from the sea are still necessary? If so I must ask the Admiralty'.[4]

That rest was short, however, for that same day came intelligence that a serious attempt seemed intended by the enemy's navy, and major German units were in the North Sea heading south. The Germans did indeed come out, but only to bombard the coast around Lowestoft and Yarmouth. Without asking permission, Hood took his destroyers back to Dover to be on hand if the Germans came down the Channel or attacked the fleets in port. He telegraphed Churchill: 'I hope that this action has met with your approval, it seemed right to me'.[5] Not many admirals would have taken independent action so quickly and without recourse to orders from on high.

That night the Belgian army once more asked for help from Hood's ships as they wanted to attempt an advance on the Yser. The admiral raised his flag in *Crusader* and with three other destroyers raced across the Channel to oblige. He was reinforced by two old battleships, but after initial success the Belgian forces retreated in the face of a German counter-attack.

Meanwhile, also on 2 November, the British government announced to the world that the North Sea was to be considered a military area and all neutral traffic intercepted in it would be stopped and searched for goods likely to aid the enemy. Such an unprecedented act was blamed on the Germans' adoption of unrestricted mining, said to have been from ships flying neutral flags (the proximate cause was the sinking of the new battleship

Audacious on 27 October, off Tory Island, by a mine laid by the German armed merchant cruiser *Berlin*). The northern end of this North Sea blockade would be maintained by the 10th Cruiser Squadron and the Dover Patrol was required to provide the southern 'plug' by effecting a blockade of the Channel.

Despite this, Hood was once more ordered to support the Belgian left in yet another 'push'. 'You had better be on the spot,' Churchill told him,[6] 'the Belgians must certainly be supported on the flank.' Hood's disillusionment with the situation is evident from his reply. 'Do not believe there is any intention to press it home,' he telegraphed the First Lord,[7] adding a plea not to re-send him *Venerable* and *Revenge* (another old battleship, dating from 1892 and resurrected from the disposal list) as they were 'too big for these waters' (*Venerable* drew 25ft of water and so could not operate close to the shore).

By 5 November, Admiral Hood was in a sour mood, one not calculated to appeal to Churchill's gung-ho enthusiasm for the intended Belgian and French so-called advances. From his shore base in the Hotel Crusader, Nieuwpoort, he wrote 'for the last 10–14 days that we were here I believed that the situation in Nieuwpoort was critical and I fired thousands of rounds of ammunition in order to comply with the wishes of the Belgian government'.[8] But now the Germans had placed heavy artillery in the dunes on the shoreline, making it difficult for his ships to get close enough in. And he had completely lost faith in the Belgian army: 'the Belgian advance is a myth,' he communicated, 'I honestly do not believe there is the least chance of a Belgian advance from here.'[9] He very clearly thought his mission a waste of resources now and that his, and his ships', real value would be in enforcing the Dover blockade.

Made aware by the Admiralty's intelligence division that the Germans had sent *U-29* and *U-12* into the Channel to attack Hood's bombardment units, Churchill finally minuted to Chief of Staff Vice Admiral Henry Oliver on the 7th that Hood should 'leave the gun vessels under his best officer and return to Dover to resume his duties as Admiral, Dover Patrols'.[10] The penny had finally dropped, long after Hood had divined the truth.

The admiral was recalled to Dover that day, leaving his gunships under *Vestal*, and he hurriedly returned to England with all his destroyers to resume his real purpose. Two days later the remainder of his ships were also withdrawn.

So ended the three weeks of operations. The main object for which they were designed, the defence of Belgium, was lost but, with the area around the Yser flooded and the German withdrawal from its left bank, it was certain the enemy would not be able to reach Calais through Nieuwpoort and Dunkirk. Hood's ships had faced all kinds of difficulties. The movements of the ships had been greatly hampered by the shoals and banks on the coast and by the constant menace of submarines. Dunes, rising in places to 50ft high, obstructed the view. The only way to find the enemy was to locate a prominent high object, such as a tower or tree, in the neighbourhood of which the ships were informed the enemy's troops or guns were congregated, and then to search the area round that object by gunfire. Bad weather also hindered his efforts, and for much of the time it was unfavourable for air reconnaissance and balloon observation. Fire control was always difficult, owing to the slowness of communication with the shore. But he had inflicted severe loss both in guns and men on the enemy, whilst keeping his own to a minimum. All told, his casualties were two officers and ten men killed, and three officers and forty-six men wounded.

Horace Hood had shown enormous energy in exercising his command, driving himself on ceaselessly. He flew his flag in six different ships (*Amazon*, *Attentive*, *Foresight*, *Crusader*, *Venerable* and a French destroyer). He had taken charge of the submarine screen, liaised on shore with the military authorities, overseen the daily bombardments, had been everywhere and anywhere, driving his heterogeneous force on in support of the army. Altogether thirty-six ships, British and French, had served under him. Hood and his men had performed valiantly and his, and their, efforts were recognised by Sir John French, commanding British forces in France, by whom he was mentioned in despatches (gazetted 17 December 1915). Colonel Tom Bridges, writing on behalf of General French on 9 November 1914, noted that Horace's 'action undoubtedly saved the Belgian left flank and in my opinion had a decisive effect on the final success of the defenders.' He went on: 'the hearty co-operation of Rear Admiral Horace Hood and the officers and men under him in what has been a difficult and arduous task is worthy of record'.[11] And General Joffre was fulsome in his praise too, sending a note of appreciation on 3 January 1915 which was later gazetted on 9 April. Hood's friend General Archibald Hunter noted, 'Master Samuel [referring to Hood's newborn child] is still too young to quite relish what it all means. But he and his brother are going to have the pride in the future of hearing of their father's exploits spoken of with rapturous delight by their father's host of friends.'[12]

These commendations hide an uncomfortable truth. Horace had become more and more convinced that his efforts were doomed to failure and in his rather guileless way had passed this information on to Churchill, who was a great deal less than pleased to be told that his plan for helping the army and the Belgians was increasingly wasteful of ammunition and effort.

Nelson had argued that ships could not engage shore-mounted weapons with success (Nelson was particularly considering the case of forts) and Hood had come to the same conclusion. As a colleague at the time wrote later:

> There is little doubt that the presence of the flotilla under Admiral Hood assisted powerfully in checking the enemy's movement along the coast with the intention of seizing the Channel ports ... In this connection I am tempted to quote a statement written at the time by a competent eyewitness who was fully aware of the views of Rear Admiral Hood, because his words confirm my own views and those of every one qualified to express an opinion. Although in the early days of the operation the ships were able to check the advance, it is not to be believed that ships alone are ever able to defeat guns mounted on shore. As long as the enemy tried to advance along the coast, so long was the flotilla efficient for masses of troops in motion, and guns and wagons en route are good objects. As soon as the advance was checked, so soon was the enemy able, by mounting heavy guns in permanent well-concealed positions, to check the flotilla. When the enemy no longer advanced there were no more masses of troops or of transport to form a good target.[13]

Hood became frustrated by this predicament. By March 1915, he was writing to a friend: 'to the Belgian coast for a few days of bombardment but I do not do any good there now as the Germans have too many big guns in position which my ship's guns cannot reach and I cannot see'.[14]

Hood and Nelson were united. Churchill disagreed, and was unhappy to be told he was wrong. He was to repeat his mistake at the Dardanelles.

Decline and Fall, November 1914 to April 1915

The initial objectives set for the Dover Patrol had been threefold: to maintain a safe passage for men and supplies from England to France; to lay and clear mines from the Channel; and to check the cargoes of merchant ships passing through the Dover Strait as part of the blockade of Germany. But instead of these duties, Hood's attention had been perforce focused on acting as floating artillery in support of the Allied armies.

With the loss of Zeebrugge and Ostend, the strategic position of the Patrol was difficult. As another admiral described it:

The waters of the Dover Patrol extended from the Scheldt to the North Foreland, and from Beachy Head due south to the French coast. It formed a water area of about 4,000 square miles in extent. The vital front that had to be protected every night was fifty-five miles long, with Nieuwpoort and the Allied lines on the extreme right, Dunkirk, then twenty miles of trade route to Calais, then twenty miles of the mouth of the Channel, down which commerce raiders or destroyers might pass, then, on the extreme left, the Downs, with their north and south entrances, between which eighty to a hundred ships lay at anchor day and night – an attack on them being only a matter of two hours full speed steaming in a destroyer. Ostend and Zeebrugge were only sixty-two and seventy-two miles respectively from Dover Harbour, the nearest point to the English coast, and Dunkirk only twenty-three miles from Ostend. ... And the traffic to and from Dunkirk had to be maintained, as this port was the main feeding base of the northern parts of the British and French Armies.[1]

The capture of Belgian ports by the Germans now meant that they could establish submarine pens with direct access to the Channel and attack both naval and civilian targets from close at hand, as well as gain easy access to the Atlantic Ocean and Britain's supply lines. Hood and the Dover Patrol were given additional instructions – stopping the submarine menace was a priority.

Operating from bases in Dunkirk and Dover, the Patrol deployed destroyers, small anti-submarine drifters and trawlers. The fishing vessels were taken up from commercial use, either requisitioned or hired, and were manned by fishermen. Their duty, in the case of the larger trawlers, was to sweep for German mines and lay British ones as protection against German submarines. The drifters were meant to 'fish' for submarines, by entangling them in their nets. The emphasis was on the use of mines and active hunting patrols to try to intercept the submarines as they attempted to enter or exit the Strait. This was a challenging job, for there were no means of detecting U-boats once they were submerged, other than to look for their periscope wakes.

But losses to submarines mounted. On 26 October *U-17* torpedoed the French 4,590grt ferry ss *Amiral Ganteaume* off Cap Gris-Nez. The stricken vessel was attacked without warning, in con-travention of international law, and the German attacker flew no flag, again in defiance of accepted international practice. On board, were over two thousand Belgian refugees, fleeing their homeland for the apparent safety of Britain. There was widespread panic on board and had it not been for the seamanship of Dover-born Captain Robert Edward Carey of the South Eastern and Chatham Railway company's cross-channel steamer *Queen*, many more than the forty who died would have perished. She manoeuvred alongside and passengers were able to jump from one vessel to the other, where willing crewmen caught them.

The Germans were widely criticised for this action in the subsequent weeks and initially put it about that the vessel had hit a mine, a ruse only finally dismissed when pieces of a torpedo were found in the wreckage of the ship itself.

Then on 31 October *Hermes*, a seaplane carrier sent to assist Hood in the bombardment of the Belgian coast, was torpedoed whilst cruising in the Strait of Dover by *U-27* and sank with the death of twenty-two crew. This loss caused the Admiralty to issue an instruction that in daylight no vessel larger than a destroyer or, at most, a scout cruiser was to cross the Channel east of the meridian of Greenwich. Nonetheless, *Niger*, a torpedo boat of 1892 vintage, converted into a minesweeper, was sunk by *U-12* when anchored off Deal on 11 November. Lieutenant Commander Arthur Thomas Muir, captain of the vessel, remained on the bridge, despite serious injuries, until all his crew were taken off, but fifteen men were killed in the explosion.

And losses had been suffered farther afield as well. On 1 November, off the coast of Coronel in the Pacific Ocean, the Admiralty and Churchill conspired to sacrifice Rear Admiral Kit Cradock and 1,600 men through poor dispositions and misleading orders.

There had been change at the Admiralty at the end of October. First Sea Lord Battenberg, under the triple pressure of Churchill's continued interference, a press campaign against him given the lack of naval success and his German ethnic background, and gout, suffered a nervous breakdown and tendered his resignation. At the month end, and not without a fight from the King, Churchill brought back to the First Sea Lord's office the 73-year-old Jacky Fisher. Hood had served under Battenberg in *Cambrian* and worked closely with him as Churchill's naval secretary. On leaving office Battenberg wrote to Hood, whom he rated highly, 'it was an awful wrench, but I had no choice from the moment it was made clear to me that the Government did not feel themselves strong enough to support me by some public pronouncement'.[2] Not for the last time, a sailor was the necessary sacrifice to protect Churchill's reputation.

Hood now got into a renewed correspondence with the Admiralty about the use of old battleships in the Channel. It will be recalled (see above) that he thought them too large and vulnerable for such work. On 14 November the Admiralty raised the issue again. 'It is necessary to have the battleships at Dover,' their telegram informed him, 'temporary measures must be taken to protect any ships exposed to torpedo fire through the Western Entrance either by nets or putting colliers alongside them. *Revenge* should remain for the period. It is understood that there are five battleship berths. *Russell*, *Duncan* and *Exmouth* have sailed for Dover.'[3] Hood must have been pulling his hair out. His reply, sent the same day, was remarkably restrained. 'Am taking steps to obey your 197 [the previous telegram] but I wish to state that Dover is open to submarine attack through the Western Entrance and is in my opinion unsuitable for battleships. Shall I send *Revenge* to Portsmouth tomorrow?'[4] He had put down a marker, at least.

If Admiral Hood thought that he had seen the last of the Belgian coast, he was proved incorrect. The French CinC, General Joffre, had sent a message to the Admiralty stating that, since Hood's squadron had ceased operating on the Belgian coast, the enemy's guns east of Nieuwpoort were becoming increasingly more active and hostile. General Foch was, in fact, being subjected to a violent artillery barrage which he had no means of countering, and Joffre begged that the Admiralty resume bombardment operations. Once again, Hood's attention was to be dragged away from the anti-submarine campaign. On 19 November he was summoned to London for a conference with Churchill and Fisher. Further assistance for the French and how to counter U-boat incursions into the Channel were on the agenda. Speedy action followed the receipt of Joffre's plea, and on the 20th Hood telegraphed Adams and Johnson to send six destroyers and four trawlers to Dunkirk and that he would fly his flag in the Tribal-class destroyer *Crusader*. The faithful *Bustard* also sailed and the Admiralty attached Hood's bête noire, *Revenge*, as well. At Britain's request, four French destroyers and a torpedo boat based at Dunkirk were additionally placed under his command.

The French asked Hood to attack German gun batteries at the mouth of the Yser. However, the targets were difficult to locate, the enemy was now well established on the coast and the weather was steadily deteriorating. Hood noted to the Admiralty that 'conditions are quite different from what they were from the first ... Today there was heavy fire from guns which I could not locate or damage.' He added, 'I don't think *Revenge* is safe through the Zirdcoote Pass and I really don't think at the moment there is any justification for it'.[5] In any event, the job was apparently over almost before it had begun. General Foch informed Hood on the 22nd that 'the task assigned to the ships consisted of reconnaissance to prove the existence or non-existence of German batteries ... The existence having been established by the engagement of the ships of Admiral Hood on November 22nd the task demanded of the naval forces is for the moment completed'.[6]

The 22nd was also the day when the second outcome from Hood's trip to London was enacted. A new system of anti-submarine patrols had been devised. A region bounded to the southwest by a line Dungeness–Gris-Nez, to the north by the parallel 51.15° N, to the east by the Ruytingen Shoal and the eastern half of a line joining the Goodwins buoy to the Pointe de Gravelines was now divided into eight patrol areas. Each was to be continuously occupied by a British destroyer with a light cruiser and flotilla on call at Dover. The submarine menace was being belatedly recognised.

Additionally, attention now turned to trying to deny the German submarines the use of their new bases. On the 23rd the Admiralty, oblivious to Hood's frequent protests, sent him the battleships *Russell* and *Exmouth* and together with light forces they bombarded Zeebrugge, which was used by German submarines on passage from their base at Bruges. They fired over four hundred rounds in what Dutch observers called a successful attack, but which actually achieved very little.

On 9 December the French requested further bombardment support. Hood was not in favour but was overruled by the Admiralty and once again *Revenge*, *Excellent* and *Bustard* were sent to oblige. There was now great difficulty in screening the big ships from potential torpedo attack, for the destroyers and torpedo boats sent to do the job were frequently driven from their positions by shore-based gunfire.

Desultory action continued into December until, on the 15th, the old battleships *Revenge* and *Majestic* were engaged in attacking positions around Zeebrugge. *Revenge* took two 8in shell hits, one of which penetrated her hull below the waterline and caused a serious leak. Hood was forced to withdraw her from the gun line and send her back to port for docking and repair, and *Majestic* was also recalled because of the risk to a single bombarding ship. The monitors could not, in Hood's opinion, do the job by themselves and so on 16 December the operation was called off and he and his ships returned to Dover.

But this was not the end of Hood's travails. On the 17th the French reported that three of their destroyers from Dunkirk were bombarding the coast, and they wanted Hood's monitors to support them. This time the admiral put his foot down and told the Admiralty that unless the Allies made a significant advance he thought that the random bombardment of the coast was pointless. The risk from submarines was significant and his escorts could not remain in position.

Still the French requested his support and on the 20th he was forced to write to Their Lordships that this casual routine kind of bombardment 'was absolutely useless and was fraught with the greatest danger to the ships, for the enemy's guns rendered it necessary to employ battleships, and battleships were certain to be sunk by the enemy submarines unless their visit was unexpected and of short duration'. He added that 'General Foch on one occasion had asked for and got ships when he had not the least intention of pressing an attack home [on the Germans], and had explained later that he only wanted them to draw the enemy's fire in order to ascertain if the enemy's guns were really there.'[7] He also later expressed the view that the army regarded the naval units as so many field guns to be moved around the sea like land-based artillery pieces, ignoring the dangers of mines and torpedo attack.

The Germans had not had it all their own way, however, and the Dover Patrol's mining efforts – in which they had laid 3,064 mines off Zeebrugge and across the Dover Strait by the end of 1914 – paid at least two dividends with the sinking of the U-boats *U-11* and *U-5* off the Belgian coast on 9 and 18 December respectively, both lost with all hands.

Despite these efforts, submarines continued to be a menace. On 1 January 1915 the battleship *Formidable* was sunk by *U-24* off the coast of Dorset with the death of nearly six hundred crew. The U-boat had traversed through the patrol zones easily, as the stress of constant operations had reduced the available destroyers to the point where all patrol zones could not be simultaneously covered.

New year, new problems

The year 1915 had started with what must have seemed to Hood like a bad case of déjà vu. On New Year's Day he once again beseeched the Admiralty, having tried as best he could to find a safe berth for the old *Revenge* at Dover, 'please send no more big ships to Dover for the present'.[8] The constant overriding of his requests concerning the obsolete but heavily manned battleships must have become very wearing.

But January caused him other frustrations too. In the opening months of the year the Admiralty had requisitioned or hired a large number of trawlers and drifters, primarily for minesweeping and submarine-hunting work.

With regard to drifters, no general tactical doctrine had been promulgated and there were thus many views as to what role they should fulfil. Hood had trawlers attached to his force, but Dover was also base to an independent command of drifters under Captain Edmund Clifton Carver RNR. Carver was a typical product of the Vicwardian navy. Born in 1878, he had joined the training school *Britannia* aged thirteen and by 1906 had attained the rank of commander. He took the War College course in 1910, where he was assessed as fifth out of twelve commanders, but Carver then resigned from the Royal Navy and joined the merchant service, qualifying as a master mariner in 1912. When war was declared he volunteered for service and was made a captain RNR and given a flotilla of drifters to command. He set about arming them, fitting them with gun shields and fire control arrangements and training the boats to operate offensively off the Belgian coast – as might be expected from a man imbued in pre-war naval doctrine of offensive action.

Both the existence of the command in his port but not under his control, and their activities and tactical intent, vexed Hood greatly. On 10 January he telegraphed the Fourth Sea Lord, Captain Cecil Lambert (in charge of naval supplies), to put a stop to Carver's continued request for arms. He criticised the deployment of the drifters off the Belgian coast, stating that 'the boats are quite unsuitable for this work. They could not exist for ten minutes unless supported by heavy guns'.[9] Hood had a better use for them, for he was already forming in his mind the proper tactical disposition of such vessels. 'The drifters will be of great use here in connection with the indicator nets in the Channel, also to patrol the Strait and protect the approaches to Dover.'[10] Indicator nets were at that stage being experimented with and Carver intended to test deployment of them off Zeebrugge. Hood again demurred. 'In my opinion trials in the Strait of Dover are far more important and I have demanded suitable nets and will conduct the experiments myself.'[11] Hood also wanted Carver's vessels out of his harbours, unless, of course, they came under his control. His message to Lambert ends with a peremptory 'I will call you up at 4.45pm to discuss'.[12] As will be seen, Hood eventually got this way.[*]

On 4 February 1915 Germany declared unrestricted submarine warfare. This meant that ships, naval or civilian, would be torpedoed and sunk on sight and without warning. This was a direct

---

[*] Carver's aggressive instincts found other outlets: in 1916 he was mentioned in despatches for his actions as a beach-master at Gallipoli, and in 1917 he was awarded the DSO, after which he joined the Royal Flying Corps.

attempt to disrupt the Allied supply chain and, in part, retaliation for the increasingly successful Allied blockade of Germany.

As previously noted, a large minefield had been laid in October 1914 to the northwest of the Sandettie Bank and towards the North Goodwin light vessel. However, it proved useless, and an immediate and better anti-submarine barrier was now urgently required. On 6 February Hood visited the Admiralty to discuss his plan to deploy a new type of barrage, indicator nets, a net and buoy barrage system across the channel to detect the presence of submarines and to prevent their egress. The following day Hood telegraphed Lambert that he would forward a detailed scheme that day, by hand of officer, which would include the employment of drifters.

The plan was to use indicator nets of various depths, deployed to capture enemy submarines by entanglement. These were a rather primitive arrangement: indicator nets were a light steel wire net, sections of which were stopped by a jackstay buoyed with bottle glass floats and shot and laid by the drifters. They could be up to 100ft long, made into longer lengths by clipping together. Some were kept extended by a drifter proceeding at low speed, others permanently moored. If a submarine fouled a net, the drifter was supposed to attack it with a lance bomb (a sort of giant hand grenade on a pole) and call for assistance from the nearest destroyer.

Experiments with these nets had been previously conducted and deployment gear had been devised by which they could be run out quickly. They were operated by special flotillas of drifters, which, being largely lightly armed or not armed at all, were escorted by patrol yachts or other vessels furnished with guns and explosive sweeps. The drifters were under the command of Captain Humphrey Wykeham Bowring, a full navy captain (not the irritating Carver who had been reassigned) and were organised into divisions of six or so vessels, with each division having an RNR lieutenant or sub lieutenant in charge. Two days after commencement, seventeen miles of these nets were deployed across the Dover Strait.

The nets were augmented by minefields, also at various depths. Finally, destroyers were used to patrol the area. In total, Hood now had under his command no less than 140 vessels of various types.

These arrangements met with some success. On 20 February a submarine which had passed through the minefields was caught in the nets near the Varne, but though two of the escorting destroyers followed the movements of the buoys and exploded charges, the submarine tore its way through and escaped. Part of the problem seemed to be that no satisfactory detachable clip for joining the individual nets together had yet to be supplied. But better luck obtained on 4 March.

At 1315 the destroyer *Viking* signalled sighting a submarine near the Varne buoy and followed its tracks, as highlighted by the movement of the floats, whilst paying out her explosive sweep. On receipt of the signal the rest of her destroyer division, under Captain Johnson, was ordered to close; forty-five minutes later another buoy movement alerted *Viking* and a periscope came to the surface again as though a submarine was in trouble with the nets. *Viking* ran up to the spot and exploded her sweep to no obvious effect, except that for a moment the periscope reappeared. An hour later a periscope was again seen, this time by *Maori* further to the westward. The submarine was clearly moving down Channel, and Captain Johnson directed *Ghurka* to work her sweep across the track. At 1700 it was exploded. The submarine shot up to the surface nearly vertically and stem first. The destroyers opened a rapid fire at her conning tower, which quickly encouraged her crew of four officers and twenty-five men to surrender, and ten minutes later she sank.

She proved to be *U-8*, the first boat that had set out from Heligoland to enforce the new war zone. It was her first patrol (in which she had sunk five ships with a total of 15,049 tons) and she had returned to Zeebrugge for repairs; she had been trying to break out to continue her work of commerce destruction. Hood and his men were delighted. But the Admiralty made a serious error. Trying to make a point, and following the dictum of Admiral Sir Arthur Wilson VC that submariners were pirates, they ordered that the crew were to be segregated in detention barracks and treated not as prisoners of war, but as pirates awaiting trial. This immediately caused reprisals from the Germans, who replied with sanctions against captured military officers, and the order was soon rescinded. But the explosive sweeps had proved their worth, and Hood requested that one drifter in every four should be furnished with one.

However, Hood was beset by two problems. First, the French, with Admiralty complicity, continued to request 'casual bombardments', for example on 20 January and 9 March. Hood's reaction was outspoken. On 15 March he wrote to the Admiralty:

I am personally of the opinion that the expenditure of ammunition is greatly in excess of the moral effect obtained. The ships will do excellent service when a real advance is intended ... but to demonstrate when no advance is intended is, I honestly believe, a mistake ... The removal of destroyers from the Dover Patrol practically prevents the proper watching of the Strait and of the indicator nets. I endeavoured to obtain other destroyers but they were not available. For four days [of the latest bombardment], therefore, the destroyer force in the Strait was perceptibly weakened, and this at a time when the new organisation appeared to be bearing fruit.[13]

It would seem a fair point.

But at the Admiralty, it was taken as clear that the Dover nets and minefields were not stopping all submarines, for two at least were known to have got through. Explosions were heard in the barrage minefield, but it was thought likely they were due to the defects of the mines themselves. They were proving very unsatisfactory and were constantly breaking adrift. Nor were the nets much better, owing to defective clips, floats and buoys, and the constant trouble of tides and wind.

Additionally, in order to defeat the nets, U-boats developed the use of net cutters. In response, the British began to attach small EC (electro-contact) mines to the nets. The electric current to the detonators was provided by a battery on the drifter and the nets were not 'live' until that was connected. But the Germans were not deterred and developed new tactics to defeat the barrier. U-boat commanders found they were able to transit the Strait of Dover with relative ease. Either they timed their arrival at the line of barrage to coincide with a westerly tide and the hours of darkness, and slipped through one of the many gaps available to them in the darkness and sped by the tidal rush, or they lay on the bottom to the north of Ruytingen Bank and proceeded submerged when a favourable stream started to run.

Nevertheless, in the last two weeks of March only five British, one French and two neutral ships were sunk, while merchant masters were growing so skilful in acting on the Admiralty anti-submarine instructions (which included trying to ram any U-boat which intercepted them) that no less than ten British ships foiled efforts to attack them.

The mercurial Horace Hood was, however, far from happy with things. The indicator nets were still giving constant trouble. On 7 April he reported that almost every day some of them were being carried away by submarines without the buoys indicating. But he kept trying; a new type of glass ball was now being trialled for floats and an improved indicator buoy had been sourced.

But some believed that better methods should be employed, and at the end of February it was decided at the Admiralty to throw a boom right across the Strait of Dover. The plan was to run an anti-submarine steel net, of harbour defence strength and quality, suspended from buoys, from a point just east of Folkestone across the Varne Shoal to Cap Gris-Nez, with a 'gate' at either end. Such devices were already in use to protect major fleet anchorages, but no one had tried them in the open sea. The work of laying the boom finally began in April, initially under the command of Captain Donald Munro (who had laid a similar, but much shorter, net in the Cromarty Firth to help protect the naval base at Invergordon), and an enormous amount of material and labour was expended on the project.

Separately, in an attempt to prevent U-boat exit from the Flanders ports, it was decided to lay net barriers close to the harbours of Ostend and Zeebrugge themselves. On 8 April two new cross-channel steamers, *Prince Edward* and *Queen Victoria*, fitted for laying wire nets at high speed, made their first attempt off Ostend, under escort of two destroyers. It was successful and by dawn they had run out about one and three-quarter miles of nets in twelve minutes, all within range of the German shore batteries. So quickly was the work done that it was completed before the guns opened fire, and both net-layers got away untouched. Things were definitely improving.

However, from the perspective of Whitehall, British merchant shipping losses mounted (from a total 47,981 tons in January to 80,775 tons in March) and the Admiralty had received intelligence that U-boats were slipping through the Dover Strait at will. By March they were operating freely in the strategically important Western Approaches. Once again Churchill found himself under public and parliamentary pressure. The solution was easily found. On 13 April Hood, who had already incurred Churchill's displeasure over the bombardment dispute and battleship deployments (see above), was ordered to strike his flag. He had been fired.

In fact, the Admiralty's information regarding U-boat transit was entirely erroneous. In early April 1915 *U-32*, heading west towards the Irish Sea, came close to being lost when she became entangled in a net and was forced to dive and sit on the bottom till nightfall. On surfacing, she found that the net was foul of the conning tower and struggled to free it. On her return, her commander (the magnificently named Freiherr Edgar von Spiegel von und zu Peckelsheim) decided to return via Scotland and the North Sea rather than risk another adventure in the nets. *U-33* suffered likewise. After their reports, the Dover route was absolutely forbidden by the German naval command. All submarines were now to go by the northern route and operations in the southern area were confined to a new class of small submarine known as 'UB' and 'UC', of which a Flanders Flotilla was being formed at Ostend and Zeebrugge. Three of these 'UB' boats were at work in the first half of the month with some success, and five were on station by the end of April, but their design proved faulty and they had to be withdrawn for overhauling.* Hood and his men had actually stopped the rot. He had been fired despite his success.

The generally reported reason for Hood's dismissal is that he was not preventing the U-boats' passage through the Strait and had perhaps 'blotted his copybook' with Churchill, as above. However Lord Charles Beresford, writing in 1917 to Admiral de Robeck stated, 'I am informed that Hood was relieved because he wanted to get rid of a most useless officer ... Churchill's brother-in-law [Lieutenant W O Hozier]; that Hood wrote to Churchill begging that this officer should be superseded ... [and was] himself superseded in twenty-four hours.'[14]

This, indeed, may have had a bearing on the decision. Hozier's service record shows him to have been described by some of his commanding officers as 'slow' and 'lacking in tact and discretion', characteristics that would not have appealed to Hood. He may well have wished to be rid of him. Certainly, he would not seem to be an especially capable officer. Between January and June 1915 Hozier was in command of the destroyer *Nubian*. His Admiralty record

---

* They were painfully slow when submerged and on the surface (5 and 6 knots respectively), exhausted their batteries after an hour under water, had a tendency to lose trim after firing a torpedo, and were nicknamed 'tin tadpoles' by their crews. The vessels of the 'UC' class were the first operational minelaying submarines in the world and, as they were based on the 'UB' design, suffered from most of its disadvantages.

shows that he was replaced in command on 4 June because of the escape of an enemy submarine in the Strait of Dover. 'This officer considered to have missed an opportunity of ramming her and superseded in command of *Nubian*.'[15] He was sent off to the old cruiser *Edgar* which was by now serving as floating artillery in the Dardanelles.*

Hood was given the less than prestigious post of commanding Cruiser Force 'E', a collection of old and obsolete vessels on trade inspection duties off the Irish coast, with his flag in *Juno*, a ship laid down in 1894. He was crestfallen. But, typically, his thoughts were for those who had worked under him rather than himself. He wrote to the Admiralty on 4 May asking for recognition for the men of the Dover Patrol. 'I allude equally,' he wrote, 'to retired and reserve officers and to those who were in appointments outside of the ordinary run of the service. Officers on the active list in regular appointments are always, more or less, in the limelight but this is not always the case with some of the officers who served and served well in the Dover Patrol'.[16] He went on to recommend three retired captains and one retired lieutenant commander who, on recall to the colours as RNR, had done sterling service.

Hood also wrote to Fisher asking for an explanation for his dismissal and received back a near illegible scrawl in Fisher's usual green ink: 'as you well know Flag Officers appointments are the prerogative of the First Lord and I endeavour to avoid meddling in his business'.[17] From Scapa Flow, Jellicoe wrote to Hood expressing his surprise at the treatment meted out: 'such strange things have happened in the matter of changes since last August that I have ceased to be surprised at anything'.[18] Hood sent the letter to his wife with a note, asking her put it in 'the glass case. Jellicoe is a big man,' he noted.[19] And his successor, Reginald Bacon, later wrote, 'The Patrol never forgot its first Admiral, and no subsequent events ever dimmed the pride of those who were privileged to have served under him'.[20]

Fortunately, help was at hand. Hood's friend David Beatty was now (acting) vice admiral commanding the Battle Cruiser Fleet, based at Rosyth. He was incredulous: 'Hood has been treated abominably,' he wrote to his wife.[21] Beatty was entitled to have

---

* Hozier reached the rank of lieutenant commander in 1917 and was placed on the retired list in 1919, to die two years later aged only thirty-three.

three rear admirals under him, commanding his three squadrons. He only had two. Beatty told Hood to write to him stating that he (Hood) wanted the vacant position. This Hood did, after Beatty had told the Admiralty it was Hood he wanted and Hood that he intended to have. Beatty wrote to him: 'Dear Bertie. I was glad to get your letter. I think you have been treated abominably and I simply cannot understand it … I have taken the opportunity of applying for you without asking you'.[22]

Beatty's machinations coincided with a period of great upheaval at the Admiralty. Churchill's arrogation to himself of the powers which had traditionally belonged to the First Sea Lord became a matter of great contention between the Sea Lords and Churchill, and for Jacky Fisher himself. The Dardanelles affair brought things to a head. Churchill increasingly issued orders for ships and equipment to be sent, without Fisher's prior consent. At 0500 on 15 May, Fisher received four minutes from Churchill, calling for yet more reinforcements to the Dardanelles. It was the straw that broke the camel's back. Before he ate his breakfast, Fisher sent his resignation to both Churchill and Prime Minister Asquith. The Titan had fallen.

Fisher's resignation set in train a run of events that Churchill and Asquith found themselves powerless to resist. His departure, coupled with the breaking news concerning a shortage of high-explosive shell, threatened to topple the Liberal government. *The Globe* newspaper of the 18th headlined 'Lord Fisher must not go', and opened its article with the line 'Lord Fisher or Mr Churchill; expert or amateur?'

To stave off opposition attacks Asquith was forced to agree to a coalition. And the Conservative Party's price for coalition included the sacking of Churchill. On the 20th Asquith wrote to Churchill asking him to take it as settled that he would no longer be at the Admiralty, which Churchill reluctantly accepted the following day.

The coalition government was formed on the 25th, with the great patrician A J Balfour as First Lord of the Admiralty. As his First Sea Lord he had a compromise candidate, everybody's second choice, Sir Henry Jackson – a good administrator but lacking much verve.

The navy was generally pleased to see the back of Churchill and welcomed Balfour. Beatty (whom Churchill had considered a friend and whose career he had arguably saved) wrote to his wife, 'the navy breathes freer now it is rid of the succubus Churchill',[23] and Jellicoe declared, 'Mr Balfour is absolutely sound in his views'.[24]

Meanwhile, Churchill, now about to depart the Admiralty, wrote to Hood on 22 May. He had by now been appraised that the intelligence that U-boats had been slipping through the Strait in numbers was faulty. He was man enough to recant. Churchill wrote:* 'I am glad to be able to appoint you to command 3BCS. I should have been sorry to leave the Admiralty without marking my sense of the excellent work you did off the Belgian coast in the Strait of Dover.'[25]

---

* After the war, Churchill blamed Fisher (now dead and unable to deny it) for the decision to remove Hood from the Dover Patrol. 'Injustice was done to this officer when, upon Lord Fisher's advice I transferred him.' There may be an element of truth in this as Fisher had informed Bacon that 'the tenure of the Dover Command varied, with the number of submarines sunk'. But it was still Churchill's decision.

PART THREE
Bacon

Bacon was about the ablest and cleverest officer I have ever known.
Admiral of the Fleet Sir Henry F Oliver, *Memoirs*, vol II, pp170–1.

9

Reginald Bacon

Horace Hood's replacement at Dover was Rear Admiral Reginald Bacon (known throughout the service as 'Porky'), a protégé of Fisher's, and a materiel and technical expert, brought back from retirement. He had been over in France with an experimental battery of 15in howitzers. Of his recall to Dover he noted, 'I left the next morning for Dover and found that Rear Admiral Hood was no more anxious to go ... than I was to relinquish my guns.'[1]

Reginald Hugh Spencer Bacon was in many ways the antithesis of Horace Hood, but they had one thing in common: they were both considered to be very intelligent men. Born in 1863, he joined the navy in 1877, and as a lieutenant had specialised as a torpedo expert (which in those times also included mines and all things electrical), showing a considerable flair for engineering and mechanical problems.

In 1897 he served as a member of the Benin punitive expedition (where he won the DSO), and then in 1899, while serving as a commander in the Mediterranean Fleet, met Admiral Jacky Fisher and was swiftly drawn into the circle of young officers employed by Fisher as an informal staff and known as 'the Fishpond'. Fisher became his mentor and Bacon was promoted to captain in 1900. Owing to Fisher's influence, Bacon was appointed to the new position of Inspecting Captain of Submarines, and given the task of introducing and developing the Royal Navy's earliest submarine boats. In August 1901 came the accompanying appointment as captain of *Hazard*, which had recently been converted into the world's first submarine depot ship (and which he would meet again in 1915 as part of the Dover Patrol). The appointments gave Bacon the imprimatur of Fisher and the Admiralty as a most promising officer.

In 1906 Fisher had specifically selected him to be the first captain of the revolutionary *Dreadnought*. A newspaper of the time wrote:

> To be only forty-three and command the world's greatest battleship must surely come near to the summit of every sailorman's desire. Captain Reginald Bacon, DSO, the Commander of the *Dreadnought*, has not attained his distinguished command without a fairly hard struggle upwards. Submarine training had formed a good part of his training, and submarine work, as the outsider knows, is not exactly child's play. Commander Bacon while serving as lieutenant on the *Camperdown* was awarded a medal by the Italian government for saving life at the wreck of the *Utopia* in the Bay of Gibraltar, ... he has also written a text book entitled 'Manual of Electricity and Electric Lighting for the Navy' ... A fitter man for this important could hardly, therefore have been found.[2]

He was, however, a divisive character, being a poor delegator, and giving the arrogant impression that he could manage without help from anyone. According to Arthur Marder, he 'had not the gift of drawing loyal service from his officers and men ... and was not a popular figure.'[3] He was a polarising character, like Marmite. People liked him or hated him and he was certainly not a friend to all and sundry.

In August 1907 he was appointed to the position of Director of Naval Ordnance, succeeding Jellicoe. However, his close association with Fisher, and the revelations that he had privately submitted letters to Fisher when serving in the Mediterranean under Beresford, which were held to be uncomplimentary to his CinC, and which became a cause célèbre at the hearings held in 1909 to lance the boil of the Beresford–Fisher open 'war', went against him. Accused of 'spying' for Fisher, questions about the probity of Bacon's actions in writing the letters were asked in Parliament, and eventually he felt that he had no option but to leave the service, which he did in November the same year, after criticism which he felt was tantamount to dismissal.

That his technical abilities at least were a loss to the navy can be seen in the views expressed by the then Commander-in-Chief on the China Station, Vice Admiral Sir Hedworth Lambton (later Meux), who wrote to First Lord McKenna on 11 May 1909 that 'Bacon is in a great many ways the ablest man in the Service & I can say no more than that, should I ever command a fleet in war, I think I would rather have him for my second in command or "Captain of the Fleet" than any other man I know'.[4]

In civilian life Bacon accepted the post of managing director of the Coventry Ordnance Works (a privately held company jointly owned by Cammell Laird & Co, Fairfield Shipbuilding and Engineering Company and John Brown & Company), to which his work as Director of Naval Ordnance and his own proclivities well suited him.

He had married into the wealthy and aristocratic Surtees family and was clearly a man of means. In November 1912 he had bailed out one Henry Surtees, bankrupt after a messy divorce and who had been required to mortgage his ancestral home and lands at Redworth Hall. Together with Robert Lampton Surtees, Bacon provided a mortgage for the property of £1,200.

The outbreak of war brought Bacon's recall to active service and he was granted a commission as a colonel second commandant in the Royal Marine Artillery, in order that he might test and develop, in live conditions of warfare, a 15in siege howitzer of his own design made at the Coventry Ordnance Works.

On 13 April 1915 he was appointed to command of the Dover Patrol, 'to the astonishment of many of his naval contemporaries and the fury of some',[5] and hoisted his flag in the second-class protected cruiser *Arrogant*. His association with Fisher no doubt played a role in his appointment, as did his familiarity with things technical, an attribute that would be increasingly important in the development of the mine and barrage defences of the Channel. As Churchill wrote of him, 'in everything that concerned machinery, invention, organisation, precision, he had few professional superiors'.[6]

One of those who may have expressed 'fury' was the notoriously offensively minded Reginald Tyrwhitt (known to his men as 'Black Jack'), commander of Bacon's near Dover Patrol neighbour, the Harwich Force. To Tyrwhitt*, Bacon became a worse enemy than the Germans, unwilling to take risks and 'our bugbear ... the Streaky

---

* There may have been an element of sour grapes in Tyrwhitt's comments, however. In 1916 Tyrwhitt proposed an attack to block Zeebrugge which was rejected, and led him to suggest a more ambitious operation to capture the mole and the town, as a prelude to advancing on Antwerp. Bacon was asked to give his opinion and rejected the plan, and thus so did the Admiralty.

One has obsessed everyone at the Admiralty and does exactly what he pleases with them ... You will understand me when I say he is not a white man'.[7]

Thus it was that a retired officer, successful in civilian life and who had left the navy under something of a cloud, returned to the colours as a rear admiral on the retired list, aged fifty-two, and ready to take on the challenge of stopping the U-boat menace.

Sea Adaptability, April to December 1915

The role of the Dover Patrol was by now mainly focused on preventing German submarines passing through the English Channel, and shore bombardment, which was sometimes the same thing, and to facilitate the despatch of supplies, both men and materials, across to the Western Front in France. Few, if any, merchant ships carrying freight consigned to Germany tried to burst through the confines of the Channel defile, although many vessels still had to be checked for prohibited trade.

By mid 1915, Germany held twenty-seven miles of Belgian coast from Nieuwpoort (eight miles east of the French border) to neutral Dutch territory at the mouth of the Scheldt. Furthermore, German submarine flotillas from Antwerp, Zeebrugge and Ostend (the latter two housed in protected ferro-concrete shelters at Bruges, now designated an 'imperial port', eight miles inland and joined to the North Sea by a canal), together with those from the High Seas Fleet, were a constant problem in the narrow sea. They preferred to be able to break out to the Atlantic through the shorter Channel route, rather than having to go round the northern top of Britain, passing though the North Sea, the Northern Blockade and into the Irish Sea, from where they could attack Britain's Atlantic trade. And the reason for this preference was very clear – going the long way round severely reduced their operating time in the Atlantic hunting grounds. Additionally, the Channel and Downs sea areas were hugely important for British coastal trade, supply to France and shipping into the port of London. Zeebrugge was, after all, only sixty miles from the Kent coast. Free access to all these areas for U-boats could play havoc with Britain's supply chain.

The activities of the Patrol in preventing transit by submarines were thus a very important part of trade defence, as was trying to kill the problem at source by attacking the German submarines' shore installations and harbours. Equally important was the effort to keep the Channel open for legitimate British and Allied trade and defend the supply chain from British ports to France. Minesweeping and detecting minelayers, as well as laying protective British minefields, was also now an important part of the duty, as was anti-submarine work in the Channel waters themselves.

As Bacon took over his new position, the Germans commissioned the 1st Flanders U-boat Flotilla, comprising initially six operational boats. These were 'UB'-type craft, small coastal vessels, intended specifically for work in the shallow and narrow waters of the Flanders coast. They were prefabricated in Germany in fifteen pieces and then sent by rail to Bruges for assembly. From here they made their way by canal to the exit ports of Zeebrugge and Ostend. The competition for control of the Strait was warming up.

It did not take long for Bacon to suffer his first loss of a ship. On 7 May the Tribal-class destroyer *Maori* was off the Belgian coast, laying marks to guide the shooting of the battleship *Venerable*. At 1515 *Maori* hit a mine and almost immediately afterwards was attacked and hit by a shore battery. She was clearly doomed and the crew abandoned ship in the boats. Her buddy ship, *Crusader*, also sent a boat to the rescue, but was herself forced to retire by an intense cannonade from onshore. All seven officers and eighty-seven men reached the coastline where, along with the unfortunate boat crew from *Crusader*, they were taken prisoner and served out the rest of the war as POWs, including *Maori*'s captain, Benjamin Wingate Barrow, who was a cousin of General Sir Reginald Wingate, Kitchener's successor as Sirdar of Egypt.

U-boats were now being regularly sighted in the Thames Estuary and the Dover Strait and on 1 June Bacon temporarily lost a further vessel when the destroyer *Mohawk* was mined. She was towed into Dover harbour with her decks almost awash and later repaired. Mines were becoming a serious problem for the Patrol. The mine had been laid by *UC-11*, one of a new type of submarine minelayer, the 'UC' class, which the Germans were starting to deploy in the Channel and North Sea. These were fitted with vertical tubes, charged with mines which could be ejected as necessary.

Minefields started to appear all over the Patrol's operational area. On 18 June mines were discovered off Dover and on the 30th, off the mouth of the Thames, where they claimed the old destroyer *Lightning*. On 13 July another field was found off Dover and another close to Calais, beyond the net barrier. From this point, minesweeping flotillas were in constant use, keeping open the main channels of trade, and the Patrol's destroyers added mines to their to-do list.

However, artillery support for the army was still a regular task for the Patrol. Bacon's bombardment resources were substantially increased by the arrival from August onwards of the large 12in-gunned monitors of the *Lord Clive* class, armed with guns taken from decommissioned *Majestic*-class battleships and hence some twenty years old. *Prince Rupert*, *Sir John Moore*, *Lord Clive* and *General Craufurd* had all been intended for the Dardanelles, but the new team at the Admiralty had other ideas and allocated them to the Dover Patrol. These were joined by the smaller *M-15*-class monitors, which had been inspired by the success of Hood's 'Brazilian' ships. They were rushed into production, utilising old guns from decommissioned vessels. These ships were creditably completed in around six months of build time, driven in part by Fisher's enthusiasm for the type, as part of his pet plans for Baltic amphibious landings. They packed a punch. The *M-15* class carried a single 9.2in gun taken from the old *Edgar*-class cruisers and could get close inshore, but their speeds were leaden, around 6.5 knots at best, which necessitated a large escort, and their gun range not over-long; Bacon quickly had them rearmed with more modern 6in and 7.5in weapons (see also Appendix 3). Monitors *M-23* to *M-28* served with the Patrol from this time.

Bacon used the monitors, as Hood had, to continue support for the army. Beginning in July, he based a force of two small monitors, a scout cruiser and several destroyers at Dunkirk, where they could be ready at short notice to provide covering fire, as well as defend the approaches to Dunkirk harbour from German surface attack. He also busied himself with preparing his disparate fleet for new bombardment operations, this time aimed not at German artillery batteries and troops, but at the U-boat bases. And whilst Bacon planned how to use his new resource, he was advanced to the rank of vice admiral on the retired list.[*]

---

[*] On 15 July 1915.

With regard to submarines, Bacon did not believe that hunting them with his smaller ships held much possibility of success, and he believed that the best way to deal with the U-boat problem was to destroy their bases. He had further convinced himself that the optimum method was by bombardment. To this end he had designed a novel form of observation platform for spotting the fall of shot. These comprised iron tripods made from railway rails, 44ft high and fitted with observation platforms (just 6ft 9in by 5ft 4in in area) and instruments mounted at the apex. Signalling fall of shot was by an acetylene lamp. The tripods were carried on specially fitted colliers and deployed by planting them on the seabed in shallow waters. Now he was ready to execute his plan.

In the evening of 22 August Bacon took three of the new 12in-gunned monitors, *Lord Clive*, *Prince Rupert* and *Sir John Moore*, together with no less than seventy-six other small vessels for anti-mine and anti-submarine defence (including two minesweeping gunboats, *Seagull* and *Spanker* sent from Harwich, and ten shallow-draught paddle minesweepers), to attack the submarine facilities and pens at Zeebrugge. Drifters formed a protective wall of nets on three sides of the monitors and for two hours he bombarded the port. However, gun-mounting problems and other technical issues bedevilled the monitors and the admiral did not get off the weight of shell he had intended. *Lord Clive* fired only thirty-one shells, of which four were considered to have landed close enough to the target to cause damage. *Sir John Moore* suffered some ruptured pipes after shooting off nine rounds and had to cease fire. And *Prince Rupert* had an electrical circuit failure which meant that communication between the turret and the ship's gunnery officer depended on a chain of voice commands and she got off only nineteen rounds.

Withdrawal was also difficult. The German batteries got the range and *Lord Clive* was hit four times, one of which dislodged a 3pdr gun on deck and sent it flying across the ship, injuring several sailors; another carried away the flag halyards, entangling Bacon's chief of staff, Captain Bowring, in a rat's nest of lines, and causing a block to strike *Lord Clive*'s captain, Commander Norman Hunter Carter, on the head.

Nonetheless, Bacon was pleased with the results of the raid. In his report to the Admiralty he noted:

It was satisfactory that extreme accuracy was obtained with the gun fire at the long ranges necessary for the best attack of such defences. This accuracy fully justifies the novel methods used and the careful training in attention to details to which the vessels are subjected. A similar organisation was employed in subsequent attacks.[1]

The Germans, however, did not seem to be particularly inconvenienced.

The paddle minesweeper *Albyn* had been part of the flotilla, sweeping ahead of the bombardment force and as she returned to Dover the following day, she was attacked by a German seaplane, which dropped bombs. These were only avoided by her RNR captain through frantic course and speed changes. With their distinctive broad beam, the paddle steamer minesweepers had become a favourite target for German pilots, who could readily recognise them from above. By 1916 they were generally bombed every time one went to sea.

On 7 September Bacon ventured out again, this time to target Ostend and Westende simultaneously. He took with him a vast and 'curious medley of a fleet, an old-fashioned battleship, several monitors and cruisers, a large force of destroyers, a spotting balloon ship devoid of masts, a cross channel steamer, converted into a seaplane base [and carrying three Short 184 seaplanes], and a huge flotilla of trawlers, drifters, armed yachts and motor launches'.[2] It was about this time that the Patrol gained the soubriquet 'Fred Karno's Army'.

Bacon had taken five monitors, but only two of the 12in-gunned ships, *Lord Clive* (flag) and *General Craufurd* (the other two having been sent to Chatham for overhaul), to attack Ostend, but was met with heavy shellfire in return from a new German heavy gun position, the Tirpitz battery. It fired twenty-two heavy rounds at Bacon's flagship and sixteen shells which landed within 30yds of his other ships. Meanwhile, Westende suffered the attentions of some old friends – *Bustard*, *Excellent* and *Redoubtable* (the new name for the *Revenge*). One of the monitor captains, Lieutenant Commander B H Ramsay of *M-25*, would find fame in the same areas twenty-five years later, as the organiser of the Dunkirk evacuation.

For the Westende bombardment, Bacon had deployed a kite balloon for gunnery spotting purposes, flown from *Menelaus*. She was a hired and converted merchant vessel, originally built in 1895 in Greenock for the Ocean Steamship Company of Liverpool. She broke down and had to be towed home to Dover by the trawler *Peary*, a modern (1913) Hull-registered boat, used as a minesweeper.

The overall operation was not a success. Two of the tripods were discovered by the enemy and destroyed, and the only verifiable success was the wrecking of Ostend lighthouse and some naval-looking sheds. During the attack, *Attentive*, out in support of the big gun ships, was attacked from the air by a German Albatros C1, and a bomb hit a 4in gun, killing two men (a marine and an officer's cook), and wounding another seven.

In truth, neither operation had caused the Germans much hardship, but Bacon was upbeat about the performance of his ships, nonetheless. Writing to Winston Churchill, now confined to the sinecure position of Chancellor of the Duchy of Lancaster, on 5 October Bacon stated that:

> the drifters with nets did excellent work protecting the ships and all did well and behaved splendidly ... I venture to say [it was] one of the best pieces of naval shooting ever undertaken. The scheme, you may remember, involved the use of observation stations which was very successful ... not bad for a first shoot with the monitors.[3]

It is difficult at this distance to know whether this gloss was Bacon's normal arrogance, or just wishful thinking.

The attention of the Tirpitz gunners had been an unpleasant surprise for Admiral Bacon. The battery consisted of four modern 11in guns and was sited just to the west of Ostend. Importantly, it outranged the British monitors, and proved worryingly accurate. By June and August 1917 respectively, the Germans would install two other long-range batteries – at Knokke, east of Zeebrugge (the Kaiser Wilhelm), and east of Ostend (known as the Deutschland). These provided an even greater and severe risk to any bombarding vessels.

So concerned was Bacon at the effect of the Tirpitz battery in preventing his short-range monitors from bombarding the ports, he designed and implemented a plan to land a long-range 12in naval gun at Dunkirk, and moved it using specially adapted mountings by road, using low-loader bogies he had himself designed. These were pulled by three large tractors coupled together to do the towing.

This battery was known as Dominion, as it was installed largely by Canadian engineers at St Joseph's Farm near Adinkerke. This was about 27,000yds from the Tirpitz battery, while being outside the accurate range of other nearer German guns. It carried out a continual duel against Tirpitz, obtaining hits which, however, did not result in long-term damage, but rendered the harbour at Ostend much more dangerous to use by the enemy (a post-war inspection by a US army team revealed that there were innumerable shell holes around the battery, but not one decent hit).

On the 19th it was back to the shore bombardments that had so frustrated Horace Hood, when the army called for support from the sea, and Bacon responded with attacks against several batteries on the Belgian coast, again using his monitors, now joined by the newly commissioned 15in-gunned vessel, *Marshal Ney*. Her debut was eventful. The German Tirpitz battery soon got her range and she was forced to retire after firing only seven rounds. Trying again, she fired sixteen rounds, with one reported hit on the Aachen battery of four 150mm guns, but the blast from her gunfire blew out the securing slip for the port anchor, which ran out and stopped the ship. It proved impossible to raise the offending object and, for good measure, the starboard engine stopped and would not restart. To cap it all, the German battery found her range and surrounded her with shell bursts. Eventually her commander, Captain Hugh Justin Tweedie, managed to get her off the sandbank to which she had become anchored, to then discover that her rudders were jammed and that she would only proceed in circles. Eventually, she was saved from premature disaster by the destroyer HMS *Viking*, which towed her back to Dover: not an auspicious beginning.

Yachts

There was a royal occasion on 23 September when King George V visited Dover and the Dover Patrol. The drifters of the Patrol were anchored in three long lines off the dockyard wall, and the crews were paraded ashore for His Majesty's inspection. The drifter *Clover Bank*, with her nets and all gear complete for shooting, was moored alongside the wall for the King's inspection. A keen sailor himself and ex-Royal Navy commander, the King went on board her, inspected the gear and went down to the after-cabin with her skipper, taking a great interest in the life and work on board.

On 24 September Admiral Bacon again took his monitors and escort craft out to bombard the coast around Zeebrugge and Ostend, in response to a request from the army to create a diversion whilst they carried out an offensive on the Western Front (the Battle of Loos).

Amongst the escort craft was the Admiralty drifter *Great Heart*, only hired in the June, and on duty streaming anti-submarine netting. Two miles off Dover harbour, she hit a mine (laid by *UC-6* two days previously) and sank immediately, taking her skipper, William Davidson RNR, and seven RNR ratings with her.

Another escort vessel was the armed steam yacht HMY *Sanda*, 300 tons, built in 1906 as *St Serf* for the linoleum king Sir Michael Nairn of Rankeilour. Now armed with two 6pdr guns, her captain was 67-year-old Henry Thomas Gartside-Tipping. Born on 11 June 1848, he had joined the navy in 1860 and had made sub lieutenant by 1867. He was promoted lieutenant in 1870 after a tour in the Royal Yacht *Victoria & Albert*, and left the service for 'private reasons' in 1874. A wealthy man, with properties on the Isle of Wight, Bolton (Lancashire) and in Ireland, Gartside-Tipping was a keen yachtsman and a stalwart of the lifeboat service. He held the post of Inspector of Lifeboats (Irish District) between 1879–92 and was awarded the Royal National Lifeboat Institution Medal, the citation for which read 'in high appreciation of his zealous and efficient services ... in acknowledgement of the risk of life he frequently incurred in the Lifeboat service.' He was also the inventor of 'Tipping plates', named after him, which enabled a heavy lifeboat to be transported on her carriage over deep and soft sand.

At the outbreak of war, Gartside-Tipping had badgered the Admiralty to give him a role, despite his age, and his reward was the *Sanda*. He was the oldest naval officer afloat[*] and one who, as Bacon recorded, served at sea as a lieutenant commander with 'undemonstrative patriotism'.[4] Gartside-Tipping had become something of a celebrity by virtue of his age, and had been presented to King George V during the King's inspection of the Patrol.

At 0700 on the 25th, *Sanda* was off the coast of Zeebrugge in company with the monitors *Prince Eugene* and *General Craufurd*,

---

[*] This was the claim of the newspapers, but it depends on the definition of 'afloat'. He was not the oldest officer with an operational command, see Chapter 11.

when she was hit near the deckhouse by an 8in shell. Her executive officers, including Gartside-Tipping, were killed instantly. The old man of the sea had gone forever.* Only thirteen of her complement of twenty-six survived her sinking. The dead included, at the other end of the age spectrum to *Sanda*'s commander, fifteen-year-old signal boy Clement Kendrick from Sheffield, and from faraway Isle of Lewis, William Macleod RNR lost his life in waters strange to him until now. Gartside-Tipping was not, incidentally, the oldest man serving. That distinction went to ex-Chief Gunner Israel Harding VC, who had retired from the navy in 1885, but returned to the colours at the outbreak of war. Although now aged over eighty, he served in the minesweepers until a mine blew up under his ship, breaking his left leg.

Bacon made further coastal bombardments throughout the remainder of September and again on 2 and 3 October, when his forces were subjected to sustained but ineffective submarine attacks. On the 6th his ships were back in position off Nieuwpoort, when the paddle minesweeper *Brighton Queen*, previously an excursion steamer and hired in September 1914, struck a mine (laid by *UC-5*) under the paddle box, broke in two and sank within minutes. Eight men died in the explosion. She was the first of the paddle minesweepers – pleasure boats and ferries before the war – to be lost in action.

As the episode of the *Sanda* demonstrated, yachts were dangerous places to be in 1915. On 31 October *Aries*, an oceangoing steam yacht, serving as a patrol vessel and under the command of Lieutenant Commander H R D Calder RNR, a merchant captain from Leith, hit a mine (again laid by *UC-6*) off Leathercoat Point. She sank immediately and her captain and twenty-two of her crew (many of whom were MMR – Mercantile Marine Reserve) went down with her. There were only five survivors. She had been rushing to the rescue of a cargo steamer, SS *Toward*, which had itself just blown up on a mine.

Minesweepers were called up, including *Othello II*, a minesweeping trawler built in 1907 and in peacetime based out of Hull. She had been on patrol in an area between the Goodwin Gate

---

* This was not the end of the Gartside-Tipping tragedy. Shortly after her husband's death, Henry's wife, Mary Gartside-Tipping, joined the Women's Emergency Corps for service in France, where on 4 March 1917 she was shot by a French soldier whose mind was 'disordered'. The French military authorities did everything possible to express their sympathy: the Croix de Guerre, which had been withheld from women since November 1916, was conferred on her at once and a full military funeral followed.

and the Gull Lightship. There was a strong gale running from the south-southeast and she was having to battle her way through heavy seas towards her new station when, at 1155, she hit a mine. The mine detonated amidships and the explosion caused extensive damage to her port side and distorted the cabin door and wheelhouse windows such that that neither doors nor windows would open fully. John Millet, the second hand, skipper Duncan McLachlan and the helmsman (all RNR) in the wheelhouse managed to squeeze and push the cabin boy through a window opening, but they could not get out themselves and went down with the ship. The lucky lad was the only survivor of the ten men on board. Amongst the dead was Frederick Butt, a reservist from faraway Newfoundland.

However, from tragedy came learning. The quotidian heroism of McLachlan and Millet had one positive effect. Their struggle to get free caused Bacon to order all the wooden doors in the Dover Patrol trawlers and drifters to be replaced with canvas screens.

And then just over a week later, on 9 November the Dover Patrol lost the yacht *Irene*, previously a Trinity House lighthouse tender and commanded by Master Mariner Hugh Leopold Phillips. She was another armed yacht employed looking for submarines and hit a mine laid by *UC-1*, sinking with the loss of all her twenty-one-man crew, which included fifteen-year-old apprentice John Reading, indentured just one year previously.

More bombardments

Bombardment raids carried on throughout November, despite deteriorating weather conditions. The force was strengthened by the arrival of *Ney*'s sister ship, *Marshal Soult*, and the admiral could now deploy six 12in-gunned monitors and two 15in, together with four of the smaller *M-15* class.

Bacon was pleased with the results of his activities. He noted:

concerted operations of considerable magnitude have been carried out on six occasions, and on eight other days attacks on a smaller scale on fortified positions have taken place. The accuracy of the enemy's fire has been good. The damage inflicted on the enemy is known to include the sinking of one torpedo boat, two submarines and one large dredger, the total destruction of three military factories and damage to a fourth, extensive damage to the locks at Zeebrugge and the destruction of thirteen guns of considerable calibre, in addition to the destruction of two ammunition depots and several military storehouses, observation stations and signalling posts, damage to wharves, moles and other secondary places. Further, a considerable number of casualties are known to have been suffered by the enemy.[5]

Bacon didn't hesitate to praise the efforts of the men of the Patrol, especially the volunteers, but he could not help making the point that it was as a result of the training that he had instigated:

I cannot speak too highly of the manner in which the officers and men under my command have carried out the duties allotted to them. The work has been varied, and to a great extent novel, but in all particulars it has been entered into with a zeal and enthusiasm which could not have been surpassed. The gunnery results have exceeded my expectations.

Bacon went on to comment:

Their Lordships will appreciate the difficulties attendant on cruising in company by day and night, under war conditions, of a fleet of eighty vessels comprising several widely different classes, manned partly by trained naval ratings but more largely by officers of the Naval Reserve, whose fleet training has necessarily been scant, and by men whose work in life has hitherto been that of deep sea fishermen. The protection of such a moving fleet by the destroyers in waters which are the natural home of the enemy's submarines has been admirable, and justifies the training and organisation of the personnel of the flotilla. But more remarkable still, in my opinion, is the aptitude shown by the officers and crews of the drifters and trawlers, who in difficult waters, under conditions totally strange to them, have maintained their allotted stations without a single accident. Moreover, these men under fire have exhibited a coolness well worthy of the personnel of a service inured by discipline. The results show how deeply sea adaptability is ingrained in the seafaring race of these islands.[6]

The Tribal-class destroyer *Amazon*, Hood's occasional flagship in 1914.
(AUTHOR'S COLLECTION)

Broke, Commander 'Teddy' Evans's ship at the Second Battle of the Dover
Straits, 1917. She was originally built for the Chilean navy.
(AUTHOR'S COLLECTION)

Mersey, one of the three 'Brazilian' monitors that were 'commandeered' by Rear Admiral Hood. (AUTHOR'S COLLECTION)

Swift, *Broke*'s consort at the Second Battle of the Dover Straits 1917. (AUTHOR'S COLLECTION)

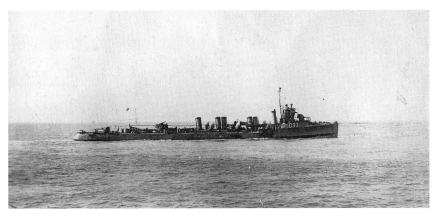

Viking, the only British destroyer in the war to have six funnels.
(AUTHOR'S COLLECTION)

Prince Eugene, a *Lord Clive*-class 12in monitor. (AUTHOR'S COLLECTION)

A scale model of the monitor *Marshal Soult* which clearly shows the
enormous 15in gun turret and shallow draught of the type.
(© IMPERIAL WAR MUSEUMS MOD 434)

Either the monitor *Lord Clive* or *General Wolfe* firing her 18in gun during 1918, photographed from a motor launch of the Dover Patrol as the monitor engages targets on the Belgian coast. (© IMPERIAL WAR MUSEUMS HU 130296)

Glatton after being sunk in Dover harbour.
(COURTESY OF DOVER MUSEUM AND BRONZE AGE BOAT GALLERY)

The Tribal-class destroyer *Zulu* which later became one half of *Zubian*.
(AUTHOR'S COLLECTION)

Nubian being salvaged off South Foreland after the First Battle of the Dover
Strait. Her aft section was mated with the fore section of her sister 'Tribal'
Zulu (mined 8 November 1916) in 1917 to form a new destroyer, *Zubian*.
(AUTHOR'S COLLECTION)

The armed yacht *Ombra*. (AUTHOR'S COLLECTION)

One of the P-boats or sloops, designed for submarine-hunting, *P-48*. (AUTHOR'S COLLECTION)

HM Hospital Ship *Dover Castle*; note the stripe which was green. (COURTESY OF DOVER MUSEUM AND BRONZE AGE BOAT GALLERY)

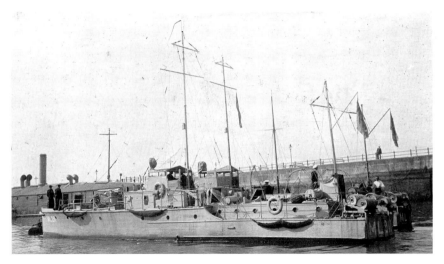

ML-211, a typical example of the motor launches that worked in the Dover Patrol. (Naval-History.net)

Motor launch *ML-22*. This vessel took part in the raid on Ostend on 23–24 April 1918. (© Imperial War Museums HU 130287)

Vice Admiral Sir Roger Keyes in 1918.
(AUTHOR'S COLLECTION)

A rather unflattering portrayal of Admiral
Hood (inset) on a postcard of a Dover
Patrol trawler. (AUTHOR'S COLLECTION)

Commander 'Teddy' Evans in a publicity photograph for his lectures in 1914. (AUTHOR'S COLLECTION)

Captain Alfred Carpenter VC, in command of *Vindictive* at Zeebrugge. (AUTHOR'S COLLECTION)

Rear Admiral Horace Hood, the first admiral to command the Dover Patrol. (AUTHOR'S COLLECTION)

Edwin Farley, Mayor of Dover 1913–1918. (AUTHOR'S COLLECTION)

An artist's impression of Dover harbour in 1914 on a postcard.
(AUTHOR'S COLLECTION)

A Dover resident's town pass dated 1917, used to gain entry and exit. (COURTESY OF DOVER MUSEUM AND BRONZE AGE BOAT GALLERY)

A view of Dover harbour showing the high level of congestion which made entry and exit difficult for the Patrol.
(COURTESY OF DOVER MUSEUM AND BRONZE AGE BOAT GALLERY)

A view of Dover harbour. In the foreground is the 'P'-class sloop, *P–52*. According to her pennant, the destroyer in the mid-ground is *Rowena*, which held that pennant from January 1918, but she was with the 15th Destroyer Flotilla in the Grand Fleet all of her service. It is possible that she was visiting, or had been briefly loaned, to Dover. (J MANNERING)

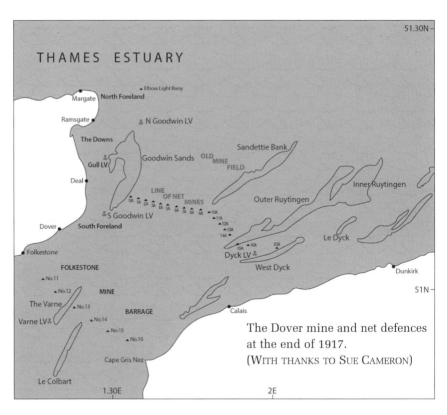

THAMES ESTUARY

51.30N

Elbow Light Buoy
Margate · North Foreland
Ramsgate · N Goodwin LV
The Downs
Gull LV · Goodwin Sands · OLD MINE FIELD · Sandettie Bank
Deal
LINE OF NET MINES · Outer Ruytingen · Inner Ruytingen
6A 6A 6A 6A 6A 6A 7A 6A 6A · 10A
S Goodwin LV · 11A
Dover · South Foreland · 12A · Le Dyck
13A
14A
Folkestone · 15A 16A 20A · Dyck LV
West Dyck · Dunkirk
FOLKESTONE · 51N
No.11
No.12 · MINE · Calais
The Varne · No.13
Varne LV · BARRAGE
No.14
No.15
No.16
Cape Gris Nez
Le Colbart
1.30E · 2E

The Dover mine and net defences
at the end of 1917.
(WITH THANKS TO SUE CAMERON)

A copy of a painting by Charles John de Lacy (1856–1929) of *Vindictive* at
Zeebrugge mole. (ORIGINAL AT THE BRITANNIA ROYAL NAVAL COLLEGE)

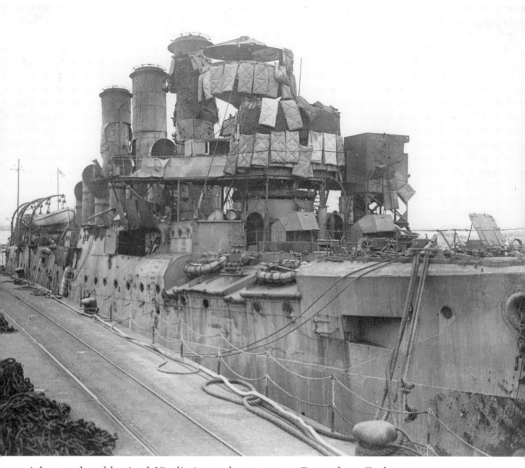

A battered and bruised *Vindictive* on her return to Dover from Zeebrugge.
Note the mattresses used for additional side protection.
(COURTESY OF THE NATIONAL MUSEUM OF THE ROYAL NAVY)

Group photograph
of unknown date:
Commander
Godsal is back
row, second from
right; Lieutenant
Crutchley front,
second left with
pipe. (AUTHOR'S
COLLECTION)

The concrete U-boat pens at Bruges.
(COURTESY OF THE NATIONAL MUSEUM OF THE ROYAL NAVY)

The gap in the Zeebrugge mole caused by the blowing up of *C-3*.
(COURTESY OF THE NATIONAL MUSEUM OF THE ROYAL NAVY)

RN blockships at entrance to canal: *Intrepid, Iphigenia* and *Thetis*.
(COURTESY OF THE NATIONAL MUSEUM OF THE ROYAL NAVY)

A grappling hook used by *Vindictive* at
the Zeebrugge mole, preserved outside
the Maison Dieu in Dover.
(AUTHOR'S COLLECTION)

The River Mersey ferries *Iris* and
Daffodil. (COURTESY OF DOVER
MUSEUM AND BRONZE AGE BOAT
GALLERY)

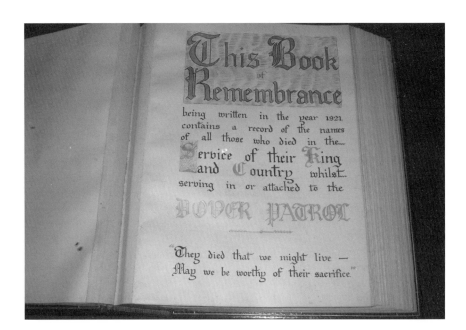

Above: The Book of Remembrance in St Margaret's Church, to the 2,000 men of the Dover Patrol who died between 1914 and 1918 securing the Narrow Sea. (AUTHOR'S COLLECTION)

Right: The dedication ceremony for the Dover Patrol memorial at Leathercote Point, 1921. (COURTESY OF DOVER MUSEUM AND BRONZE AGE BOAT GALLERY)

The motor launch

During the latter part of the year, Bacon began to receive a new type of vessel to help him in these duties, one which would be almost entirely the preserve of the volunteers he praised, the motor launch, or ML. These were of American design and construction, made by the Elco Company of Bayonne, New Jersey, conceived by Elco general manager Henry Sutphen in conjunction with representatives of the Royal Navy, and designed by Elco's chief naval architect Irwin Chase.

They were twin-engine, fast (19 knots), just about seaworthy (they were 'lively' ships), armed with one 3pdr gun (and Type 'D' depth charges when available) and carrying a crew of nine, two RNVR officers, two engineers and five deckhands. They were conceived as anti-submarine vessels, the precursors of the American 'sub-chaser' classes, but found themselves maids of all work, undertaking escort duty, boarding merchant ships, detonating mines and smokescreen laying, amongst many other tasks. Fifty were ordered on 9 April 1915 and a further 500 on 8 June, all of which had been delivered by 3 November 1916. Altogether, the Royal Navy would operate 580 of these little vessels (forty later transferred to the French navy), which were known to their crews as 'Movies' (which had something to do with their liveliness in any sort of sea). Three VCs would be won in these craft by the Dover Patrol, and they became a versatile and flexible part of the Dover Patrol's workforce, operating out of Dover harbour and serviced by depot ships.

The U-boats withdraw

Bacon possibly had time and resources for the number of bombardments conducted in the latter part of the year because of the self-inflicted problems the Germans were experiencing as a result of their unrestricted submarine warfare campaign. It will be recalled that Germany had declared unrestricted submarine warfare on 4 February 1915. Although much maligned at the time, it was not an illogical decision. The international rules pertaining at the time (from various Hague conferences and the unratified Declaration of London of 1907) maintained that merchant ships could not be sunk on sight.

Commerce warfare was planned to be conducted under so-called 'cruiser' or 'prize rules'. These, originally drafted at the Treaty of Paris in 1856 and subsequently re-ratified at the Hague Convention of 1899 and 1907, stated in essence that passenger ships may not be sunk, crews of merchant ships must be placed in safety before their ships can be sunk (lifeboats were not considered a place of safety unless close to land), and only warships and merchant ships that were a threat to the attacker might be sunk without warning. Alternatively, the vessel could be taken by a prize crew to a port where passengers or crew could be discharged and the cargo inspected.

Jacky Fisher saw that submarines would find adherence to prize rules impossible, for a simple practical reason: a submarine could not capture a merchant ship, for it would have no spare manpower to deliver the prize to a neutral port, neither could it take survivors or prisoners, for lack of space. There was nothing a submarine could do except sink her captive.

Hence, when the threat from German surface raiders had been largely eliminated, the German attack on Allied trade could only proceed through submarines, and without adherence to prize rules or convention rulings.

In this decision lay the kernel of a problem, for the German establishment was keen to avoid antagonising neutrals such as Italy and America, in an attempt to keep them out of the war. Thus it was that when on 7 May *U-20* torpedoed RMS *Lusitania*, a passenger liner on the Atlantic run, with the loss of 1,198 passengers and crew – including 128 Americans – the protests of the US government gave some cause for concern in Berlin. President Woodrow Wilson condemned the killing of Americans, stating: 'no warning that an unlawful and inhumane act will be committed can possibly be accepted as an excuse of palliation'.

Next, the liner SS *Arabic,* outward bound from Liverpool to the USA, was sunk on 19 August off the coast of Ireland by *U-24.* Forty-four passengers and crew were lost, including three Americans. This time the American diplomatic protest was so sharp that the Imperial German government felt constrained to act and the German navy was prohibited from attacking liners of any nationality without giving due warning and ensuring the safety of passengers. U-boats were told to use guns only and not to attack liners.

However, stop and search, as now prescribed by 'playing by the rules', was far too dangerous for the U-boats, and exposed the submarines to considerable risk. Thus on 18 September the decision was taken to withdraw them from Atlantic waters altogether and from the Channel in large part.

Nonetheless, during 1915, the Flanders Flotilla had sunk 131 ships for a total tonnage of 90,295 and the loss of only two boats. The U-boats attached to the High Seas Fleet had sunk 390 vessels totalling 700,782 tons, for eleven lost.

Hospital ships and the loss of *Anglia*

The wounded and dying, ferried back from the slaughter of the Western Front by hospital ships, were not spared from the U-boats' depredations. The responsibility for the provision, despatch, protection and unloading of hospital ships fell to the transport division of the Dover Patrol. Their ships were an eclectic collection, as were some of their commanders. Shortly after the war's beginning, the hospital ship 'fleet' comprised SS *St Petersburg* and three Great Western Railway steamers, *St David*, *St Andrew* and *St Patrick*, which had been built between 1906 and 1908 for the Fishguard to Rosslare service.

These were supplemented by three private yachts and a trawler. The yachts had once been glamorous in the extreme. *Liberty*, a beautifully fitted vessel, was owned by Lord Tredegar, Courtenay Charles Evans Morgan. He had only just purchased the vessel and accompanied her to war as her commander. *Grainaigh* was owned by Lord Dunraven, a keen yachtsman, and owner and co-owner of the 1893 and 1895 America's Cup yachts *Valkyrie II* and *Valkyrie III*. He too now skippered his boat at Dover, aged seventy-three, as a lieutenant RNR. The Liberal politician Henry Graham White had contributed *Paulina*, with his brother in command. And the trawler, *Queen Alexandra*, once a Mission to Seamen vessel, was skippered by Captain Sir Charles Chadwick Hardy. Now painted white with yellow funnels, a stripe of green round the sides and with a row of green lights (if assigned to carrying navy casualties they sported a red stripe and red lights) these disparate ships carried men home from (predominantly) Calais and Boulogne.

By early 1915 these vessels had been further supplemented, as a result of high and unexpected casualty levels, by SS *Cambria*, *Dieppe*, *Brighton* and *Newhaven*; shortly they were joined by the French *St Denis* and the Belgian *Stad Antwerpen* and *Jan Breydell*. And in May HMHS *Anglia*, a converted merchant steamer of 1,862grt and previously owned by the London and North Western Railway Company, was added to the 'fleet'. She had gained unlikely prestige on 1 November when she brought the King back from France, where he had been injured whilst reviewing troops; his charger had reared up and fallen, pinning the unfortunate George V underneath it.

On 17 November *Anglia* was bringing home 386 wounded soldiers, following the specially marked-out channel for hospital ships. As per the Geneva Convention, she was identified by a huge red cross, painted white with yellow funnels and a broad green band round her sides. One mile east of Folkestone Gate she struck a mine in the special channel, laid by *UC-5*. Captain Lionel Manning, *Anglia*'s commanding officer, had just gone below for his gloves. When he reappeared on deck, he was blown off the bridge by the force of an explosion and was then appalled to discover that the engine room telegraphs and voice pipes no longer worked and he was unable get the ship to stop; furthermore, the radio room was wrecked and he could not issue an SOS. Down by the head and with the starboard propeller out of the water but still driving her, she would surely sink quickly. Some men managed to get into the lifeboats and the collier *Lusitania,* sailing from London to Lisbon, closed to pick them up, lowering her own boats. But as her boats returned she too hit a mine and exploded, quickly sinking stern first. On board the hospital ship, desperate nurses strapped lifebelts onto wounded men and helped them over the side.

The explosions had been heard in Dover harbour and the old and much abused gunboat *Hazard*, with the River-class (or 'E'-class) destroyer *Ure* in company, steamed out to assist. Lieutenant Commander Henry Percy Boxer, commanding *Ure*, faced a seemingly impossible situation. The hospital ship was going round in circles at 8 knots and sinking at the same time. *Hazard* was too big a vessel to close the stricken hospital ship but, displaying outstanding seamanship, Boxer matched *Anglia*'s evolutions and got near enough for his crew to be able to manhandle many men to safety. Not satisfied with that, and having been forced to haul off, Boxer repeated the manoeuvre. *Hazard* (commanded by the son of Vice Admiral Doveton Sturdee, the victor of the Battle of the Falklands) stood off and attempted to pick survivors out of the water. More vessels set out from Dover to help.

Within fifteen minutes of the explosion, *Anglia* sank. She went down bows first and took 164 men, many badly wounded and in cots below decks, with her. One nurse, Sister Alice Meldrum, later described her experiences:

I personally was in the water about forty minutes before being taken on a destroyer. That would be about the time the majority were in the water. The kindness of the men on the destroyers we shall never forget, their helpfulness was beyond words. Imagine our delight, on reaching Dover, to find many of the patients lying on the Admiralty Pier; they had last been seen floating in the water, and had been picked up by other destroyers. Many were the handshakes, kindly greetings, and expressions of real thankfulness at meeting again on terra firma.

She added that 'it was a never-to-be-forgotten sight to see armless and legless men struggling in the water, very many of whom were eventually saved'.[7] Over a hundred of *Anglia*'s survivors were taken to the County of London War Hospital at Horton, Epsom, from whence Mary, Lady St Helier (a noted society hostess and London County Council alderman) made a public appeal for funds to feed and clothe them.

Manning himself, not having a life preserver, floated on his back in the water until he felt tired (a classic symptom of the onset of death by exposure). He was plucked unconscious from the sea by *Hazard*.

The Folkestone Gate was part of the clearly marked hospital ships' channel. At first it was believed that the U-boat may have mined the area in error. But an announcement from Berlin confirmed that it had been mined deliberately, as the Germans suspected Britain of using hospital ships under false pretences, something emphatically denied by the British government.

For his seamanship and bravery in the rescue attempts, Henry Boxer received an 'Expression of Their Lordship's appreciation for services rendered' in January 1916. And Captain Manning stated, 'I cannot speak too highly in praise of the work of HMS *Hazard* and HMS *Ure*'.

11

Barring the Strait and Difficult Times, 1915–1916

It was believed at the Admiralty that the towed net, indicator net and float systems devised in 1914 and early 1915 to prevent the egress of submarines from the Dover strait were inadequate, and that a more permanent, continuous and solid barrier should be constructed. Work on this project had started under Admiral Hood in April 1915, and it had become Bacon's task on his succession to the post.

The original proposal had been to use buoys and wooden baulks to support heavy harbour defence-type nets which had proved useful in defending harbour entrances. The difference, of course, was that harbour entrances were of limited width – the intention at Dover was to stretch across the whole of the English Channel and down to a depth of 120ft. The job was entrusted by Bacon to one Commander George Bernard Eldridge, who replaced Munro and was clearly a luckless fellow, condemned to work hard at deploying the barrage as envisaged. However, the task transpired to be impossible. The action of the tide caused frequent problems; the wooden baulks would break off, the trailing lines of cable left conspired to wrap around the buoys causing further stress, and as quickly as a new length of barrage was installed, another piece would break up. Bacon went out in a trawler to investigate the situation on the spot and could only agree with Eldridge that the operation was impossible. 'I was forced to report to the Admiralty,' he later wrote, 'that the whole scheme was impracticable, and that the remnants of the boom were becoming a real danger to navigation by strewing the waters of the Channel with vagrant floats and mooring-buoys, some of which fetched up on the coast of Essex and some off Ostend.'[1] Admiral Sir Henry Jackson, Fisher's replacement as First Sea Lord, had to agree and the task was abandoned.

We live from day to day

Bacon and Eldridge may well have been depressed by their problems, but in this they were not alone. The nation's morale was suffering too and voluntary enlistment in the services was well down, particularly in the West Country and in Kent. By the middle of 1915 there was an air of despair over the progress of the war. What had been expected to be a short, sharp shock, 'all over by Christmas', had turned into a war of attrition. In 1914 the British had suffered 90,000 casualties, of whom 50,000 were killed. That effectively wiped out the pre-war British regular army. The year 1915 brought a litany of failure. In March, Neuve Chapelle cost 11,200 British casualties; April and the Second Battle of Ypres 59,275; May saw 11,619 casualties at Aubers Ridge and 16,648 at Festubert, where Sir John French withdrew on the 25th, citing shortage of ammunition and with no gains to set against his not inconsiderable losses. Coupled with the later Battle of Loos (59,247), these encounters caused the loss of most of the pre-war reservists and territorials.

Also, by May it had become clear to the public that the Dardanelles naval campaign had failed. The French were stridently demanding more British troops on the Western Front. Furthermore, the great seas were no longer safe for transit, and no major British naval victory had lifted the inherent threat of the German fleet or the nation's confidence.

And on 28 July, the anniversary of Austro-Hungarian declaration of war against Serbia, Prime Minister Asquith announced to the House of Commons that the British total of men dead, wounded and missing since the war began was 330,995, including 9,000 from the navy.

On 5 May Horace Hood, now commanding Cruiser Force 'E' (11th Cruiser Squadron) off the coast of Ireland, and usually so optimistic, was concerned for the future. That day he had written to Thomas Perkins, the husband of his wife Ellen's best friend in America, asking Perkins to look out for his family if anything happened to him. Perkins replied on the 20th. 'Of course it is useless to dodge the very obvious fact of the risk – all I may say is that you may be sure that I shall do everything I possibly can for Ellen and the children if you get killed.'[2] Hood's family's wellbeing and his own potential mortality were clearly on his mind.

And his chances of survival in his flagship, the ancient cruiser *Juno*, protected rather than armoured, slow when built and slower now, did not appeal to him. 'I don't see how *Juno* can escape [being torpedoed],' he wrote.[3] Referring to the *Lusitania* sinking, he noted 'it was just murder'.[4]

Hood's mood did not change with his transfer to the 3rd Battlecruiser Squadron. In August he wrote criticising the pre-war peace movement politicians who 'knew Germany was preparing for war',[5] but failed to build the necessary ships or prepare the people. 'Spies and enemy aliens still flourish in Great Britain,' he added, 'I think we shall get a very bitter lesson.' And again he worried about his own fate as well as that of the country. 'I am concerned that we must win and if we don't I shall not see it ... We live from day to day'.[6] He saw no merit in the political leadership of the country either, undermined as it was by continued losses of men, a shell shortage scandal that rocked the country and the failure of the Gallipoli adventure. 'In such circumstance an autocratic, patriotic [person] must rule the world.'[7]

Commander W B Forbes was likewise concerned. After joining the Dover Patrol from the Gallipoli campaign, on 31 July 1915 he wrote in a letter home: 'this is nearly the end of a year of war and things look black for our great Cause and it's no use running away from the facts; better that it all be known and then those worth their salt will come and do their bit when the worst is put before them.'[8]

Others were more sanguine. Writing in the *Daily Telegraph* of 3 August, the naval correspondent Archibald Hurd was relentlessly upbeat:

> This [unrestricted submarine] campaign was initiated with the fixed determination, publically and officially proclaimed, of 'starving England'. Has England starved? Has our intercourse with the markets of the world been interrupted? Have we suffered serious losses? A number of ships have been sunk and over 500 merchant seamen have been done to death. But has our ability to fight the enemy been reduced? That is the only test.[9]

One reason for the mood of depression among civilians was the frequent and largely unopposed Zeppelin night-time bombing attacks on English soil during the latter part of 1915, seemingly without opposition. This led to a most curious use of the monitors. Between December 1915 and January 1916, all the Dover Patrol's monitors were ordered to the Thames Estuary to shoot at Zeppelins.

The smaller vessels used their searchlights to illuminate the airborne intruders and the larger ships fired shrapnel from their big guns at maximum elevation, hoping that the falling lead shot might puncture the dirigibles' skin. The operation was not a success.

King George V's choice of Christmas card, announced in November, seemed, perhaps inadvertently, to capture the prevailing mood. It depicted *Revenge* under Sir Richard Grenville fighting the whole Spanish fleet at the Battle of Flores in 1591. Brave, gallant, unyielding, but he lost. Was the King worried too?

Nets off the Flanders coast and a monitor saves the day

By March 1916, the Germans had ended their self-imposed exile from the English Channel. U-boats again sailed from Zeebrugge and Ostend and increasingly found that they could readily pass through the barrage, with many even coasting along the surface of the Channel under cover of darkness.

In an attempt to curtail the submarine menace, an operation was conceived and approved in early 1916 to lay a coastal mine and net barrage off the Belgian coast, between Nieuwpoort and the entrance to the River Scheldt, aimed at restricting the movements of the Flanders U-boat minelayers. A significant force was put together, including six divisions of net drifters (to lay the nets), four large minesweepers (to clear the passage in and out) and escorting destroyers, six minelaying trawlers, two monitors (to provide a diversionary bombardment), with the addition of a division of Harwich Force destroyers and the Flanders coast patrol from Dunkirk. The ships were in place by 0400 on 24 April, and by 0730 had laid a fifteen-mile double-line of mines and thirteen miles of mined nets, 5,077 mines in total, twelve miles off the coastline. No small achievement.

War makes enemies of friends, however. The Admiralty drifter *Clover Bank* was an Aberdeen-registered boat, hired by the Admiralty in January 1915 and inspected by the King during his visit to Dover in the same year. She was skippered by Alonzo Strowger RNR, with a crew of seventeen. Owing to an error of placement, a line of nets which should have been laid seaward of a line of mines had been positioned on the shoreward side. After fulfilling her net-laying tasks, *Clover Bank* sailed the wrong way, detonated a newly laid British mine and blew up off Zeebrugge. Her skipper and all the crew were killed. Accident, miscalculation or stupidity, the result was all the same. Eighteen reservists died, a long way from home.

There now broke out a nasty little destroyer action. The minelayers had returned to port, but the drifters and supporting ships were required to keep a watch over the newly laid nets. Here, the force was attacked by German aircraft without result. But at about 1445, three German destroyers came out of Zeebrugge to offer battle.

The British escorting destroyers *Medea*, *Murray* (which had the slight distinction of being commanded by naval author 'Taffrail', otherwise Captain Taprell Dorling*), *Melpomene* and *Milne* engaged them, but came too close to the shore and were all taken under fire and hit by German shore batteries. *Murray* was struck on the forecastle by a 6in shell which passed through the ship's side, luckily without exploding, but she was able to clear danger with the help of a smokescreen by about 1550.

Melpomene (built originally for the Greek navy and, ironically, named for the muse of tragedy) was hit at about 1540 by one of the 4.1in shells fired by the German destroyers, a shell which ricocheted into her without exploding, but flooded the engine room, and she lost way. *Milne* took her in tow, but then tangled the towing cable in one of her own propellers. *Murray* went ahead through the mined nets, followed by the now limping *Melpomene* with *Milne* on her port side and *Medea* to starboard, offering both protection and motive power to their stricken sister. Seeing an easy prize, the German destroyers came out from under the shelter of their shore batteries and closed to 8,000yds, at which point *Murray* dropped back to lay smoke to cover the retreat of her brethren.

At this critical point, the brave and dangerous (given her slow speed and lack of manoeuvrability) intervention of the monitor *Prince Eugene* settled the case. Her commander, Captain Ernest Wigram DSO, a veteran of the Falklands and Gallipoli campaigns, opened fire on the German destroyers with her twin 12in guns, massive artillery which would utterly destroy the enemy vessels if her shells hit home. The German vessels turned and ran for home.

Once more the shore batteries opened fire, and *Medea* was struck by one shell on the quarterdeck, a second close to her funnels, and

---

* Author of, among other things, *Endless Story, Being an Account of the Work of the Destroyers, Flotilla Leaders, Torpedo Boats and Patrol Boats*, written in 1932.

then by a third, but continued at full speed, and all the ships were clear after about six minutes under fire. *Medea* lost two men. *Milne* went into the floating dock in Dover to have the cable unwound from her port propeller, *Murray* received a temporary patch on her bow until her next refit, *Medea* went to Chatham for repairs, and *Melpomene* was dry-docked in Dunkirk to be patched up before sailing for a full English dockyard repair job. The navy could ill afford to lose so many ships from service at the same time.[*]

This was not quite the end of the incident, however, for the following day the Lowestoft registered drifter *Au Fait*, under skipper Arthur Bridge RNR, was attending to the new net barrage when three German torpedo boats burst out of the early morning mist to shoot up the supporting buoys. The drifters (the 9th Drifter Division) were chased off to the north and ordered to scatter. But *Au Fait* had been hit several times and fell behind; the chasing pack captured her, took off the crew and sank the boat. All the crew survived to become prisoners of war for the duration.

A new barrage

Throughout the spring of 1916 there was a spirited debate between the higher echelons of the German High Command and the diplomats around Chancellor Hollweg as to the desirability of restarting unrestricted submarine warfare, given the probability of such a move offending neutral, and especially American, opinion. The Imperial Navy was agreed on the necessity and general principle of restarting the U-boat campaign but they were, for the moment, unable to make their views prevail. In a fit of pique, on 24 April Admiral Scheer recalled all his submarines from the trade routes and refused to allow them to carry on commerce raiding whilst constrained by prize rules.

This withdrawal coincided, of course, with the laying by the Dover Patrol in April of a new and continuous explosive net and mine barrier off the Belgian coast (see above). With the temporary cessation of U-boat activity, Bacon drew the unfortunate conclusion that his barrier had worked and immediately began to plan and execute a new and similar barrier across the Dover Strait. As Churchill later put it, 'an immediate diminution of losses to merchant ships and U-boat activity followed', but the apparent

---

[*] Attention at home was distracted – this was the same day as the Easter Rising in Dublin.

success was due to Scheer's frustrated withdrawal of U-boats from the commerce campaign, rather than Bacon's mine barrage.[10]

It was clear to the admiral that such a barrier could only be built if it was of a much lighter construction than the first attempt. As his model, he therefore took the barrage which had been laid in 60ft of water off the ex-Belgian ports, which used much lighter mesh materials and which he had incorrectly deduced worked perfectly. Additionally, Bacon proposed that the proper position for the barrage was between the Goodwin Sands and the opposite coast at Snouw Bank. The distance between the Goodwins and the French coast was longer than between Folkestone and Gris-Nez; the maximum depth of water was about the same; the tides were approximately equal in strength. This more easterly position was probably more difficult to defend, but had the advantage of protecting the coastal routes to the Downs and to Dunkirk as well.

It proved absolutely impossible to use nets of anything approaching 120ft in depth because of the severe strain brought on the clips by the tide. Nets 80ft deep were tried, but had to be abandoned; 60ft net depth proved possible on the less strong tides, 40ft in the stronger. In the localities where the tide ran with strength, vertical wire uprights with mines, but without nets, had to be used. Every 500yds along the line there was a buoy, each of which was numbered. To compensate for the lack of depth of the barrier, Bacon filled in the gap below the nets with a mine barrage. The entire span was complete by the end of the year.

The drifters were the key to this enterprise. They deployed, maintained and repaired the system. New sections were always required to replace old ones; and every day, summer and winter, when the sea and tide allowed, old sections were taken in and new ones laid out. It became a wall of nets, moorings, and batteries (to power the mines), in length equivalent to the distance between Windsor and London.

The drifters, small trawlers designed to catch herring in a drift net, steam-powered with an auxiliary sail, were an important part of the Dover Patrol's armoury – or un-armoury, as they were seldom armed with much more than a rifle or two or a 3pdr gun. The first of them had arrived at Dover in January 1915 under the overall command of Captain Humphrey Bowring; Bowring then became Bacon's chief of staff and was replaced by the unvaryingly cheerful Captain F G Bird, an RNR officer who exercised his command from the drifter *East Briton*. By June the drifter patrol had reached its maximum strength thus far of 132 drifters and three yachts, manned by upwards of 1,500 officers and men, all bar a dozen of them volunteers, new to the navy in the preceding six months.

Not all of them were based at Dover; there were also some thirty or so armed drifters which were harboured at Ramsgate. Here they served four days at sea then two days in harbour, turn and turnabout, under the command of a naval officer who reported to the senior naval officer for the port. For four weeks in the summer of 1915, the officer in charge of the Ramsgate drifters was a remarkable sailor – remarkable because he was the oldest operational serving officer in the navy.

William Balfour Forbes was born in 1845, the son of Arthur Forbes-Gordon of Rayne, and retired from the navy in 1888. He volunteered for service at the outbreak of war, aged seventy, was commissioned with the rank of commander and given charge of a dummy battleship which, when torpedoed off Mudros, had success-fully completed its intended function.

Forbes was then appointed to the Ramsgate drifter command, having received 'Their Lordship's appreciation' for his efforts abroad, and took up his position on 8 July. On 12 August he retired as a result of a sudden and serious illness and returned to his home in County Carlow. The Admiralty advanced him to the rank of captain on the retired list in recognition of his service.

But despite the presence of so many auxiliary vessels at Dover and elsewhere, there were many issues. Bacon himself wrote:

Troubles of a grave nature were encountered. In the first place, the buoys dragged their moorings in south-westerly gales, with a strong east-going tide. This was overcome by using larger chains at the anchors and light pendants to the buoys, but at times the task seemed almost hopeless. Nothing but the cheery energy of Captain Bird and the dogged pluck of the drifter crews enabled the Barrage to be maintained. Chafe of the chains in the trunk of the buoys gave trouble. This was got over by fitting filling-pieces in the trunks to steady the chain and prevent chafe. The clips broke, the electric circuits chafed and made earth, the battery boxes leaked – in fact, every item gave trouble, but by steady plodding the whole was rendered fairly efficient.[11]

At night the barrier was lit by light buoys every three miles (which, it transpired, the Germans used as navigation beacons).

The nets worked by ensnaring a submarine in the mesh. Each was held lightly by steel clips in a frame of flexible wire rope. Incorporated into each net were two mines, which were powered from a battery moored in a convenient separate receptacle. When a submarine struck the net the clips broke, and the net was carried on by the submarine's forward movement. The stream lines of the water forced the net close to the submarine, and the mine was drawn against the U-boat's side and an explosion caused.

But the reality was that the barrage was by no means impassable, not least on account of the unreliability of the available mines (see above). Further, the nets had been laid in an uneven pattern, which allowed gaps through which a U-boat could weave its way. Bird himself thought that it was only ever 25 per cent efficient. Nor was the area patrolled as often as was necessary, owing to a shortage of available destroyers or other patrol craft, and competing demands on their usage. The navy was stretched everywhere and the perception was beginning to form in the minds of serving men and public alike that the war was not necessarily running in the Allies' favour.

Whilst he recognised the limitations of the system, Bacon was convinced that the barrage was working: that this was misguided is shown by the fact that towards the end of 1916 about 300,000 tons of shipping was being destroyed monthly in the North Atlantic.

Additionally, the Germans regularly attempted to disrupt or destroy parts of the barrage system. Explosive bullets were fired at the buoys, cutters were used to sever the net supports and the drifters were often attacked by German destroyers or torpedo boats. And if it wasn't the German destroyers that were a menace to the men and ships of the Dover Patrol, it was her minelaying submarines.

On the Defensive: Minesweeping and the First Battle of the Dover Strait, 1916

The Germans continued to sow mines in the Channel, both in new fields and singly, through the activities of their *UC-I* minelaying submarines, now supplemented by the highly successful *UC-II* type. These carried eighteen mines in six minelaying tubes, and an 88mm deck gun, as well as a complement of torpedoes. They laid their mines in the North Sea and the Channel with relative impunity.

On 29 January 1916 HMS *Zulu* was on patrol when she saw a sudden and huge column of black smoke. John Brooke, her captain, took her at full speed to investigate and found *Viking* in flames and with her after section glowing red. She had hit a mine. Two of her four officers were dead, the captain (Commander Thomas C H Williams) and a sub lieutenant, and another, the gunner, badly wounded. Eight ratings had also been killed and another seven wounded. *Zulu* took her in tow and with great difficulty got her charge to harbour. Sub Lieutenant Harold Courtenay Tennyson, who was the youngest son of the 2nd Baron Tennyson and the grandson of the poet and laureate, had only joined *Viking* on 9 November the previous year, having gained his single stripe two months earlier. He died aged nineteen. He was, noted *The Times*, 'a high minded and capable officer who had a strong literary instinct inherited from his grandfather'.[1] But mines treated all alike.

On 27 February the P&O liner *Maloja*, 12,431grt, was outbound for India with 122 passengers and a crew of 301 officers and men, when she was mined on her starboard quarter within two miles of the entrance to Dover harbour. She had run into a new minefield laid by *UC-6*. Immediately afterwards, the Canadian vessel *Empress of Fort William*, bound for Dunkirk with a cargo of Tyne coal, was mined going to her assistance. The liner sank in twenty-four minutes, the *Empress* in forty.

As a precaution against enemy attack, *Maloja* had been steaming with her lifeboats already swung out on their davits so that they could be lowered more quickly. When the explosion occurred her master, Captain C D Irving RNR, immediately had her engines put astern to take off her forward motion and stop the vessel so that her boats could be lowered. He also sounded her whistle as a signal to prepare to abandon ship. But her engine room was flooded and the engines proved impossible to control; once moving backwards, she continued to go astern at 8 knots and also developed a list to starboard. The combination of these factors ruled out the launching of the starboard lifeboats.

Many small vessels headed out of Dover harbour to help her, including the two Port of Dover tugs *Lady Brassey* and *Lady Crundall*, the Admiralty trawler *Lord Minto*, dredgers and a destroyer. But as *Maloja* was still steaming astern and unable to stop, the rescue vessels could not get alongside to take off survivors. A heavy sea was running and the hundreds who crowded her decks could only put on a simple lifejacket, jump overboard and try to swim clear. The waters were bitterly cold and many who took this route died of exposure. They were mainly the Lascar (sailors from Asian or Arab countries) crew.[*]

The rescuing boats pulled people from the sea and took many of the survivors to the hospital ships *Dieppe* and *St David*. Others were brought ashore and Royal Navy ambulances took them to the Lord Warden Hotel before being transported to London by a special train.

From about 1130 the dead began to come ashore. The chief constable of Kent took charge of the bodies and made the Market Hall a temporary mortuary. Forty-five bodies had been recovered, but over a hundred people were unaccounted for. 'The crew behaved splendidly,'[2] said Captain Irving; this did not prevent many of them losing their lives. But as tradition would befit, Irving was the last man to leave the ship and was in the waters for thirty minutes before rescue. When the reckoning was complete, 155 lives had been lost, including four children aged three, five, six and eight.

---

[*] P&O later erected a monument to twenty-two of the Lascars in the cemetery of St Mary the Virgin, Dover.

The next day *Lord Minto* and the Grimsby-registered hired trawler *Angelus* left Dover harbour at 0550 to attempt to find and clear the minefield. They did not have to wait long to do so, for at 0740 *Lord Minto* caught a mine in her sweep in the harbour's western entrance. Having exploded it, she caught another, entangled in her kite, at 0845; this mine detonated and carried away the kite, forcing the trawler to return to Dover to fit a new one. By 1430 she was back sweeping again, once more in partnership with *Angelus*. Around 1715 both vessels took in their sweeps, but as *Angelus* was doing so she hit a mine. She began to settle very quickly. *Lord Minto*'s skipper slipped his sweep and launched his small lifeboat, towing it into position to pick up the survivors. He saved six men, one badly scalded, and landed them ninety-five minutes later at Prince of Wales pier. *Angelus* lost two men, her skipper Richard Saunders and deckhand John Boyle, both RNR. That same day and sweeping the same minefield, the Milford Haven-registered trawler *Weigelia* was lost to a mine. Trimmer John Thompson RNR was killed. And the field claimed yet another victim that day, when a Dutch steamer foundered after being mined.

February and March 1916 were bad months for the Patrol's minesweeping trawlers. On 21 February the Grimsby trawler *Carlton* was lost to a mine off Folkestone; on 4 March the Hull-registered *Flicker* was sunk just outside Dover harbour with the loss of all fourteen of her crew; and on the 28th *Saxon Prince*, from North Shields and with a crew of twelve, disappeared forever during a storm in the Strait.

Minesweeping was essential to keep the seaway free for both trade and supply to the Western Front and the trawlers were in the thick of it. Clearly, it was also extremely dangerous. One such minesweeping trawler was *Corona* and her story is typical of the many. She was a modern Grimsby-based trawler built by the Dundee Shipbuilding Company in 1912 (the same company that had built Scott's *Discovery*), and operated by the Grimsby and North Sea Fishing Company under the registration number GY684.

For just over two years she had plied her trade as a fishing vessel before she was requisitioned by the Admiralty in February 1915. To a man, her crew were taken into the Royal Naval Reserve (RNR), the vessel itself was fitted with two guns, a 3pdr and a 6pdr, and given the new identity of Her Majesty's Trawler (HMT) 1137. Now her job was sweeping mines, not hunting fish. An RNR lieutenant, James

Irvine, was appointed to command her, and her previous skipper, Frank Thornton, stayed on as second in command.

On 23 March 1916 *Corona* was minesweeping in the Dover Strait, off Ramsgate, when – in an occupational risk of her new trade – she hit a mine. She sank quickly and took all thirteen of her crew with her. One moment they had been fishermen, the next they were the first line of defence of the Channel supply chain, and soon after they were dead. Amongst the dead were her two engineers, trapped in the engine room, one of whom, George Allbones, transpired on later investigation to have been a bigamist, no doubt giving the paymaster's department a problem. *Corona*'s story was by no means unusual in this war of attrition in the Narrow Sea.

The mines had again been laid by *UC-6*, commanded by Matthias, Graf von Schmettow. He profited little from it, however, as the Dover Patrol extracted its revenge the following May, when his boat became entangled in one of the nets off North Foreland and triggered a mine which sank it, taking all sixteen crew to the bottom of the English Channel.

Although the German U-boats had been effectively prohibited from attacking Allied passenger vessels in the area around the UK since September 1915, the Germans announced a new campaign on 11 February 1916, in which enemy merchantmen within the war zone would be considered as fair game. Outside of this area, they could only be sunk without the application of international rules if armed, and passenger liners were not to be interfered with in any way. The effects of this intensified campaign would soon be felt – by the German government.

On 24 March 1916 ss *Sussex*, the regular cross-channel packet between Folkestone and Dieppe, was torpedoed by *UB-29*. The entire bow forward of the bridge was blown off. Some of the lifeboats were launched, but at least two of them capsized and many passengers were drowned. The Dover destroyer *Afridi*, with her captain Lieutenant Commander Percy Percival showing magnificent seamanship, placed herself alongside and took on board all who could make it, but of the fifty-three crew and 325 passengers, at least fifty were killed. She remained afloat long enough to be eventually towed stern-first into Boulogne harbour and beached.

Amongst her dead were the Spanish composer Enrique Granados and his wife Amparo. Granados, in a lifeboat, saw his wife struggling in the water and jumped in to help her. Neither were seen again. Several Americans were injured, although no US citizens were killed. Nonetheless, following on as it did from the *Arabic* and *Lusitania* affairs, and given that the German ambassador to the USA was providing assurances that passenger vessels would be spared henceforth, the incident inflamed public opinion in America. The subsequent heated diplomatic exchanges between the US and German governments during May 1916 led to Germany issuing a declaration, the so-called *Sussex* pledge. The key elements of this undertaking were that passenger ships would not be targeted; merchant ships would not be sunk until the presence of weapons had been established, if necessary by a search of the ship; and merchant ships would not be sunk without provision for the safety of passengers and crew. It effectively represented the suspension, once again, of the unrestricted U-boat campaign and led to the eventual suspension of U-boat activity in the Strait (see Chapter 11).

Despite the losses and problems he faced, Bacon seemed pleased with his performance so far. In a despatch of May 1916 he noted:

> Over 21,000 Merchant Ships, apart from Men-of-War and Auxiliaries, have passed through this Patrol in the last six months. Of these twenty-one have been lost or have been seriously damaged by the enemy. The losses in Merchant Vessels, therefore, have been less than one per thousand. On the other hand, to effect this very considerable security to our Merchant Shipping I regret that over four per cent of our Patrol Vessels have been sunk and the lives of seventy-seven officers and men lost to the Nation. No figures could emphasise more thoroughly the sacrifice made by the personnel of the Patrol and the relative immunity ensured to the commerce of their country.[3]

He might have been less pleased had he known that the total operational number of submarines available to the Flanders Flotilla was only four in October 1915 and the same in November. By March 1916 it was still only seven.

The year of 1916 was good for Bacon personally. On 1 January he had been appointed an Additional Member of the Second Class, or Knight Commander, in the Military Division of the Most Honourable Order of the Bath (KCB) and hence became Sir Reginald; and on 15 August he was appointed a Knight Commander in the Royal Victorian Order (KCVO).

He may have been less pleased, however, to have incurred the wrath of the implacable Margot Asquith, wife of the prime minister, outspoken socialite and the 'spur to his [the prime minister's] ambition'. Asquith, with some of his senior ministers, primarily McKenna (Chancellor of the Exchequer), Isaacs (Lord Chief Justice), Cunliffe (Governor of the Bank of England) and Montagu (Minister of Munitions), together with Colonel Maurice Hankey (secretary to the Imperial War Cabinet), sailed to Calais on 24 August 1916 to confer with President Briand over British ongoing financial support for France and the war effort. They travelled on an unescorted ship and on their return were held outside Dover harbour from midnight for three-quarters of an hour, as standing orders forbade entry to the harbour at night for an unescorted ship.

Margot was incensed on her husband's behalf. 'The Germans would have had a rich bag if Henry's ship had been torpedoed,' she confided to her diary and added that, 'Admiral Bacon behaved like a perfect fool'. Hankey wrote a note of protest to the Admiralty.[4]

P-boats

Admiral Bacon was always asking for more ships and during 1916 a new class of vessel, P-boats or patrol boats, began to reach the Dover Patrol. They were a sort of coastal sloop, designed to replace destroyers in coastal operations. Twin screws, a large rudder area and a very low freeboard gave them a small and fast turning circle, and with ram bows of hardened steel they were primarily designed to attack submarines. Indeed, a resemblance to large submarines had been deliberately designed in to give the boats a chance to close the range and sink a German U-boat by ramming or gunfire. A low, sharply cut-away funnel added to that impression.

They carried a crew of fifty, could exceed 21 knots and were armed with one 4in gun, one 40mm anti-aircraft weapon and two 14in torpedo tubes, taken from older torpedo boats. Twenty-four ships of this design had been ordered in May 1915 and another thirty between February and June 1916, although ten of this latter batch were altered in December before launch for use as Q-ships (ships which looked like an unarmed merchantman to lure U-boats to the surface, but which carried concealed weapons) and were renumbered as 'PC'-class sloops. Eighteen shipyards were involved in building them and they supplemented the navy's larger Flower-class sloops.

It had been intended that they would be supplied to the Dover Patrol to enhance its anti-submarine resources, but in fact most of them were taken by Jellicoe for use as minesweepers with the Grand Fleet. As Chief of the Admiralty War Staff Henry Oliver confided in his memoirs, 'as soon as I got a sloop to hunt submarines, Jellicoe would want it'.[5] The Dover Patrol had only five by January 1917, rising to six, twelve months later. One was *P-23*, which served with the Patrol from June 1916 for the rest of the war, under the command of Lieutenant John Morrison Smith. She had been built in Sunderland by Bartram's and owner William Bartram continued to be interested in her progress. When she got a piece of net around her port propeller and bent her turbine blades, Bartram hurried down to London to where the boat was docked at Limehouse to see if he could assist. There, Lieutenant Smith declared that *P-23* was the best boat at Dover because she had less vibration than the other P-boats and that her engine room arrangements and cabins were better. This must have delighted Bartram because he recorded the remarks in his diary entry for 22 August 1916.[*]

The First Battle of the Dover Strait
Following the Battle of Jutland on 31 May 1916, the German High Seas Fleet was confined to port by orders and necessity. As an American journalist had written, the German fleet had 'assaulted its gaoler but remains in jail.' This lack of activity, and a desire to damage the Dover Barrage, thus easing the passage of U-boats, led the German navy to transfer two full flotillas of destroyers and torpedo boats from the High Seas Fleet to the Flanders Flotilla.

The units so assigned were the 3rd Flotilla, which comprised the 5th and 6th Half-Flotillas, thirteen vessels in total, generally mounting 4.1in guns and six torpedo tubes; and the 9th Flotilla, which was composed of the 17th and 18th Half-Flotillas, eleven vessels armed with three 4.1in guns or three 22pdrs, and six torpedo tubes. Up until that point, there had been little enemy activity near the barrage of the Belgian coast for some time, in part because the Flanders Flotilla had limited surface capacity. Now the balance of power was changed. It was estimated that by July the Germans had twenty-two destroyers in the Flanders flotillas, half of them of the newest types.

---

[*] A scale model of this vessel can be seen at Tyne and Wear Museums (Discovery Museum) and the diary of William Bartram is in their archives.

The Admiralty gained knowledge of the concentrations and warned Bacon, but his problem was that he did not have the resources to be strong everywhere. He decided that such forces that he possessed should be concentrated around the Downs, the area where shipping carrying supplies into the Port of London assembled. This, it seemed to him, was the most likely target. He was reinforced by ships from the Harwich Patrol, but took little care to alert the vessels maintaining the Dover Barrage of the possibility of action.

The expected strike came in late October. Under the command of Kapitän Andreas Michelsen, the commodore of the High Seas Fleet flotillas, the German forces split into five groups, all ordered to attack, not in the Downs, but at various points along the Dover Barrage itself and against the transport line between England and France. From now on, confusion reigned.

Their first victim was the empty transport vessel *Queen*, the same ship that had rescued the survivors of the sinking of *Amiral Ganteaume* in October 1914 and was now carrying nothing more lethal than the cross-channel mails. German destroyers steamed rapidly up on each side of the ship and stopped her. An officer came on board and allowed the captain and the crew to get into the boats, whereupon *Queen* was sunk by gunfire.

Queen had been observed, as had the German destroyers, by the hospital ships *Jan Breydel* and *St Denis* in transit between England and France. Neither reported the presence of the enemy forces because they were bound to take no warlike part under the Hague Convention part X of 1907. Article four outlined the restrictions for a hospital ship:

> The ship should give medical assistance to wounded personnel of all nationalities; the ship must not be used for any military purpose; ships must not interfere or hamper enemy combatant vessels; belligerents as designated by the Hague Convention can search any hospital ship to investigate violations of the above restrictions.

So they kept quiet and neither did the Germans molest them. This was not always the Germans' behaviour; at least sixteen British and Commonwealth-flagged hospital ships were sunk in the war by mine and U-boat torpedo.

The German 5th Half-Flotilla sailed to the Dover Barrage and soon came into contact with the drifters of the 10th Drifter Division tending the anti-submarine nets. This comprised five boats, under the command of *Paradox*. Just after 2200 on 26 October, the leading drifters sighted a number of destroyers. These strangers did not answer the challenge and the drifter captains fired rifles at them. The leading destroyers took no notice and passed on, but those in the rear switched on searchlights and opened fire. The drifters *Spotless Prince*, *Datum* and *Gleaner of the Sea* sank at once, *Waveney II* was damaged and set on fire, but *Paradox* escaped and made off to the northwest.

The drifters' escort was the old destroyer *Flirt*, launched in 1897 and armed with one 12pdr and five 6pdr guns, plus two torpedo tubes. She had, in fact, already sighted some of the enemy forces, but in the darkness mistook them for Allied ships. On hearing the firing, her commander, Lieutenant Richard P Kellett, turned her back to the sound of the guns and found his drifters on fire or sunk. Again believing the destroyers to be friendly, he flashed a recognition signal which they repeated back. Seeing men in the water, Kellett stopped, and lowered a boat. Just as the boat got clear of the ship, the Germans opened a heavy fire on *Flirt* and, hit multiple times, she sank in only a few minutes, taking all on board with her; only the men in the rescue boat and their officer escaped with their lives. After sinking *Flirt*, the Germans continued to attack the barrage, sinking two more drifters from the 8th and 16th Drifter Divisions before they withdrew.

Commander W H Owen RNR, commanding the armed yacht *Ombra** was the first to give the alarm. He was somewhere near no. 11A buoy when the 10th Drifter Division was attacked; and as soon as he sighted gun flashes to the west of him, he reported by wireless that enemy warships were twenty miles east of Dover. Bacon immediately ordered the Tribal-class destroyers *Viking*, *Mohawk*, *Tartar*, *Nubian*, *Cossack* and *Amazon* to slip and proceed in haste to the barrage line. This they did at 2250.

If a credulous simplicity had done for the *Flirt*, then a similarly crass ignoring of standard naval procedure would sink and injure other British forces. Instead of keeping his Tribals concentrated,

---

* *Ombra* was once owned by the Anglo-German bankers, Baron John Henry William Schroder and Baron Bruno Schroder, of the eponymous banking firm.

Commander Henry G L Oliphant, the senior officer and in *Viking*, split his forces into two. As a result, *Nubian*, *Amazon* and *Cossack* ran separately into the whole German 17th and 18th Half-Flotillas. *Nubian* had been out in front and she it was who made first contact at 0021. Commander Montague Bernard, her captain, again thought that the destroyers she saw were friendly. Accordingly, he challenged by light and put his helm over to avoid them. A moment later the 17th Half-Flotilla passed along his port side and poured a heavy and destructive fire into him. Hardly a shot missed, but bravely Bernard turned to try and ram the last vessel in the enemy's line. His luck was out; a torpedo struck under *Nubian*'s fore-bridge and blew the bows off his ship. The fires of the vessel's funeral pyre made a beacon in the centre of the Strait, marking the battle for all to see.

Amazon's commanding officer must have sighted the gun flashes of *Nubian*'s action, and heard the firing, but because Oliphant had not concentrated his forces, his commanders had, of necessity, to identify every vessel they met in case they fired on a friendly ship. Thus *Amazon*, on reaching German destroyers at 0045 and finding them firing on him, still believed them to be British and signalled with recognition lights. *Amazon*'s torpedo operator actually had his sights on a German vessel and was about to fire, but was ordered not to as 'the captain says they are ours'.[6] The Germans sailed past *Amazon* at 30yds range, each firing as they went.

Officers' cook W G Evans had been in his hammock when *Amazon* proceeded to sea at speed. He had quickly run to his action station, which was in the after magazine flat serving ammunition to the aft gun. As his ship came under attack he heard the aft gun fire, but then there was a sudden explosion above him. An enemy shell had scored a direct hit on the gun platform overhead, killing or wounding the gun crew and causing flaming cordite to be blown into the magazine flat, which set a fire to flare up in the magazine itself. This was the sort of incident which could spell disaster, as it had for the British battlecruisers at Jutland earlier in the year. Evans didn't hesitate. 'I leapt up from the shell room into the flat, jumping and stamping,' he wrote. 'In the smoke and dim light from a small blue lamp I could see two bodies motionless on the deck.'[7] He stamped at the burning cordite and shouted at the top of his voice, 'Magazine flat on fire.' And in return heard a lone voice, which he recognised as one of the gun crew, retort, 'Put it out you silly beggar,' which, as

Evans later put it, 'I was trying to do'.[8] Eventually, the stokers' fire party arrived and finished the job. They were swiftly followed by the first lieutenant, himself wounded, bleeding and with his binoculars case shot to ribbons by shrapnel. After assessing that Evans was uninjured, he said, 'I'll see what I can do for you'.[9] The following day Evans discovered that, despite the first lieutenant being taken off to hospital, he had been mentioned in the captain's report and recommended for the Distinguished Service Medal (DSM).

In fact, a total of three shells had found their mark on *Amazon*, two exploding in the after boiler room and one destroying the aft gun. The trawler *H E Stroud*, still in the area, was also hit and her skipper, Lieutenant James Richard McClorry RNR, killed. The destroyer *Swift* later put her doctor on board to tend to three wounded crewmen, and another who died of 'illness'.

The German 17th Half-Flotilla had now completed a successful night's work, but the 18th was near at hand and eager for action. *Viking*, *Mohawk* and *Tartar* were approaching them and, amazingly, Oliphant in *Viking* hesitated over their identification. He challenged them – and they crossed his bows and opened fire, then passed down his starboard side, firing as they went. *Mohawk* was badly damaged and fell out of line. *Viking* fired one shot from her forward 4in gun, which then jammed. With this, the action effectively ended.

Nubian was lying disabled near 5A buoy. At 0100 she was sighted and taken in tow, stern first as she had no forepart. But the weather conditions worsened and the tow parted. She started to drift uncontrollably towards the shore between the South Foreland and St Margaret's Bay. Seas were sweeping over her, and it was clear that without some divine intervention her crew were probably doomed. Fortunately, a hero was to hand. Whilst *Nubian* was drifting helplessly towards the shore, and in rising sweeping tides, Thomas William Smith, master of the tug *William Gray*, steered his ship alongside and took off the wounded. It was a remarkable piece of seamanship, both brave and skilful; when he placed himself alongside *Nubian*, the two vessels were only about 100yds from the shore.

British losses were one destroyer and six naval drifters sunk, three destroyers, a naval trawler and three drifters damaged. *Flirt* had sixty dead with only nine survivors, *Amazon* five dead, *Nubian* fifteen dead and six wounded, *Mohawk* four dead; thirty-seven RNR sailors died, nearly all of them fishermen until the war had supervened. The Germans sustained no losses. It had not been a good night for the Royal Navy.

Amazon was taken into Chatham for repairs. A female dockyard worker looked her over and, according to Evans, said, 'Cor lummee, ain't they copped it'.[10]

Bacon supported the performance of his captains in his official report. But the Admiralty begged to differ. Courts of inquiry upon the losses were convened at Dover the following month and the conduct of the various divisions involved considered. The Tribals were criticised for a failure to concentrate; Bacon demurred.

There was a sort of happy ending, though. The German forces were soon reduced by being returned to the High Seas Fleet; and Bacon was reinforced, it being recognised that his destroyer numbers were inadequate for the tasks set, by three divisions of destroyers from the Harwich Force – a decision that did nothing to improve relations between its commander, Tyrwhitt, and Admiral Bacon, between whom there was already bad blood. On occasion, destroyers of the Harwich Force had been seconded to the Dover Patrol as a temporary measure and Tyrwhitt frequently complained that Bacon used his ships and crews too hard. For his part, Bacon accepted the reinforcements grudgingly, despite complaining constantly about his lack of ships, for he thought he should have them permanently. As a result, he was not believed to have the regard for them that he showed for the destroyers that had been at Dover since the outbreak of war.

But there was no end to the losses. The Tribal-class destroyer *Zulu* met her end off the French coast on 8 November 1916, when she hit a mine laid by the U-boat *UC-1*. Her captain had just related to the officer of the watch that the ship's lucky black cat had deserted that morning, when there was a terrific explosion which fractured the destroyer's back. The after part of the ship broke off and sank, but not before Chief Stoker Walter Kimber and ERA Michael Joyce had shown conspicuous bravery by jumping into the mass of broken machinery, steam and oil that had once been her engine room to rescue an injured man from certain death. For this selfless gallantry, they both received the Albert Medal. The citation read:

> Immediately after the explosion Joyce and Kimber proceeded to the engine room, the former having just come off watch. The

latter had just left the boiler room, after he had seen that the oil-burners were shut off and everything was in order, and had sent his hands on deck. Hearing the sound of moans coming from inside the engine room, they both attempted to enter it by the foremost hatch and ladder. As the heat in the engine room was intense and volumes of steam were coming up forward, they then lifted one of the square ventilating hatches further aft on the top of the engine room casing (port side) and climbed into the rapidly flooding compartment over the steam pipes, which were extremely hot. Scrambling over the debris, they discovered well over on the starboard side Stoker Petty Officer Smith, with his head just out of the water. A rope was lowered from the upper deck, and with great difficulty Smith, who was entangled in fractured pipes and other wreckage, was hauled up alive. At the same time Stoker Petty Officer Powell was found floating, in the water on the port side of the engine room. The rope was lowered again and passed around Powell, who, however, was found to be dead on reaching the deck. The water was so high that further efforts to discover the remaining Artificer left in the engine room would have been useless, and the attempt had to be abandoned.[11]

Ordinary men doing extraordinary things.

The forepart of the ship was somehow towed back to harbour and eventually joined at Chatham dockyard with the aft section of the wrecked *Nubian* to make a new ship, *Zubian*, which served from mid 1917.

There seemed no end to the war. By November 1916, casualties had already topped a million men and the war was costing Britain £5 million per day, half of which was being raised in the USA. Additionally, Britain was forced to financially support its Allies, especially Russia and France. On the 13th of the month, the Conservative leader in the Lords and Minister Without Portfolio in the government, Henry Petty-FitzMaurice, 5th Marquess of Lansdowne, a man not known as a pacifist, circulated a paper which asked the Cabinet to consider a negotiated peace. He suggested that Britain's manpower and industrial resources might not be able stand the strain of the war. He was not alone in holding such views, which were shared by some other politicians, not least Lloyd George. But the Cabinet decided against such an approach. The war would continue and the search for victory with it.

New Ships and a New Barrage, 1917

At the beginning of 1917, Bacon had twenty operational destroyers (of mixed types), together with two torpedo boats, four P-boats and four 'M'-class monitors available to him as patrol vessels. In addition there were six minesweepers, eight submarines, two submarine depot ships, a scout cruiser and eight heavy monitors, five 12in and three 15in, and countless auxiliary vessels. But, tellingly, he had a further twelve destroyers in dockyard hands for repairs, along with a torpedo boat and a patrol boat.

But losses to enemy mines, torpedoes or simple misfortune were constant. On 8 February *Ghurka* struck a mine and sank. All of her crew were lost, excepting one officer and four men. Her captain, Lieutenant Harold Courtenay Woollcombe-Boyce, went down with his ship. The surviving officer was Lieutenant Commander G E Lewin, the flotilla gunnery officer, who happened to be aboard at the time. He seized a Kisbie lifebuoy and kept afloat several men who grabbed hold of it until they were picked up by a trawler. Lewin then insisted that the ratings were taken on board first, although he had been a long time swimming in the cold sea. Chivalry was not yet dead.

On 13 March the 'M'-class destroyer *Meteor*, which had joined the Patrol only a month earlier, hit a mine near no. 4A net buoy. It exploded both her depth charges and caused her to catch fire aft. She had to be towed into harbour but survived to fight again; the same day the French paddle minesweeper *Elizabeth* was sunk by a mine directly in front of Calais.

Then on 10 April, at 1143 just off Le Havre, the hospital ship *Salta* (7,728 tons) hit a mine laid by *UC-26*. She had been in an escorted convoy of three hospital ships in a cleared shipping lane.

Her pilot didn't obey the 'Follow me' sign from *Diamond* and pulled to port to let the other ships pass first. This proved a fatal error, as she immediately struck a mine. The explosion smashed the hull astern and she sank in ten minutes. She had been headed for Le Havre in order to pick up a fresh contingent of wounded for transfer to Dover, and of her 205 crew and nursing staff on board, nine nurses, forty-two RAMC and seventy-nine crewmen died. In the heavy sea conditions of that day, only three boats were successfully launched before she went down, and all were swamped immediately. Many of those who died had been first picked up by the sloop *P-26*, which subsequently hit another mine and sank with the loss of nineteen of her own men, mainly from the boiler room, and all but one of the *Salta* survivors that she had plucked from the sea. Lieutenant Charles Edward Rathkins RNR, commanding *P-26*, was later mentioned in despatches: '[he] acted very properly and gallantly going to the assistance of ... *Salta*.'[1] And then a day later the minesweeping trawler *Amy* hit another mine off Le Havre and sank with the loss of nine men, all RNR, including skipper Thomas Dales.

It wasn't just the enemy that the Dover Patrol had to fight; the weather was a constant threat in the narrow defile of the Channel too, with short, sharp seas and funnelled gales. On 21 January the destroyer *Syren* collided with a Swedish steamer she was trying to intercept in bad weather and *Crusader* lost her gunner, washed overboard in heavy seas. And on 7 March *Fawn* nearly foundered in rough weather and some hands were washed over the side: all were rescued, bar one stoker who drowned, and *Broke* had to tow her into harbour.

The skimmers

The beginning of 1917 saw the advent of new types of vessel on both sides of the Dover Strait. The introduction of the coastal motor boat or CMB, popularly known as 'skimmers', followed the idea developed by officers of the Harwich Force that a very fast, shallow-draught vessel would be ideal for attacking German ships in their harbours. It would be able to pass over the defensive minefields without triggering one and its high speed would allow rapid strike and escape.

There followed a staff requirement requesting designs for a coastal motor boat for service in the North Sea. These boats were expected to make use of the lightweight and powerful petrol engines then available. The speed of the boat when fully loaded was to be at least 30 knots, and sufficient fuel was to be carried to give a considerable radius of action. A variety of armament was envisaged, including torpedoes, depth charges or mines, together with light machine guns, such as the Lewis gun. The weight of a fully loaded boat was not to exceed the weight of the 30ft long motor boat then carried in the davits of a light cruiser: ie, about 4.5 tons.

The Thornycroft company designed the craft and fitted them with V-12 aircraft engines made by Sunbeam and Napier. From the end of 1916 they entered service with the Dover Patrol, giving a new raiding option to Bacon and his staff. Very fast (they could hit 40 knots and average 35) and able to skim over the top of minefields, they were the navy's equivalent of the fighter plane, manned by young and adventurous men (usually a crew of four) and were dangerous and difficult to handle. For example, their petrol-powered engines were prone to catching fire (five CMBs were lost through fire, three of them whilst still in harbour*); and the restriction on weight meant the torpedo could not be fired from a normal torpedo tube but was instead carried in a rear-facing trough. On launching, it was pushed backwards by a cordite firing pistol and a steel ram, and entered the water tail-first. A tripwire between the torpedo and the ram head would start the torpedo motors once pulled tight after release. The CMB would then turn hard over and get out of the way. Clearly, this was an operation fraught with danger – but there is no record of a CMB ever torpedoing itself. And they were beautiful little craft that excited envy from even hardened navy men. One officer wrote: 'I do not know who invented the CMB but this little vessel was a masterpiece of ingenuity, so much so that I wept with envy when I saw the first one go over from Dover to Dunkirk'.[2]

They were involved in a number of operations during the year, but their limitations were also exposed. On 19 June a Dunkirk-based Short 184 seaplane, with two escorting Sopwith Baby seaplanes, took off to carry out a reconnaissance of the Belgian coast. Ten miles northeast of Nieuwpoort they were attacked by three German seaplanes. One German and two British planes were shot down, and

---

* CMBs *10*, *2* and *39B* 'accidentally caught fire in harbour' and were lost; nos *11* and *47* caught fire at sea.

a French destroyer, together with *CMB-1* and *CMB-9*, sailed to rescue the pilots.

But the Germans got there first. Four German torpedo boats of the Flanders Flotilla arrived on the scene. *CMB-1*, under the command of an RNR lieutenant, took a direct hit and blew up off Ostend. All the crew survived to become POWs, but two aircrew died.

As a consequence of this particular action, air-sea rescue missions were abandoned if Allied aircraft crashed too close to the enemy coast, a decision perhaps not designed to increase the likelihood of pilots wanting to fly such missions.

The navy did not, however, desert the pilots altogether. Another such example was during a minelaying operation in the southern North Sea over the night of 25/26 September. A number of ships were out to support the minelayers, including the seaplane carrier *Vindex*. Two of her planes failed to return and on the afternoon of the 27th CMBs *8* and *13* were despatched to look for them.

CMB-8's steering gear broke down at 1800 and *CMB-13* took her in tow but now came under fire from the shore. To add to their problems, they spotted ships' smoke, which proved to be from German torpedo boats. Then at 1640, *CMB-13* had engine problems and came to a halt, causing *CMB-8* to overrun the tow, which consequently became tangled in her propellers and killed off her engines. The crew were taken off, a demolition charge exploded and she sank off the Belgian coast. *CMB-13* returned safely with both crews and with no lives lost. Meanwhile, the search had been abandoned.

New minelayers

Up until early 1917, minelaying had been undertaken by a polyglot collection of converted merchant vessels, trawlers, motor launches and even CMBs. Now they were joined by another innovation.

Meteor had become part of the Patrol in February 1917, but had almost immediately been mined (see above). She was an 'M'-class destroyer, launched in 1914. As built, she was a fast (36 knots) vessel with three 4in guns and four torpedo tubes. However she had been converted to be one of thirteen destroyer fast minelayers, a process which involved the removal of their aft gun and, in some instances, one of the two sets of twin torpedo launchers.

She returned to Dover after repairs at Chatham in early July, to join up with the similarly converted destroyers *Ariel*, *Ferret* and *Legion* and, fresh from the Grand Fleet, *Tarpon*. They were intended to operate off Ostend and Zeebrugge, extending and relaying the minefields which had been laid in April the previous year. On the night of 13/14 July, their first full sortie, *Tarpon* hit a mine and had her propellers blown off, badly damaging her stern. She was towed to Dunkirk and hence to Britain for repairs, but was not fit to go to sea again until early 1918.

But *Meteor* served with the Patrol for the remainder of her service, laying mines off Cap Gris-Nez in November, and placing forty of the new magnetic mines off Ostend in a solo operation in August 1918. In her minelaying career, she was to lay 1,082 mines in the Strait and off the Flemish coast.

New monitors

In addition to the CMBs, Bacon received other new ships in the shape of two monitors, *Erebus* and *Terror*. Both ships were named for two bomb ketches sent to investigate the Northwest Passage and subsequently lost in 1845. They were armed with two 15in guns, similar guns to the *Queen Elizabeth*-class battleships then in commission, and could deliver a 1,938lb shell from each barrel. Like all their sisters, they were ungainly, but had a reasonable turn of speed and were very effective as a shore bombardment platform.

But they were not immune from attack. *Terror* had been on bombardment duty and was anchored up off Dunkirk for the night of 18/19 October when she was attacked by three 'A'-class German torpedo boats and struck by three torpedoes, one from each raider. Two of the hits considerably damaged her bow, which was opened to the sea, whilst a third exploded against the torpedo bulge.

With help from a tug, Captain C W Bruton beached her to the north of Dunkirk and Bacon's salvage expert, Captain Irons (a civilian and also the harbourmaster of Dover), was sent for. With the assistance of two powerful salvage tugs from Dover, they managed to float her into Dunkirk harbour for temporary repairs. Irons determined that they could take her to Dover under her own steam, but the longer voyage to Portsmouth would have to be undertaken stern first. Bruton refused to countenance such an unbecoming method of sailing. They reached Dover safely, but when she set out for Portsmouth on 23 October, the inevitable happened. Whilst on passage, she began leaking badly in heavy seas and high winds. Her crew were taken off by a trawler and *Terror* was abandoned off Hasting, 8,500 tons of barely floating ship. Next day, Captain Bruton was able to reboard his ship and she was brought back into harbour. On the 27th they made a second attempt. Bruton again refused to go stern first, so Irons left the ship in a huff and Bruton then changed his mind. He sailed to Portsmouth backwards, aided by tugs, and only turned her round to enter harbour. It took ten weeks to repair her.

The Germans too had come up with a new weapon of war, one which in some ways harked back to the days of fire-ships and additionally required a 'combined arms' approach to deploy it. The distance-controlled explosive boat (DCB) was an unmanned vessel, operated from shore by electrical signals sent along an unreeling cable and directed by spotting seaplane. It carried a 1,540lb charge, thus delivering a weight of explosive nearly equivalent to five British or German torpedoes. Lieutenant R R Ramsbotham on HMS *Kempenfelt* noted that 'the Hun produced several electric motor boats which were operated from the shore. We had several narrow squeaks and tried to avoid them as the personnel ashore could direct them and did so very well.' He added, 'We did, however, sink one and although we launched a whaler [to recover it] it sank before we could secure it'.[3]

And two new weapons clashed on 28 October, when *Erebus* was hit by a DCB nine miles off Ostend. It blew a 50ft hole in her anti-torpedo bulge, but did little damage to the hull. Two seamen were killed and fifteen wounded by the blast, mainly members of the crew who had been standing on deck, watching the approaching boat and wondering what it was! Her anti-torpedo bulge suffered most of the impact, but it still took two days to nurse her back to harbour at Dover, from whence she was sent to Portsmouth for repairs. She returned to service on 21 November.

Another new barrage

Despite Bacon's belief that the barrage and the Patrol were acting to stop the passage of submarines into the western hunting grounds, and likewise preventing minelaying within the Channel, his views were not universally shared, nor were they true. The reality was that British attempts to block the Strait of Dover were proving ineffective, with the U-boats learning to pass the Strait on the surface at night with relative ease and find gaps under the surface too. A more effective barrier would force them to take the much longer route around Scotland to their hunting grounds in the Western Approaches.

This was proven beyond doubt when in August 1917, Rear Admiral 'Blinker' Hall, in charge of naval intelligence, obtained information from a sunken German submarine, *UC-44*, which had been mined by its own side off southeast Ireland, attempting to lay a minefield where a previous German visitor had already laid one. This intelligence was in the form of orders which instructed U-boat commanders to transit to the Atlantic via the Dover Strait. It read:

> Pass through at night and on the surface without being observed and without stopping. If forced to dive, go to 40 metres and wait. Avoid being seen in the Channel ... on the other hand, those craft which in exceptional cases pass around Scotland are to let themselves be seen as freely as possible in order to mislead the English.[4]

Hall sent the information to Bacon, who dismissed it.

The salvaged documents also seemed to indicate that 190 passages had been made in the six months between 23 December 1916 and 6 June 1917. These were chiefly carried out at night, and during these six months there were only eight reports of touching a net and eight reports of being forced to dive to avoid patrols. In this intelligence began the foment of a conspiracy.

The Germans had renewed unrestricted submarine warfare on 1 February 1917, citing amongst other things the success of the British blockade (which was causing severe food shortages in Germany during the infamous Turnip Winter of 1916/17) as reason. They were able to deploy a much stronger force than previously, with thirty-three U-boats available to the Flanders Flotilla under Korvettenkapitän Bartenbach. And the U-boats were proving to be a dangerous weapon. In 1915 they had, in total, sunk 1,307,996 tons of Allied and neutral shipping. By the end of 1916 the losses had risen to 2,323,326 tons. And in January 1917 they sank 368,521 tons, the highest monthly total of the war. Something must be done. It was becoming daily more apparent that nets were not stopping submarines in the Channel.

But a really good minefield might. Despite his professed belief in the effectiveness of his current measures, as early as February Bacon had proposed a deep mine barrage. His conception was that it would stretch from Folkestone to Cap Gris-Nez in France, and was to be up to seven miles wide north to south and would comprise mines laid at depths of 20, 40, 60 and 80ft. As he himself described it:

> Now, supposing the required distance to be 150 feet, and the diameter of a submarine to be 20 feet, the only method of placing mines so that a submarine must hit a mine at any particular depth, is to have eight lines of mines all at the same depth, and all with their mines 150 feet apart. Each line is 'staggered,' so that, looking at the eight lines from a distance, a mine would be seen at every 20 feet. But this only holds good for one depth. If, as in the Dover Strait, the mean depth is about 18 fathoms, or 108 feet, five such groups of lines would be required, one 20 feet from the bottom, another at 40, and so on, to form a solid wall. From this rough description it will be seen that five sets of eight lines, or forty lines, would be required.[5]

The engineer in the admiral was to the fore again.

However, there was one small problem. Bacon calculated that it would need some thirty thousand mines, and no mines were presently available and supply was not expected before the end of the year. Nonetheless, he pressed ahead with his ideas and presented them to Jellicoe (who had become First Sea Lord in November 1916) and Henry Oliver (Deputy Chief of the Naval Staff) at the Admiralty, who agreed to the idea, assuming mines could be made available, and the Operations Committee were briefed in. In view of the impracticability of the scheme at the time, the committee put forward a separate suggestion for mining from Dungeness to the French coast with a line of patrol vessels to force submarines to dive. The tone of Bacon's response to this proposal gives an insight into the reason why some people found him easy to dislike:

> This was an absurd scheme from a practical point of view. The length of line chosen was needlessly, and at the same time hopelessly, long. I was strongly opposed to having the line marked by a patrol in the first instance, and also anxious to let submarines be destroyed without the enemy having the slightest inkling of how they were lost.[6]

In September Bacon heard that mines would be forthcoming by November and the detailed planning started. Minelaying began on schedule and the barrage was nearly complete by end of the year. Between 21 November and the end of December 1917, 39,000 H.2 and H.4 contact mines were laid. Two gaps were left on the British and French sides, to allow merchant ships to pass.

Five different deterrents across the Channel had now been tried in seeking to prevent German submarine movement: the original minefield laid in the early days of the war; the towed nets and indicator nets; the aborted barrier of 1915; the net and mine barrier of 1916; and now the new deep mine barrier between Folkestone and Cap Gris-Nez. And this is not to mention the net and mine barriers laid off the Flanders coast. Surely now the U-boats would be stopped. The latest attempt was certainly a significant feat of engineering. Only time would tell if it was effective.

This is not the end of the story of Admiral Bacon and the Dover Mine Barrage and we will return to it shortly. But first it is necessary to examine some actions of the Dover Patrol in 1917 on the surface of the Narrow Sea.

Fighting Back: The Second Battle of the Dover Strait and the Bombardments of Zeebrugge and Ostend, 1917

During 1917, criticism of the navy began to grow in some quarters, over what was seen as its overly defensive posture. Many in the navy itself shared that view. There were two drivers of these feelings. First, it seemed to some observers that the measures taken by the navy to prevent the sinking of an increasing number of merchantmen were unsuccessful. Secondly, neither the public nor many naval officers understood the doctrine of blockade and the impact that a slow strangulation of the German economy, and particularly its food supplies, was having on the country and the morale of its people. A new Trafalgar was still sought in many quarters. Within the Dover Patrol, the attrition continued, but nonetheless there were actions fought and plans developed in which the navy's offensive spirit was plain to see.

With the resumption of unrestricted submarine warfare in February 1917, the Germans redoubled their efforts against the barrage and its guardians. During the night of 25/26 February 1917 German destroyers and torpedo boats attempted another raid against the Dover Barrage and Allied shipping in the Dover Strait. The plan was for one flotilla to attack the barrage and a half-flotilla of torpedo boats would seek targets of opportunity off the Kent coast. In total, eleven vessels sortied from Zeebrugge and having evaded British patrols, six of them were accidentally intercepted by the destroyer HMS *Laverock*, armed with three 4in and one 3pdr guns and two sets of twin 21in torpedo tubes. She was commanded by

28-year-old Lieutenant Henry Armstrong Binmore, who did not hesitate to engage and fought his ship with such vigour that the Germans thought they were fighting at least three enemy destroyers. Nor did *Laverock* lose a man. The German force withdrew and satisfied itself with shelling Margate, Westgate-on-Sea and North Foreland wireless station before retiring.

Then on the night of 16/17 March a flotilla of German torpedo boats made another raid. Signalman G E Haigh on board *Swift* at Dover saw fire and rockets at 2300 and all the available warships in port put to sea. *Paragon* and *Llewellyn* engaged eight German TBs and *Paragon* was sunk by a torpedo. Her captain, Lieutenant John Francis Bowyer, survived but seventy-five of her crew were lost, including Bowyer's elder brother, Richard Grenville Bowyer, also a lieutenant and serving alongside his sibling. *Llewellyn* rammed a ship, 'probably a German destroyer', and the monitors supported the ships with 12in gunfire.

Laforey had joined the Dover Patrol less than a fortnight previously on 5 March, having previously served with the Harwich Force. Attracted by the sight of an explosion, she moved in to investigate and, finding a field of debris, started to search for survivors, signalling *Llewellyn* to join her. Neither ship noticed that the German vessels were still in attendance, and two German ships, *G-87* and *S-49*, launched torpedoes against the British ships, one hitting and damaging *Llewellyn*, and then escaped unseen in the dark. But the overall result was inconclusive for both sides. As Haigh's diary entry recorded, 'no definite results'.[1]

A week later on 23 March, *Laforey*, now in company with her sister ships *Lark* and *Laertes*, was on escort duty, taking several cargo vessels to Boulogne. This was a regular duty for the Patrol, sailing from Dover early in the morning, picking up transports at Folkestone and escorting them to Boulogne. On the return leg they would frequently sail up the coast to Calais to accompany hospital or escort vessels back to Dover. Then they would make another Folkestone–Boulogne crossing, before the ships returned to Dover in the early evening to take up night patrol positions.

On this occasion, the destroyers safely delivered their charges at 1630, but as the two destroyers began the return trip there was a sudden loud explosion amidships on board *Laforey* and she broke in half, the stern half sinking immediately, whilst the bow remained tantalisingly afloat and *Laertes* attempted to take off survivors. It was to little avail, for the bow went under too after a few short minutes. *Laforey* had been sunk by a mine: a British mine, swept but incorrectly disposed of. Of her seventy-seven crew, sixty-four perished, including her captain, Lieutenant Arthur Edwin Durham. He and his ship had been with the Dover Patrol for eighteen days.

But in April there was a welcome success for the Patrol through the CMBs. In a planned operation, Bacon ordered Zeebrugge to be heavily bombed by the RNAS late on the 7th. As he had expected, the German vessels in harbour stood out to sea to avoid the bombing and anchored up for the night. At 0115 on the 8th, Lieutenant Walter Napier Thomason Beckett led a force of five coastal motor boats from the 3rd CMB Division at speed into the harbour roads and the Wielingen channel and attacked the resting ships, launching their single torpedoes as they turned away. The modern (1915) German torpedo boat *G-88* was hit amidships and sank, killing eighteen sailors, and another vessel was damaged. Beckett and his force then retired over the German minefield. His own boat filled up with smoke and gas owing to an exhaust problem, and another boat was heavily shelled by a German destroyer. But all made it back to Dunkirk safely and there were no British losses. Beckett received the Distinguished Service Cross (DSC) for his planning and execution of the mission.[2]

The Second Battle of the Dover Strait

The Germans continued to ramp up the pressure. On the evening of 20 April, twelve German torpedo boats set out from Zeebrugge with the intention of attacking the net barrage and associated drifters and support vessels. Defensive minefields prevented them reaching their objectives so, instead, they contented themselves with attempting a bombardment of Dover and Calais, six vessels to each target port.

The six ships operating against Dover were the 5th Torpedo Boat Half-Flotilla under the command of Korvettenkapitän Gautier, armed with three 4.1in guns and six torpedo tubes. Gautier found his target and made an attack around midnight, firing 350 rounds, and then withdrew, heading for home. He had, in fact, done little damage as most of the shells fell either on the cliffs or inland above the town.

Two Royal Navy flotilla leaders, *Swift* and *Broke*, had been assigned a patrol duty off Dover. The captain of *Swift* was

Commander Ambrose Maynard Peck, while *Broke* was led by Commander Edward Ratcliffe Garth Russell Evans, known to his friends as 'Teddy', and a famous polar explorer. He had been seconded from the navy to the *Discovery* expedition to the Antarctic in 1901–1904, when he served as second officer on the relief ship, and afterwards planned his own Antarctic expedition. However, he suspended this intention when offered the post of second in command on Captain Robert Falcon Scott's disastrous expedition to the South Pole of 1910–13. Specifically, he was to be the captain of the expedition ship *Terra Nova*. He accompanied Scott to within 150 miles of the Pole on foot, but became seriously ill with scurvy and only narrowly survived the return journey. In one way he was lucky, for although he nearly died, he at least survived, unlike the entire group which had continued towards the Pole, including Scott himself. Called back to active service in 1914 from the lecture circuit, he always sailed with a stuffed penguin mascot strapped to the mast of his vessel, in recognition of his exploits. A nation's hero once already, he was about to gain renewed fame.

Broke had been built for the Chilean navy and was purchased by the Admiralty at the outbreak of war. Armed with two 4.7in guns, two 4in, two 2pdrs and two torpedo tubes, she had already had an interesting war, being involved in the night action at Jutland, losing her bow in a collision with *Sparrowhawk*. *Broke* (and her sister *Botha*) was a much prized berth because the Chileans, unlike their Royal Navy brethren, had spared no expense on the officers' accommodation, which included silver-plated chandeliers in the captain's cabin.

Swift, built in 1905 and unique in design, was at that time armed with one 6in gun, which had been fitted in 1916 at the expense of two forward 4in, two 4in, and two torpedo tubes. The 6in proved to be a disaster, as it was impossible to train, and needed two men on the muzzle to help move it.

Amazon, meanwhile, had been ordered to Calais to collect a VIP (who later turned out to be none other than Lloyd George), but when the gun flashes of the German bombardment were spotted, the transport duty was cancelled. *Swift* and *Broke* were ordered to intercept the German vessels, and *Amazon* to patrol to prevent the enemy approaching Dover again.

It was a calm, intensely dark night and visibility was poor, but at 0145 and about 600yds range, the two British intercepting ships sighted the six Germans near the Goodwin Sands, trying to hurry home unseen in the dark. Confusion reigned as the usual problems of identification were considered, but this was resolved when in answer to Commander Peck's recognition signal, the British vessels heard fire gongs and the German ships opened fire with every available gun. Fortunately, every shot was an 'over'.

Commander Peck, leading the British line, immediately swung his ship and attempted to ram the foremost German vessel, missed, and spun round to launch a torpedo, which found its mark in SMS *G-85,* and then essayed another ramming attempt, causing his intended victim to cease fire and rush off into the darkness. *Swift* had been hit portside below the bridge in the stokers' mess deck, and another shell had carried away her wireless aerial without exploding. In return, she had achieved one hit with her temperamental 6in, which had struck the second ship of the German line in the engine room, 'cutting her practically in half'.[3] Peck continued the chase until his ship lost speed, owing to her injuries, and made his task futile.

Meanwhile, *Broke* was caught up in the sort of engagement which was as old as naval warfare. Evans had opened fire on the German line, which was now at full speed and belching smoke and flame from their funnels. They returned the fire, wounding Evans's helmsman, Able Seaman Rawles, four times in the legs. Despite his wounds, he was able to follow orders to port the helm and, at 27 knots, *Broke* squarely rammed the enemy third in line, *G-42,* commanded by Kapitänleutnant Bernd von Arnim. *Broke's* bows embedded themselves in the German ship's hull and the two vessels found themselves locked in a deadly embrace. The crash as *Broke* 'buried her bow into the enemy ... reverberated around the hills and cliffs, followed by firing in the night, was something I will never forget,' noted an eyewitness.[4]

Commander Evans ordered a rapid cannonade, sweeping the German's decks with gunfire, whilst his enemy did the same. Men were mown down on both sides, including von Armin himself. Of the eighteen men working *Broke's* forward guns, soon only five were left standing. But Midshipman Donald A Gyles RNR, a nineteen-year-old merchant apprentice co-opted into the Royal Navy, kept one gun in action, despite a severe shrapnel wound to his eye and wounds to his leg and arm.

The Germans now tried to board *Broke* to end the carnage, and swarmed over her forecastle. Gyles, armed only with a pistol, stood tall and fired at them; one German sailor, 'a regular giant', flung himself onto Gyles from behind and tried to take the pistol off him, but was in turn run through with a cutlass by a British rating. To the call of 'Repel boarders', a pitched battle of pistols, rifles, sailors with cutlasses and marines with bayonets raged on *Broke*'s decks, which ended with Evans's men proving triumphant and sweeping the German attackers into the sea, except for two who lay down and feigned death. Throughout the action Evans bellowed to his crew, 'Remember the *Lusitania*, men'.[5]

Finally, Evans managed to extract his ship from his victim, leaving it sinking, to seek new prey. He fired a torpedo at one German vessel and engaged another, before attacking the only two remaining torpedo boats he could see. This proved an overweening ambition, for *Broke* took a shell in her boiler, which significantly reduced her speed and left her powerless to sustain a chase. Even now *Broke*'s troubles were not over, for Evans saw an enemy vessel on fire in the distance and the crew calling for help. Evans ordered his ship to limp towards them, only for the Germans to reopen fire on him. He returned fire and pulled back into the night, whereupon his boilers finally gave out.

In the darkness, *Swift* had stumbled on a sinking German vessel, her crew mustered on deck and crying out for assistance. Peck approached with caution, for two of the enemy's crew were closed up by a torpedo tube, when suddenly the enemy vessel heeled over and sank. *Swift* lowered her boats and began to pick up survivors. The German vessel turned out to be the one rammed by *Broke*. *Swift* then had to wait for daylight as she had lost her bearings; additionally, Peck had to flood the starboard side to keep the hole in her port side above the water. But on the 22nd she was out on patrol again.

Broke was eventually found by British destroyers sent from Dover and taken under tow to the eastern arm of Dover harbour. As she entered port, all the drifters, with whom Evans was something of a cult hero, began sounding their sirens and hooters. Amid the cacophony, an officer ran along the harbour wall calling for the row to stop. 'Go to 'ell,' was the reply, 'it's Teddy'.[6] Her crew received a huge welcome in the town and many received a free drink in the pubs that night.

Two British ships had attacked six German vessels and sunk two of them, despite suffering some damage themselves. In the dark days of early 1917 it was a welcome victory and riposte. Both Evans and Peck were speedily awarded the DSO and promoted to the rank of captain, and Evans was feted by the press and the propaganda machine as 'Evans of the *Broke*'. Gyles too became a temporary hero. On his release from hospital in Deal, he went home to Hornsey where newspapers made much of his ordeal. His quondam headmaster at Stroud Green elementary school, H W Christmas, described him, with no doubt some vested interest and pride, as 'a typical product of the modern elementary school'.[7] Gyles was also featured, in an etching of his personal battle, on the front cover of *War Illustrated* in May.

Midshipman Gyles was awarded the DSC; Able Seaman Ernest Ramsden Ingleson, who had saved Gyles's life, received the DSM. *Broke*'s helmsman Able Seaman William George Rawles was awarded the Conspicuous Gallantry Medal (CGM).

Broke lost twenty-one men killed and had another thirty-six wounded. *Swift* had one fatality and four wounded. But the German appetite for such actions was clearly reduced – there were no more German surface raids in the Strait for ten months.

National newspapers published long articles about the bravery of the men of *Broke* and *Swift*. The *Daily Sketch* front page headline was 'They Died Defending Our Shores', with pictures of the funeral procession for the British dead through the Market Square, Dover. One hundred and forty German officers and men were rescued from the sea by *Swift* and other ships of the Patrol, and they suffered the indignity of being jeered at by the good burghers of Dover as they watched them being marched off to prisoner-of-war camps. It was probably better than drowning though. And three days after the battle, thirteen German dead were also laid to rest at St James's Cemetery in the town, where a Royal Navy contingent paid their respects and laid a wreath sent by Bacon and inscribed 'To a brave enemy'. Such chivalry did not commend itself to everyone, however. Herbert Richmond noted that 'the *Daily Mail* is howling for blood and in my opinion will get it, beginning with Bacon, whose wreath to the "brave and gallant enemies" had made everyone so furious'.[8]

And British insouciance triumphed to the end. As *Broke* was lying in harbour awaiting repairs, a staff car drew up on the quayside and a staff commander jumped out. He shouted up to Evans, 'Well done.' 'Thanks,' Evans replied, 'I could not get my towing gear out in time or I would have brought her in as a prize.'[9]

Swift gained a share of the kudos too. On 3 May she was detailed to take Lloyd George, Jellicoe, Lord Robert Cecil (Minister for Blockade), Bacon and several generals to Calais, and on the 7th she made the return trip with the prime minister again on board, where he gave a short speech. Then on 9 May she was cheered into Portsmouth harbour where Queen Mary, Princess Mary and the CinC Portsmouth, Admiral Sir Stanley Colville, came on board and inspected ship.

But then two months later, on 29 July, *Swift* weighed anchor at Dunkirk at 0130 and two minutes later ran aground on Hill's Bank. *Phoebe*, following behind, rammed her astern and destroyed *Swift's* whaler and dinghy. These were the same boats which, with the addition of a lost depth charge, had been replaced after being destroyed nine months earlier, when on 28 October 1916 her helm had jammed entering Dover harbour; *Swift* had gone full astern, a big wave broke over her and the boats were wrecked. Nonetheless, *Swift* left Dunkirk and patrolled up the coast, escorting the monitors and engaging German destroyers, scoring a claimed hit. *Erebus* had also opened fire, but German shore batteries straddled her. Signalman Haigh reported that 'we sank two mines and returned to Dunkirk.'[10]

The raid of 20 April did not mark the end of the German attempts to use night attacks by destroyers to cause damage and sink ships. A week later, at 0115 on 27 April, several German destroyers opened fire on Ramsgate with high explosive and star-shell. Some sixty rounds were fired, most of which landed in open country, but two citizens were killed, with three more injured, and twenty-one houses, two stables and £6,000 of property damaged. Manston airfield also came under fire.

The German ships were – improbably – driven off by the monitor *Marshal Ney* which, having proven highly unsuitable for bombardment duties ('practically a failure', according to *Jane's Fighting Ships*) owing to the unreliability of her engines, had been stripped of her 15in guns, refitted with a 9.2in and four 6in, and permanently relegated by Bacon to be moored as a guard ship for Ramsgate and the Downs.

Despite this, *Ney* returned fire and the sudden appearance of big gun shells convinced the destroyers to retire. Probably no one was more surprised than her captain. The gunnery officer on *Ney* was Lieutenant Commander Francis Charles Cadogan, who had joined the ship the month beforehand. Cadogan was the grandson of the 4th Earl Cadogan and the son of Captain Hon Charles George Henry Cadogan, but seemed ill-equipped to be an officer on board a fighting ship. His captains certainly thought so. Captain Loder-Symonds, writing in December 1916, noted that 'he is well read and has some literary attainments but his qualities fit him more for clerical work than as executive officer of a sea-going ship.' And his captain on *Marshal Ney*, Henry Luxmoore, clearly found him unhelpful, writing 'would be better at office work than an executive officer, as he has not very good manners with junior officers and men'.[11] Nonetheless, on 27 April his guns saved Ramsgate from worse enemy fire and Cadogan remained with the ship until the end of the war, as successive captains found themselves unable to be rid of him.*

The bombardment of Zeebrugge, 12 May 1917

The official history, *The War at Sea*, recorded that 'the onset of the German submarine offensive advanced to its fullest point in April 1917'. Losses of merchant ships to submarine predation were rising rapidly following the declaration of unrestricted submarine warfare. Bacon and others continued to advance the thesis that the submarine campaign could be checked by direct attack on the ports from which they operated, Ostend and Zeebrugge.

Whilst this seemed an excellent idea, there were certain difficulties which were possibly underestimated. The defences of the Flanders coastline were exceptionally strong. As noted previously, a heavy battery (the Kaiser Wilhelm II) had been erected at Knokke to the eastward of the Bruges canal, one and a half miles to the west of Ostend was the Tirpitz battery, and two more were under construction. They were formidable barriers to Allied success. The Kaiser Wilhelm II mounted four 12in guns, range 41,000yds; the Tirpitz mounted four 11in guns, range 35,000yds. And between these batteries the coast was defended by a large number of mobile and semi-mobile guns, trenches and machine-gun nests.

Zeebrugge, translated from the Flemish, effectively means the harbour of Bruges. And in Bruges the Germans had constructed a heavily fortified base for their submarines. It comprised a massive

---

* Cadogan's daughter Henriette gained rather more prominence than her father by becoming a lady-in-waiting to Queen Elizabeth II from 1949 to 1987 as Lady Abel Smith.

concrete shelter with a 6ft thick roof and which gave protection from bombs and shellfire alike. Herein lay what Bacon perceived as an opportunity, for the Germans could only transit from Bruges by means of a canal and locks at Zeebrugge. With his engineer's mind, Bacon theorised that 15in shells from his big monitors could, if they scored a direct hit, wreck the lock gates and prevent German egress.

Owing to the strong defences on shore, this would have to be done through indirect fire, using aiming marks and with spotting from aircraft of the Royal Naval Air Service (RNAS). The problem, however, was that of hitting an invisible target 90ft long and 30ft wide from a distance of about thirteen miles. But Bacon was undismayed. He calculated that with a gun laid accurately for range and direction, one round in every sixty-three should hit a lock gate. Statistically therefore, at least 126 rounds would be required to make a hit probable on each of the two gates. Making allowances for the fact that the laying would not be as exact as with a shore-mounted gun, Bacon determined that at least twice this number, or 252 rounds, should be allowed for. This seemed academically correct, but practically very tricky. It would also require conditions of wind and weather which were infrequently found on that coastline.

Bacon allotted forty-one ships and launches of the Dover Patrol to the operation. The three 15in monitors *Terror* (flag), *Marshal Soult* and *Erebus* would be the striking force, assisted by the 12in monitor *Sir John Moore* and the *M-15*-class vessels *M-24* and *M-26*. Destroyer leaders *Botha* and *Faulknor*, with destroyers *Lochinvar*, *Landrail*, *Lydiard*, *Mentor*, *Moorsom*, *Morris*, *Mermaid* and *Racehorse* would defend the monitors. Paddle minesweepers and motor launches for smoke-laying completed the flotilla, and from the Harwich Force two flotilla leaders and twelve destroyers were ordered to provide distant cover.

Three times the force assembled in the Downs, and three times it was stood down owing to adverse weather conditions. On the evening of 11 May the vessels again formed up, but as the ships began to leave between 2300 and 0000, there was as little certainty as before that the bombardment would take place.

A buoy was laid by the destroyer *Lochinvar* fifteen miles to the northwest of the mole as a guide and a second buoy was placed in the position selected for the bombardment. A bearing was taken from the buoy to the base of the mole at Zeebrugge by *Lochinvar*, under Commander J S G Fraser, sailing from the buoy to the mole despite a mist which reduced visibility to a mile, and meant that the ship advanced dangerously close to German shore batteries. The ship returned to the buoy by 0445, with the bearing and distance. The bombardment ships had taken position, the motor launches had formed a line, ready to generate the smokescreen and the escorts formed a square round the monitors. Five destroyers zigzagged around the fleet as a defence against U-boats, the minesweepers began operating around the monitors and the covering force cruised in the distance, ready to intercept a German destroyer sortie.

At this point things started to go astray. The monitor *Marshal Soult*, never a great sailing ship at any time and capable of only 6 knots on a good day, had to be towed into position. This meant that bombardment opened late and the two Royal Naval Air Service artillery observation aircraft from Dunkirk, which had taken off at 0200, had to wait over Zeebrugge for almost two hours. These aircraft were met by seven Sopwith Pups from 4 Squadron, which patrolled the coast as six Sopwith Triplanes of 10 Squadron flew over the fleet for aerial protection. One of the spotting aircraft had engine trouble and force-landed in the Netherlands and the other ran short of petrol. Thus spotting the fall of shot, upon which successful targeting depended, was carried out by one machine with a failing supply of petrol.

The monitors opened fire around 0500 and at first fell short, with many of the shells failing to explode owing to the quality of the ammunition, which rendered the aircraft unable to signal the fall of shot. But they soon got the range and *Marshal Soult* hit the target with its twelfth shell and *Erebus* with its twenty-sixth. *Terror* was most hampered by the loss of the second spotting aircraft and dud shells; only forty-five of the 250 shells fired were reported upon and eventually the single spotting aircraft had to return because of lack of fuel at 0530, leaving the last half-hour of the bombardment reliant on estimated corrections. Two relieving aircraft had engine trouble and failed to arrive at all.

The Germans did not take the attack lying down. Anti-aircraft fire and attempted radio-jamming, to prevent the observers reporting, was the immediate response, and soon a number of German Albatros fighters arrived and were engaged by the Sopwith Pups. The British pilots later claimed five German aircraft shot down.

Flight Sub Lieutenant Albert James Enstone*, aged twenty-two, was one of the Sopwith Pup pilots. In his log book he gave a terse record of the air battle above the bombarding fleet:

> offensive patrol five miles to sea to beyond Zeebrugge protecting fleet bombarding Zeebrugge – lost formation after diving to 11,000ft after another machine. Saw H.A. [Hostile Aircraft] attacked by Hemming & nose dive & disappear into the sea. Climbed to 14,000ft & was attacked by H.A single seater & saw two more H.A above me. Shot down one H.A & was then attacked by other two. Gun jambed [sic] & with great difficulty succeeded in eluding H.A. Machine hit in twelve places & afterwards new wings fitted.[12]

At 0600 Bacon judged that his mission was compete and ordered a withdrawal, just as the Kaiser Wilhelm battery finally opened fire.

The admiral believed that, as he had fired the requisite number of rounds, the bombardment must have been successful. But aerial photographs obtained the following week demonstrated that about fifteen shells had landed within a few yards of the lock gates on the western side and on the eastern side four shells had done the same. The basin north of the locks had been hit and some damage caused to the docks. However, the mission had failed. Zeebrugge remained open to German destroyers and U-boats. Bacon blamed the failure on the lateness of getting into a firing position, which meant that the spotting planes could not stay on station.

The Dover Patrol lost no men at sea in the raid. But the Royal Naval Air Service did. Sub Lieutenant Maurice William Wallis Eppstein, flying a Sopwith Triplane Scout, was shot down by anti-aircraft fire. He was twenty years old. Eppstein was typical of the young men who took to the air. The younger son of Revd W C Eppstein, Rector of Lambourne, Essex, and formerly headmaster of Reading School, Maurice had passed through the Royal Navy's officer training colleges at Osborne and *Britannia*, Dartmouth, before electing to join the RNAS and train at the Central Flying School, Eastchurch, from where he was gazetted sub lieutenant in September 1916. According to his obituary, he was 'a very fine runner, and at Dartmouth was chief whip of the Britannia Beagles'.[13]

---

* Enstone went on to become an 'ace' with thirteen confirmed kills and survived the war, retiring with the rank of captain in the RAF and the awards of the DSC and Distinguished Flying Cross (DFC).

Operating out of bases at Dover and Dunkirk, the RNAS had been, from the beginning of the war, an important contributor to the operations of the Dover Patrol, charged with the air defence of Britain's coasts, and in particular the North Sea and the English Channel. It had entered the war with six airships and ninety-three aircraft, mostly seaplanes. A base for seaplanes had been constructed at Marine Parade, Dover, in November 1914, on the site of an ice rink. A slipway was constructed so floatplanes could be manhandled up the beach and across the road, and two rather slow and flimsy Wright seaplanes were based there. Initially, there were two seaplanes and six land aeroplanes, and they were used primarily to escort troopships and transports across the Channel.

By May, Short 184 floatplanes arrived, considered a much superior aircraft, and by October 1915, scout planes had been added too, and their duties were much more directed in favour of submarine- and mine-hunting.

Amongst the necessary additions to the original rink buildings was a pigeon loft. In the days of no, and later unreliable, radio, pigeons were used for sending urgent messages from the floatplane back to base. Each plane carried three to four birds, each base had a loft, and every pigeon was given a unique service number.

Guston airfield was operated by the RNAS for the defence of the port of Dover, and an RNAS airbase was established on Hawkshill Downs, near Walmer, in May 1917, in response to an urgent Admiralty request after torpedo-carrying enemy seaplanes had torpedoed a ship in the North Downs. Six fighter planes were initially based there. Two bases for (non-rigid) airships were also established at Polegate (near Eastbourne) and Capel (near Folkestone). These were used primarily for anti-submarine duties.

Horace Hood had deployed seaplanes for spotting purposes and aircraft later proved successful at locating submerged U-boats, which were often easier to see from on high. By the time Bacon took charge, it was commonplace to use aircraft for spotting the fall of shell from bombardment squadrons when conditions permitted.

Additionally, Bacon believed that air photography could be a great help in planning operations and was frustrated by the poor quality of British photographic lenses available to him. Tired of the lack of response from the Admiralty, he sent his head of photography to London with a blank cheque drawn on the Admiral's personal account and told him to buy the very best lens that he could find. He returned and reported that he had found one costing £120, which he would test. After a second visit, he had done still better, having found two 8in lenses in a cellar. These were purchased and Bacon had them fitted to operate through a hole in the fuselage of a reconnaissance plane to good effect. Once again, Bacon's interest in things technical proved of benefit and photo-reconnaissance became part of the everyday duties of the RNAS in the Patrol.

The navy and RNAS had developed primitive aircraft carriers (or, more accurately, seaplane carriers) by the outbreak of war: *Hermes* was one, lost serving with the Patrol in October 1914 (see Chapter 8). *Riviera* was another. She was a converted cross-channel ferry (previously owned by to the South East and Chatham Railway), fitted out to carry and deploy at sea four seaplanes. *Riviera* operated briefly with the Harwich Force and from 1916 with the Dover Patrol, where her aircraft flew spotting missions for naval bombardments off the Belgian coast. On 16 October 1916 she rammed and sank the tug *Hercules* near to Dover harbour's western entrance, but otherwise served the Patrol with distinction until ordered to the Mediterranean in May 1918.

Bacon's air commander during his time at Dover was Wing Captain Charles Laverock Lambe, the captain of *Hermes* until she was sunk, who commanded the RNAS forces around Dover and at Dunkirk. From July 1915 control of air stations was under the direct operational command of the regional naval district in which they were located, and thus Lambe came directly under Bacon's orders. It was not always a happy relationship. Bacon did not believe in frequent and speculative attacks on the German-held ports of Zeebrugge and Ostend, believing that it only caused the enemy to strengthen their defences (thus making it more difficult to attack with planned bombardment) and to retaliate against his own ships and harbours. They were, he said, 'useless' or even 'harmful to well thought out military operations'.[14] As a result he largely directed Lambe to assist the army, a role which Lambe thought an inappropriate use of the forces under him.*

---

* Bacon's view was supported by the Admiralty's own post-war (March 1919) report by Majors Childers and Morris which commented: 'Bombing was at best a secondary and very imperfect method of attack ... to sprinkle a thousand tons of explosives in something under two years over a multitude of objectives, in not one of which ... anything vital could have been subjected to more than temporary injury, could not have a decisive effect' (AIR 1/2115/207/56/1, pp70–5, The National Archives).

In spring 1917 questions had been asked in the House of Commons regarding the absence of air attacks on Zeebrugge. Bacon sent for Lambe and called his attention to them. Lambe replied that he hoped that Bacon didn't think these questions emanated from him. Bacon didn't answer, but ordered that there should be no more air attacks on Zeebrugge or Ostend for three months, thus demonstrating to Parliament (at least in his own eyes) that he would not have his strategy challenged. Captain Richmond, now commanding *Commonwealth* recorded in his diary: 'to show his contempt [for Parliament] he orders that this arm is to be immobilised ... pettiness, if nothing else, could go no further'.[15]

The bombardment of Ostend, 5 June 1917

Following the disappointments and failure of the bombardment of Zeebrugge, Bacon turned his attention to a plan to attempt to degrade the port of Ostend by a bombardment of the dockyard.

There were two advantages to this project which had been absent at Zeebrugge. Though the chance of doing some serious damage was perhaps less, the target was bigger. And Ostend was visible from the sea, unlike the Zeeebrugge lock gates, giving more chance of making accurate shooting. Bad weather delayed the implementation of the plan, but on 4 June conditions were deemed favourable and a bombarding squadron of two monitors (the 15in-gunned *Erebus* and *Terror*), two flotilla leaders (*Botha*, *Faulknor*), six destroyers, two P-boats and twelve smoke-laying motor launches left Dover at 2200.

Commodore Tyrwhitt, with four light cruisers, a flotilla leader and eight destroyers of the Harwich Force also left harbour to cover the bombardment from the area of Thornton Bank.

The force passed through a gap in the barrage (near buoy 11A) and steered for the northern end of the outer Ratel Bank. Just before 0100 on the 5th, *Lochinvar* reported a group of German destroyers to the eastward. Bacon, at sea with his forces, decided not to reinforce the ship, as doing so would deprive the bombarding squadron of its protecting vessels. However, the presence of the German vessels prevented *Lochinvar* carrying out its task of deploying a sighting buoy and Bacon was thus compelled to take up his bombarding position by dead reckoning.

Meanwhile, after reaching his station near the Thornton Bank at 0215, Tyrwhitt started his patrol on a southwesterly course. When he was about halfway between the Bligh and Thornton Banks, he sighted two destroyers ahead. They were steering to the westward, and he took them at first to be part of Bacon's bombardment group, but was disabused when they opened fire – yet another recognition issue at night. Tyrwhitt returned the fire and for a few minutes the Germans hung on to a westerly course. But the weight of metal was too much for them, and they turned and made for Zeebrugge and safety.

One vessel, SMS *S-20*, was by then badly damaged and lagging behind. Tyrwhitt now ordered a division of four destroyers (*Taurus, Sharpshooter, Satyr, Torrent*) to pursue the damaged vessel and its sister. These duly sank the crippled German vessel and chased hard after the other until they were recalled, as they were getting too close to the shore batteries. A few minutes later, Admiral Bacon opened his bombardment of Ostend, beginning at 0320 and finishing forty minutes later.

There was a spirited reply from the shore, and *Erebus* and *Terror* received a consistent and accurate fire, which fortunately did no damage. One hundred and fifteen shells were fired by the monitors, of which about twenty exploded in or near the dockyard. Later reports from intelligence officers averred that the harbour workshops had not suffered much damage, but that a lighter and a UC-boat* had been sunk, and three destroyers of the flotilla, which were lying alongside the quays, were also damaged. These reports also stated that the bombardment had made an impression on the German High Command and caused them to doubt whether Ostend was suitable as a destroyer base at all. This may well have been the case, for later in the year the Germans abandoned their use of Ostend for such vessels.

Commander Hubert Henry de Burgh, captain of *Satyr*, was later awarded the DSO for his part in the action, in which he succeeded in saving seven men of *S-20*'s crew while under heavy fire from the shore batteries and with three German seaplanes hovering overhead.

De Burgh was an interesting character, lineally descended from Hubert de Burgh (*c*1175–1243), who had entered the service of King John in the 1190s and made his reputation by his stubborn defence of the castle of Chinon in 1205. He was one of the great constables of

---

* Some authorities claim this was *UC-70* (for example Buxton, see Further Reading) but this is untrue as she survived until 28 August 1918. The author can find no record of a U-boat sunk on that day.

Dover Castle and held the office for over thirty years. In 1203 he founded the Maison Dieu in the town. Now another de Burgh was defending Dover. Hubert Henry was Irish-born and played cricket for Ireland and also India, where he played a first-class match in India for a 'Europeans' team against a 'Hindus' team in February 1906 (a right-handed batsman, he played for Ireland in a first-class match against Oxford University twenty years later).

Lieutenant Commander Edye Kington Boddam-Whetham was similarly recognised for the way he had handled his ship in the face of superior forces and under the fire of the shore batteries. And there was also recognition for some officers who had taken part in both the May and June bombardments, lacking in success though they had been. Captain Charles Samuel Wills RN, Captain Colin Kenneth MacLean RN, Commander John Stewart Gordon Fraser RN, Commander Ion Hamilton Benn MP RNVR, and Lieutenant Commander Evan Bruce-Gardyne RN were all gazetted in July 1917 with the DSO. And, much to the disgust of some officers, the Patrol had to undertake a replica of the bombardments some ten days after the event for the benefit of an official cinematographer.

Three days after the Ostend bombardment, and following the declaration of war on Germany by the United States of America on 6 April 1917, General John 'Black Jack' Pershing, commander of the American Expeditionary Force, landed at Liverpool with his staff, having crossed the Atlantic on the White Star Line vessel, SS *Baltic*. On 13 June, after he had visited Buckingham Palace for an audience with the King and then stayed at the Savoy, he and his entourage took a train from Charing Cross station to Folkestone, where they boarded a cross-channel steamer for Boulogne. The Dover Patrol provided the escort. As a correspondent from the *Chicago Times* saw it, 'swift torpedo destroyers dashed to and fro under our bow and stern and circled us constantly. In the air above airplanes and dirigible balloons hovered over the waters surrounding us, keeping sharp watch for the first appearance of the dark sea killers of destruction.'[16] The Patrol delivered Pershing safely and the long-awaited American presence on the Western Front commenced.

Operation Hush

In late 1915 Bacon had proposed a plan to the Admiralty for a naval landing at Ostend to take the town and link up with Allied ground forces. These ideas were reconsidered in early 1916 and talks were arranged between Sir Douglas Haig (newly placed in charge of the British forces on the Western Front) and the admiral. Bacon's original plan proposed to land 9,000 men in Ostend harbour from six monitors and 100 trawlers.

Haig was sufficiently impressed to appoint Lieutenant General Aylmer Hunter-Weston, who had commanded the 29th Division and then VIII Corps at Gallipoli (and thus had some experience of maritime landings) to work with Bacon on the proposal. However, Hunter-Weston rejected it, because the attack was on too narrow a front, Ostend harbour was in range of German heavy guns, and the exits from the harbour were easy to block. But he encouraged Bacon to develop a new plan for a beach landing near Middelkirke, one which was to incorporate Haig's desire for tanks to be involved.

Bacon was always happiest with problems of materiel and the requirement for a new amphibious landing was meat and drink to him. He developed a scheme to use large floating pontoons as both transport and piers, to be pushed across the Channel by two monitors to each pontoon. The monitors could then also provide covering artillery fire. Jellicoe, newly appointed as First Sea Lord, approved the plan and the naval constructor Charles Lillicrap was tasked with designing the pontoons.

They were specified to be around 550ft long and 32ft wide. Men, guns, wagons, ambulances, boxcars, motorcars, handcarts, bicycles, Stokes mortar carts and sidecars, plus two male tanks and one female tank, were to be embarked in each, and the monitors would push the pontoons up the beach. The tanks would drive off, pulling sledges full of equipment, climb the sea walls (an incline of about 30°), surmount a large projecting coping stone at the top, and then haul the rest of their load over the wall.

When the pontoons were completed, Bacon withdrew all his monitors to the Swin channel of the Thames Estuary to practise, and sequestered them in great secrecy, the crews being denied shore leave. Tested in the estuarial waters, the pontoons performed exceptionally well, riding out bad weather and being easier to manoeuvre than first expected, suggesting that they might be reused again after the initial assault to land reinforcements. Night landings were also practised, with wire stretched between buoys to guide the pontoons to within 100yds of their landing place.

Bacon was euphoric; as far as he was concerned, his plan worked. As he saw it, a landing operation would begin at dawn and an army division in three parties of about 4,500 men each would disembark on three beaches near Middelkirke, covered by a naval bombardment and a smokescreen generated by eighty small vessels. Trawlers would carry telephone cable ashore, and the tanks would disembark from the pontoons and climb the sea wall to cover the infantry landing. The infantry would have four artillery pieces and two light howitzers, and each wing of the landing was planned to have a motor machine-gun battery. For mobility, each landing party had more than two hundred bicycles and three motorbikes. In many ways, it was a faint, prescient, vision of the D-Day landings twenty-seven years later.

The plan was finally approved by Haig on 18 June 1917 as Operation Hush, and the 1st Division was chosen to make the coastal landing. But it never took place: Operation Hush was cancelled four months later on 14 October because the necessary precursor of an advance during the Third Battle of Ypres (an attack originally launched on 8 June with the capture of the Messines Ridge and with the objective of capturing and clearing the Belgian coast) did not meet the objectives required to begin the attack. It ended 'in a punch-drunk standoff'.[17] Bacon never had the chance to test his wonderful new conceptions.*

But that may have been all to the good. Although Jellicoe supported the idea, Rear Admiral Keyes (Director of Plans at the Admiralty from October 1917) thought that the operation was doomed to fail. And the military thinker and writer J F C Fuller (on the staff of the Heavy Branch of the Machine Gun Corps at the time) called the scheme 'a crack-brained one, a kind of mechanical Gallipoli affair'.[18] When in the area in 1933, he found that the sea walls were partially covered in a fine green seaweed, which the tanks might not have been able to scale.

Bacon was so disappointed in the decision not to proceed that he wrote a poem about it, which concluded:

---

* The original 1916 plan called for the blowing up and capturing of the Wytschaete Messines Ridge, then breaking out of the Ypres Salient and swinging round to capture Ostend and Zeebrugge in conjunction with an amphibious attack from the sea. Haig favoured this plan over the Somme campaign eventually, and disastrously, launched on 1 July 1916, political considerations forcing him to abandon his preferred option. Haig was finally able to launch the plan in 1917, as above, but it was doomed to failure because of an unusually wet summer and autumn, and the fact that the Germans had significantly strengthened their defences, which hardly existed in 1916. Had the original conception gone through, it may well have been a success and avoided the terrible Somme slaughter.

Then at last faint shock and grating, one great rush, and one great
    cheer,
As the tanks and living columns in the smoke-cloud disappear.
But that shout our dream has ended; broken is our reverie –
Wake to find that we've been dreaming of what never now can be.
Cruel fortune rudely shattered that matured and cherished scheme
All that might have been has faded. Nothing left us but a dream![19]

The attack of the drifters

Dover was not the only port which sustained elements of the Dover
Patrol. Ramsgate was also a patrol base and home to an armed drifter
squadron. It was this squadron that on 28 November 1917, at around
0630, sighted and engaged a German submarine *U-48*, which, while
waiting for the moon to set and recharging its batteries on the
surface, had drifted aground on the Goodwin sands. The drifters
Paramount, *Majesty* and *Present Help* attacked and were joined by
Feasible, *Acceptable* and *Lord Claud Hamilton*. A short, sharp
exchange of fire followed, in which *Feasible* stood in so close that
she bumped the sand some 30yds from the submarine. Armed only
with 3pdr or 6pdr guns, the small ships were outgunned by the
submarines' heavier 88mm (~3.5in) weapon. Shells fell all around
them and *Paramount* was hit; but just after 0700 the destroyer *Gipsy*
arrived from the north and opened fire at 2,000yds range with 12pdr
and 6pdr weapons, quickly achieving hits.

At this point *U-48* had sustained thirteen hits and was unviable.
Her commander ordered confidential books destroyed, gave the
orders to abandon ship and set scuttling charges. The crew leapt
overboard and the submarine blew up, taking her captain and twenty
men with her. One officer and twenty-one survivors were made
prisoners. There were no casualties on the drifters. The Admiralty
paid prize money of £1,000, and the destroyer captain and three
drifter skippers, all RNR, were awarded medals. Lt Commander F W
Robinson RNR of *Gipsy* received the DSO, whilst Skipper Hemp of
Paramount, Skipper Barker of *Majesty* and Skipper Lane of *Present
Help* were all awarded the DSC. Five ratings gained the DSM. The
press entitled this success 'The Battle of Ramsgate' and Bacon wrote
to express his satisfaction at the gallant way in which the lightly
defended drifters had attacked a submarine, which was armed with a
4in gun [sic]. The weapon was later salved and placed on display in
the town.

The Lure of the Offensive, 1917

Bacon had served under three First Sea Lords and three First Lords. He had taken up his command under the stormy duo of Churchill and Fisher (whose protégé he had been). The steady hand of Balfour had soon replaced Churchill, and Sir Henry Jackson took over from Fisher. This was not a dynamic partnership, Balfour being too aloof and disengaged, whilst Jackson was a workaholic technician and administrator. Bacon, a not dissimilar character, got on with him, however, and was largely left to his own devices.

The navy's reputation for caution was not disturbed by Jackson, and he was replaced in November 1916 by Jellicoe, much against the latter's wishes. On the night of 27 November, Jellicoe entertained a group of staff and other officers. He allegedly said that the submarine war was going to get so bad in 1917 that he would be blamed, and not last as First Sea Lord for more than six months. Balfour was replaced too, by the Ulster politician Edward Carson, who proved to be somewhat out of his depth. But Bacon and Jellicoe had a good relationship and again Bacon had a relatively free hand.

But throughout 1917 there were whispers building up against both men. Jellicoe had rightly divined that the submarine problem would only get worse. As previously mentioned, merchant shipping losses increased in the first quarter of 1917, January, February and March's figures being 368,521, 540,006 and 593,844 tons respectively and reaching an all-time high in April of 881,027 tons. By the end of the year, 6,235,878 tons of total Allied and neutral shipping would be sunk, up from 2,327,326 tons the previous year. And the Germans had reinstated their unrestricted submarine warfare doctrine from 1 February 1917. Despite this, Jellicoe was reluctant to introduce the system of protected convoy and this set him at odds with the politicians, especially new Prime Minister Lloyd George.

But he was also criticised, not least within the service that he ran, for his essentially defensive strategy which followed the doctrine originally adumbrated by Fisher, of distant blockade and the avoidance of risk to major units of the fleet. Beatty, now CinC Grand Fleet in succession to Jellicoe, had never really accepted it. As early as 1913 he had written to Churchill, whilst still serving as his naval secretary, to complain about both the vagueness and the lack of offensive spirit in the then newly issued fleet orders – which emphasised the distant blockade and abandonment of the North Sea. And firebrands like Roger Keyes or Reginald Tyrwhitt, in charge of the Harwich Force, regularly complained about the essentially defensive nature of the navy's activities.

Some of the press too began to chafe at the absence of publicly convincing action. As the *Spectator* magazine later put it:

defence was not, or should not have been, its [the Dover Patrol's] sole function. Englishmen by instinct and tradition regard the navy as a weapon of offence, and we may say frankly that the disappointment caused by the inability of the Grand Fleet to bring the enemy to action, save for a brief hour at Jutland, was intensified by the seeming passivity of the Dover Patrol.[1]

Eric Geddes was a successful businessman who had worked for and with Lloyd George at the Ministry of Munitions and proved to be a man who got things done. Faced with the growing losses of merchant ships, in May 1917 Lloyd George transferred Geddes to the Admiralty as Controller and Lord Commissioner and with the honorary rank of vice admiral. He was given responsibility for British shipbuilding, and charged with making up for as many of the losses as possible. Geddes found the Admiralty in disarray and wrote to his friend Field Marshal Douglas Haig about the lack of drive and positivity. On 19 June, Jellicoe, always a pessimist, confessed to the War Cabinet that they were losing the war. Haig and Geddes met with Lloyd George over a breakfast and argued for a new administration at the Admiralty. As a result, on 6 July, Carson was shoved aside and Geddes entered political life as First Lord of the Admiralty. His brief was, as before with munitions, to shake things up.

Vice Admiral Rosslyn Wemyss had been slated for command in the Mediterranean, but in September 1917 Geddes persuaded him to go to the Admiralty, first as Second Sea Lord and then, after only days in that post, as Deputy First Sea Lord. This was a blatant attempt by Geddes to work around Jellicoe and have Wemyss in place for the purposes of 'succession planning'. Wemyss quickly found the situation inimical: as his wife wrote later, 'how completely out of touch he [Wemyss] was with the spirit pervading the Admiralty which was purely defensive when he was entirely offensive'.[2] His position was made worse by the fact that Jellicoe, a man famous for his unwillingness to delegate, gave him nothing to do. 'Sir John Jellicoe could never be brought to see the utility of it [the deputy role],'[3] Wemyss commented later. Frustrated, he had a face-to-face row with the First Sea Lord. He told Jellicoe that he would complain to the First Lord, who could legally order him to delegate some of his role. 'Sir John did not agree'.[4] In the circumstances, Wemyss began to consider his position.

'To leave the initiative to the enemy, as we were doing, he [Wemyss] deemed a fatal mistake',[5] and it was to correct this perceived fault that Wemyss, with Geddes's consent, 'persuaded Admiral Keyes to leave the Grand Fleet and become Director of the newly formed Plans Division at the Admiralty.'[6] Keyes and Wemyss had become friendly serving together in the Dardanelles.

Wemyss now turned his attention to Dover where 'I found the opinion that it was impossible to do more than was being done towards stopping enemy submarines from passing through'.[7] He disagreed and 'Admiral Keyes was in agreement with me and many were the hours that we spent studying the situation'.[8] Neither man held much respect for Bacon. Wemyss thought that he 'was no sea officer and in my judgement turned his attention too much towards the military situation in devising means for landing heavy artillery etc and not enough towards stopping the passage of submarines.'[9] The old rivalry between army and navy, based on a pre-war competition for resource, resurfaced in the Deputy First Sea Lord's statement, and Bacon stood condemned for his involvement in Operation Hush and other military activities.

Amongst Keyes's new responsibilities, as defined by Geddes and Wemyss, was to establish and chair a new Admiralty committee to oversee the design, construction and use of the new mine barrage proposed by Bacon. Keyes had been rumoured to be after Bacon's job since the beginning of 1917; nobody knew where the gossip had started – but everybody knew it, including Admiral Bacon himself.

In October a friend had told him that a 'clique' at the Admiralty was conspiring against him, with the evidence salved from *UC-44* in August (see Chapter 13) forming the rational underpinning of the conspiracy.*

The Barrage Committee was convened on 17 November and submitted its report just twelve days later. It owed its genesis to the fact that, through messages intercepted and decrypted by Room 40 (the Admiralty's top-secret code-cracking team in the intelligence division), it was evident that German submarines were freely beating the barrier laid for them. Admiral Reginald Hall, in charge of intelligence, estimated that thirty a month were getting through the barrier. As Churchill later wrote, 'during 1917 the failure of the 1916 barrage across the Dover Strait had been total'.[10] Or as Wemyss later put it:

> the intelligence department satisfactorily proved to me that the enemy submarines did pass the Strait successfully and without challenge. Sir R Bacon on the other hand maintained that they did not, that his system of nets was satisfactory and that the proof of this lay in the fact that no ship had ever been torpedoed in his area.[11]

However, it might appear that Bacon's riposte rather missed the point, as it was the Western Approaches where the problem lay.

The Barrage Committee's term of reference reflected this problem. They stated, among other things:

> 1. The committee is appointed for the purpose of investigating and reporting on the possible measures for constructing a barrage across the Channel between England and France.
> 2. The committee is particularly charged with the following duties: to consider in what respects the barrage already attempted has not been successful and why.
> 3. To consider in detail the practicability from all points of view and probable efficiency of any scheme or schemes which can be put forward, showing clearly every detailed requirement which

---

* In fact, it was not just at the Admiralty. Captain Herbert Richmond had met Carson and Lloyd George, at the latter's request, in early June and strongly recommended that Bacon should be replaced by Keyes.

is involved in the construction, equipment, maintenance and defence of the barrage in the matter of personnel, plant, materials and equipment – the latter, of course, including all vessels and guns employed in its defence.

Keyes himself noted:

> I had made up my mind ... to devote my energies to stop submarines streaming through the Strait of Dover. Hall assured me that they were passing through at the rate of thirty per month; notwithstanding the assertion of the Admiral [Bacon] that the Strait was closed by his anti-submarine nets and that nothing was getting through.[12]

Thus the irresistible force of Keyes and the committee under his direction was pitted against the immoveable object of Bacon's self-belief.

The subsequent report was scathing, even going so far as to suggest that the Germans would regret the removal of the barrage, as it gave the Royal Navy a false sense of security. Papers taken from captured submarines and statements from prisoners indicated that the U-boat commanders did not see the barrage as a real obstacle, and it was estimated that the barrier had been 'navigated 334 times during 1917'.[13] One U-boat that had successfully transited the Dover Barrage as the investigating committee was forming was *U-58*, a 217ft-long oceangoing vessel sent to cause chaos in the Western Approaches. She passed through on 14 November but, alas for her, she became the first German submarine to fall victim to an American warship, being sunk on the 17th off the southwest coast of Ireland by the destroyers *Fanning* and *Nicholson*.

From his position in Dover, Bacon took huge offence at his judgements and control being so questioned and compromised. Bacon later wrote of 'the obvious fact that it was better to leave the defence of the Strait to the Admiral who had local knowledge, experience, and the whole responsibility entailed by the command at Dover, than to allow dabbling by a committee who had no local knowledge, experience, or responsibility.' He went on to add:

> it was such foolery! There was I, with a possible destroyer raid at my door, the Downs to protect, the French coast to keep from

molestation, and there at the Admiralty was an irresponsible committee, trying to get orders given to me as to how I should dispose my patrols to suit their theories.[14]

Bacon's self-belief shone through in a series of petulant letters he sent to the new First Lord. One extract will illustrate the general tone. 'I own I like my own way. I own in some matters I have firm convictions. But then I know the place and am generally right!'[15] These did not endear him to the equally self-confident Geddes. But Bacon was the man in the job, and he was supported by Jellicoe, possibly for too long for the latter's own good.

The differences between the committee's view of what was necessary and those of Admiral Bacon became entrenched and a matter of principle on both sides. Neither Keyes nor Bacon would back down. At the heart of the issue the differences were threefold. First, it was found that destroyers, never mind submarines, could pass over the barrier without damage. Bacon thought this could be resolved by tightening the jackstays holding the nets in place. Secondly, lighting: Bacon had the net lit by large light buoys at positions 5A, 7A, 9A, 11A and 13A (see map at picture section). Keyes and the committee wanted the whole net area constantly illuminated at night and swept by searchlights with additional lightships and trawlers firing flares. Bacon strongly opposed the use of such constant illumination. Finally, the committee wanted the patrol craft all concentrated in the eastern Channel guarding the net and its approaches, even to the extent of removing support from the nets Bacon had laid off Zeebrugge and the Flanders coast. Bacon did not agree and felt he had to deploy his forces to protect all the important points in his command.

Eventually, things came to a head. At a meeting at the Admiralty on 18 December, Bacon was forced into giving an undertaking to trial the illumination strategy and did so on the night of 19 December – the very night that *UB-56* was driven down into the deep mines and destroyed. From that point he was living on borrowed time.

Wemyss continued to press both Geddes and Jellicoe about Dover, and Bacon's tenure. As he put it, 'towards the end of December I brought the subject up very insistently before both the First Lord and First Sea Lord.'[16] But at least Bacon still had Jellicoe's support, and appealed to him as a last resort on many occasions. Jellicoe's view was clear. 'No suggestions of any proved value emanated from the [Barrage] Committee which had not already been put forward by Admiral Bacon and approved to be carried out as materials and vessels were available.'[17] Bacon appreciated the support. 'Thank goodness, we had a First Sea Lord who was a seaman of experience; but I imagine, from events that happened shortly afterwards, that his work was not made easy for him.'[18]

Matters reached a climax during a meeting in the First Lord's room at the Admiralty: 'Jellicoe maintained that Bacon was the best man for the job. I, on the other hand, maintained that he was not ... the First Lord was [thus] in the disagreeable position of finding his two principle technical advisors in direct opposition to each other.'[19] Frustrated at every turn, Wemyss determined to resign. But on 23 December he was summoned from wife, dinner and his London home to meet with Geddes, who told him that he had decided to remove Jellicoe and asked Wemyss to take over as First Sea Lord.

The 'events' referred to by Bacon (see above) was this termination of Jellicoe's tenure as First Sea Lord by Geddes on Christmas Eve 1917, by letter. Both the manner and the dismissal itself caused outrage in some parts of the navy. Rear Admiral Sir Dudley de Chair spoke for many when he expressed the view that 'I was surprised that any naval officer on the Board of Admiralty could remain there, as it looked as if they condoned this action of Jellicoe's dismissal. In fact, I expressed myself forcibly, and let myself go, and left after a scene which did me no good and had disastrous results'.[20]

The new First Sea Lord took office on 27 December. He was a monocle-wearing member of an aristocratic family (a cadet branch of the Earls of Wemyss and March who had inherited Wemyss Castle and 7,000 acres of land in Fife in the eighteenth century), and on good terms with royalty, having George V as a long-standing friend. He had been a favourite of Fisher's in his youth, but they became estranged, and he admired Beresford. Wemyss was a 'battleship navy' man, socially adept but no thinker. He was self-important, patrician, aloof, and possessed a low opinion of democracy and politicians, once exclaiming 'when every crossing sweeper has a voice in matters it is quite impossible for any government to rule'.[21] The economist John Maynard Keynes knew Wemyss and thought he was a 'lightweight ... with a comical quizzical face and a single eyeglass'.[22]

On the same day Wemyss took office he summoned Bacon to the Admiralty and ordered him to haul down his flag, which he did on

1 January 1918. His replacement was the man who had intrigued against him, Roger Keyes. Wemyss sent for Keyes and told him, 'Well Roger, you have talked a hell of a lot about what ought to be done in the Dover area. Now you must go down there and do it all yourself.'[23]

However, many in the navy disapproved of both Wemyss's and Keyes's appointments. Admiral Sir Arthur Cavenagh Leveson, commanding the 2nd Battlecruiser Squadron and the Australian navy, spoke for many when he said to Richmond that he did not agree with Keyes's appointment, stating that Keyes had not 'made good' and did not deserve it.[24] It was, after all, an unwritten rule that one didn't take the job of a man one had caused to lose it. Both Wemyss and Keyes had broken that rule.

Bacon's tenure in the post polarised opinions. Some thought very highly of him. The one-time Deputy Chief of the Admiralty War Staff, Admiral Sir Henry F Oliver, later recalled:

> Bacon was most energetic and tireless, he slept in his office and when anything happened at night in his command and I telephoned, the secretary would tell me he had gone afloat. He had the most exacting and arduous command of any Flag Officer in the War and was very badly treated at the end of it. Keyes intrigued against him and when Lord Westerwemyss [sic] became 1st Sea Lord he pushed him out and supplanted him.[25]

Others, as has been noted previously, couldn't abide him.

However, it was undeniable that during Bacon's tenure the Dover Patrol had achieved its primary duty of keeping the Channel open for trade and traffic. Over that period of three years, 120,000 merchant ships had passed through the Dover Strait. Fifty had been destroyed by mines. Five had been torpedoed. Just one had been destroyed by gunfire. It wasn't a bad record!

Bacon's own views on being superseded are clear from his later writings:

> The First Lord (Sir Eric Geddes, who, until the war, was Assistant General Manager of the North Eastern Railway) appointed a Barrage Committee to enquire into the Dover Barrage in 1917. I was not even represented on it. But this body, in its report to the Admiralty, was forced to agree with all I had done and proposed to do as regards the Folkestone–Grisnez [sic] mine barrage. It

recommended, however, that the barrage should be placed under one officer responsible to the Admiralty only! This meant that, in the middle of the waters I had to regulate and protect – a business that these reminiscences will show was one of the greatest complexity – an *imperium in imperio* was to be established under Admiralty control. This separate command was to control mines, some hundreds of patrolling vessels, and possibly, obstructions, while I was to remain responsible for the safety of traffic. These mines, patrol vessels and obstructions would probably have been subjected to direct attack by the enemy. This separate command and its very existence were necessarily closely linked with every portion of my command from Zeebrugge to the Downs, from Boulogne to Beachy Head. Yet officers capable of framing such a suggestion were sent to report on the Dover barrage! Needless to say, when the President of that Committee was appointed almost immediately afterwards to supersede me in the Dover Command nothing more was heard of such lunacy.[26]

And he described his dismissal in frank terms:

After my brutal – brutal is the only adequate term I can think of to apply – dismissal from Dover, the Admiralty, through their official head, took no steps to contradict statements in the press as to my work, both past and present, and the operations I had planned for the future, though they knew those statements to be untrue.

So long as silence is imposed, and most properly imposed, on officers and men during a war, so long is it incumbent and obligatory on the First Lord of the Admiralty to defend the professional honour of the personnel when publicly attacked. This duty was in my case totally disregarded, and, therefore it is necessary for me to state the facts, which, without in the least compromising secrecy, might and should have been done by the Admiralty earlier. It is this kind of treatment of officers that shakes to its very foundations the confidence of the navy in its rulers. Personally I have nothing to gain or lose; but the traditions of the navy are a national heritage, and any First Lord who impairs those traditions does a disservice to the State.[27]

In 1919 Bacon wrote his own version of the story of the Dover Patrol, from which the comments above are taken. One reviewing magazine commented:

The enemy held the Flanders coast for four years, used its ports as bases for destroyers and submarines, and might, for all we know, have prepared an invasion of our shores or, as Admiral Bacon says, a landing on the French coast south of the Yser which would have turned the left flank of the Allies. Yet, except for an occasional bombardment, the Dover Patrol apparently did not interfere with the Germans until in the spring of 1918 when it attacked Zeebrugge and Ostend and closed these harbours by block-ships. We looked to Admiral Bacon for enlightenment on this crucial matter, and we are glad to find him asserting in the plainest terms that he was eager to undertake an offensive on the Flanders coast, and that it was through no fault of his that nothing was done.[28]

PART FOUR
Keyes

'Keyes is a fine fellow but is not blessed with much brains'.

Jellicoe to Hamilton, 9 November 1915,
Jellicoe Papers I (Navy Research Society), p187.

Roger Keyes

Acting Vice Admiral Roger Keyes* was a small ship and submarine specialist who had served for much of his early career commanding destroyers and more latterly had been responsible for the submarine service as Inspecting Captain of Submarines. In this way, at least, he seemed fitted for command of the Dover Patrol.

Roger John Brownlow Keyes was born in October 1872 into a military family, the second son of Brigadier Sir Charles Patton Keyes of the Indian Army. From an early age he knew that he wanted to join the Royal Navy and, specifically, be an admiral. After an education in India and Margate, he joined the navy as a cadet in the training ship HMS *Britannia* on 15 July 1885. He did not make a good impression on everyone. His term captain remembered him as 'a miserable little squirt'.[1] Service around the world followed, but he was still not universally appreciated. As a sub lieutenant, his first captain would not allow him to stand any complicated watches alone, as he did not trust his abilities.

Nonetheless, by January 1898 Keyes had become commanding officer of the destroyer *Opossum* at Plymouth. He was subsequently posted out to China to command another destroyer, *Hart*, and in September 1898 transferred to a newer ship, *Fame*, in January 1899. In April the following year he went to the rescue of a small British force which had been attacked and surrounded by irregular Chinese forces while attempting to demarcate the border of the Hong Kong

---

* Keyes's number two at Dover, who had also been Bacon's deputy, was Rear Admiral Cecil Dampier, who had not only been a lieutenant in charge of Cadet Keyes in the dim and distant past, but was his superior in rank owing to his two years' seniority over Keyes as a rear admiral. Wemyss sidestepped this problem by appointing Keyes acting vice admiral.

New Territories. He went ashore, leading half the landing party, and while *Fame* fired on the besiegers, Keyes personally led the charge which routed the Chinese and freed the troops.

In June 1900 during the Boxer Rebellion, Keyes commanded a mission to capture a flotilla of four Chinese destroyers moored to a wharf on the Peiho River. Together with another junior officer, he took boarding parties onto the Chinese destroyers, captured them and secured the wharf; later he had to recapture one destroyer from the Russians. Shortly thereafter, he led a mission to take the heavily fortified fort at Hsi-cheng: he loaded *Fame* with a landing party of thirty-two men, armed with rifles, pistols, cutlasses and explosives. His men quickly destroyed the Chinese gun mountings, blew up the powder magazine and returned to the ship.

Not content with his growing fame, Keyes was one of the first men to climb over the Peking walls, to break through to the besieged diplomatic legations and to free the legations: for his conduct he was promoted to commander on 9 November 1900. By now, one could see the defining characteristics of Keyes's personality. He was brave to a fault, fearless and more than a little rash.

Back home, in 1901 Keyes was appointed to the command of the destroyer *Bat*, serving in the Devonport instructional flotilla, moving to *Falcon* in 1902 and then *Sprightly*. Service as naval attaché in Rome followed and in 1910 he became Inspecting Captain of Submarines, followed by Commodore of the Submarine Service in 1912. When the First World War broke out, Keyes took command of the 8th Submarine Flotilla at Harwich, where he led his forces personally in the flotilla leaders *Lurcher* and *Firedrake*. In 1915 he became chief of staff to successive admirals commanding the Dardanelles campaign. During his tenure, he personally devised and commanded an operation in the March to attempt to clear the Kephez minefield. It was a disaster, as the Turkish mobile artillery bombarded Keyes's minesweeping squadron to pieces. Heavy injury was inflicted on four of the six minesweeping trawlers, while his command vessel, the *Topaze*-class protected cruiser *Amethyst* was badly hit and had her steering gear damaged. When further minesweeping by trawlers failed, Keyes was apoplectic: 'to put it briefly the sweepers turned tail and fled directly they were fired on'.[2] He did not tolerate what he perceived as a lack of courage, but Keyes may have done better to remember that these vessels' crews were only transplanted fishermen.

In disagreement with his commanding officer (Admiral de Robeck), about the decision to withdraw from the peninsula, Keyes was given permission to return to London and lobby political opinion for staying. In this he failed, but he intrigued against his boss, persuading First Lord Balfour to offer de Robeck a 'holiday' while Keyes would replace him. De Robeck declined. Keyes went instead to the Grand Fleet as second in command of the 4th Battle Squadron. When de Robeck eventually took leave, his replacement was Wemyss, who immediately tried to resurrect Keyes's more aggressive plans.

Keyes was a keen huntsman, an excellent shot, avid polo player and a prize-winning jockey. He did everything at top speed and had loved the cut and thrust of destroyer work. He was an ardent patriot and obsessed by the gentleman's code of chivalry. But he divided opinion. Jellicoe thought him unintelligent, whilst the historian Arthur Marder described Keyes as one whose 'judgement ... was often overruled by their fiery temperament and he never looked much further than the launching of an operation': a starter, but not a planner or a finisher. Another historian described him as 'not renowned for his outstanding intellect or technical facility'.[3] Marder, however, asserted that Keyes was 'one of the most attractive of men, warm hearted and full of boyish enthusiasm – a born leader with few brains'.[4]

Churchill was unsurprisingly a fan, writing to Fisher on 21 December 1914 that 'Keyes is a brilliant officer with more knowledge of and feeling for war than about any other naval officer I have met'.[5] But Fisher himself hated Keyes, believing that the submarine service had stagnated under Keyes's command and that it was largely Keyes's fault. He had written to Churchill in early 1914 advocating Keyes's replacement with Hall or Bacon on the grounds that Keyes had never seen a submarine until he was given the post and 'we have fewer submarines now than when I left office four years ago ... and Germany then was zero'.[6] Fisher also thought that Keyes had sided with Beresford in the great internal 'war' between them; in fact, this was unfair, for it was a different officer with the same name who was to blame.

And despite Churchill's encomium, Keyes's leadership qualities were not universally admired. Lieutenant (later Commander) R T Young noted that 'he [Keyes] was an aloof figure. He didn't make it his business to be known. In the six months I served under him I never saw him. For another he was reputed to have his favourites and if you were not in the Magic Circle you might just as well pack up.'[7]

Keyes's role models were the buccaneers of the Elizabethan age with whom, like his friends Tyrwhitt and 'Kit' Cradock, he would have felt perfectly at home. This was the man now in charge of the Dover Patrol: not a planner or clever thinker like Hood; not an engineering- and materiel-orientated sailor as was Bacon, but an action man, an heroic doer.

1 7

Under Pressure: Keyes Takes Charge and the Massacre of the Drifters, 1918

Bacon had been far from unpopular with his men, being regarded as fair-minded and even-tempered, not attributes universally shared by flag officers. But Keyes wasted no time in bringing in the changes to the operations of the Patrol that he had been advocating. He effectively abandoned the cross-channel mine and net barrage between the Goodwins and West Dyck and instead focused on the deep minefields between Folkestone and Cap Gris-Nez with massed patrols and brilliant illumination at night. Keyes sent destroyers out in groups on frequent submarine-hunting patrols, especially at night, and lighted the length of the deep mine barrage with shipborne flares and searchlights during the hours of darkness – the so called 'light barrier', which was intended to prevent the U-boats exiting on the surface in the dark. Armed trawlers went out on 'flare patrol', carrying sufficient flares to light one every sixteen minutes as they cruised up and down the line of the minefield. Other vessels mounted permanently lit searchlights. Bacon had fundamentally disagreed with such changes, arguing that it exposed the ships to more danger, and that the illumination would make British vessels stand out as easy targets at night.

Keyes continued with his ideas nonetheless and, rather less admirably, persisted in belittling his predecessor's views to his quondam staff. Bacon's most recent chief of staff had been Captain Evans, last noted here commanding *Broke*. Evans, convinced that Keyes's appointment was the result of some distasteful behind-the-scenes manoeuvring, asked for an immediate transfer. Keyes agreed, on the face-saving grounds of ill health.

Captain Herbert Grant had been Bacon's intelligence officer. He and Keyes had been cadets together at *Britannia* where they had detested each other, so Keyes's appointment could hardly be expected to fill him with joy. Nonetheless, on hearing the news, Grant wrote, 'I thought the Admiralty had gone mad. Later when I was at the Admiralty, I was convinced that Sir Reginald had been ousted by as despicable an intrigue as ever occurred in the annals of war.'[1]

Keyes also continued his 'favourites' policy. His new chief of staff was Captain The Honourable Algernon Boyle (the son of the 5th Earl of Shannon), an old friend from China days, for whom Keyes gained promotion to commodore, and his new captain of the fleet was Captain Wilfred Tomkinson, who had been his first lieutenant in China. Later he had worked alongside Keyes in his role as Inspecting Captain of Submarines, and became his flagship captain when Keyes moved to the Grand Fleet in the 4th Battle Squadron. Now he was at Keyes's side again.

And Admiral Hall tried to assist and buy Keyes some time by concocting an espionage scam, whereby he sold details of an imaginary barrage across the Strait, equipped with new electric devices of destruction, to a known German agent for the princely sum of £2,000.

Keyes's tenure started with a success. *UB-35* was a German U-boat commissioned in April 1916. In her short career, she had sunk forty-two ships, damaged two and taken four as prizes, for a total of over 54,000 tons in twenty-six missions, initially in the Baltic and from July 1917 as a member of the Flanders Flotilla. On 26 January 1918 she was attempting to transit the Dover Barrage and gain access to the killing grounds where the transatlantic traffic came to British shores.

Leven was on a courier mission from Dover to Dunkirk that same day under the command of an RNR lieutenant, Arthur Percy Melsom. She was an old (1898) '30-knotter' destroyer, armed with one 12pdr gun and five 6pdrs, two torpedoes and, more latterly, depth charges. About six miles northwest of Calais, Melsom spotted a periscope and attacked with depth charges. A large explosion, a sudden oil slick and the sight of two men struggling in the water told him that he had sunk a submarine. It was *UB-35*; she would sink no more merchant ships. Twenty-six men went down with her, and although two survivors were pulled from the water, they later died.

Leven's first lieutenant was also an RNR officer, John Noble Shipton. He was typical of the sons of empire who had volunteered to serve far from their homes and families. Shipton had been born in Inverell, New South Wales, and was a resident of Subiaco, where his father worked as superintendent of the industrial school. He initially joined the 3rd Light Horse, an Australian volunteer cavalry regiment, as a sapper in November 1914, unmarried, aged twenty-six years and six months and giving his occupation as 'master mariner.'

The Light Horse served in the disastrous Gallipoli campaign and the slaughter (and to judge from his service record, the enteric fever, for he was hospitalised with dysentery) persuaded him that he would be better off fighting for the empire in the navy.

He was discharged from the Australian forces in England and commissioned into the RNR as a sub lieutenant in October 1915, being posted to *Foyle* in the Dover Patrol. His service in the Patrol proved eventful. *Foyle* was mined on 15 March 1917, losing her bows and eventually sinking near to Plymouth after an unsuccessful attempt at towing her to safety. She lost twenty-eight officers and men. Shipton, by now a full lieutenant RNR, survived and transferred to *Leven* where, as a result of the sinking of *UB-35*, he gained a 'mentioned in despatches' (gazetted 6 April 1918).[*]

The old and obsolete gunboat *Hazard* had given sterling service to the Dover Patrol. She had been a submarine depot ship, operated stalwartly as a floating artillery piece under Horace Hood, participated in the rescue of the survivors of *Anglia* and been a maid of all work under three admirals. She surely deserved a better fate than that which eventually overtook her. On 28 January she was rammed whilst steaming off Portland Bill by the hospital ship SS *Western Australia*. *Hazard* was virtually sliced in half and sank very quickly, despite attempts to effect a tow. Out of a complement of 120 men, all but three were saved (and a fourth later died from his injuries): two stokers, a carpenter and a shipwright. At the subsequent court martial, her commander, Lieutenant Commander Finlay RNR, was found to be at fault.[**]

The everyday work of minesweeping continued unchanged, and so did the risks entailed. The Aberdeen-registered trawler

---

[*] By January 1919, Shipton was still in the navy, commanding *Milbrook*. But the ship had been put under a care and maintenance party by October and Shipton returned to Australia, his duty to King and empire done.

[**] Finlay was later to die during the flu epidemic in March 1919.

Drumtochty was requisitioned by the Admiralty on completion in October 1915 and sent to the Dover Strait as a minesweeper, with a crew of Aberdonian trawlermen.

By 29 January 1918 her skipper was Brixham-born, 27-year-old George Carpenter. He had volunteered at the outbreak of the war, and soon after was transferred to the trawler section of the Royal Naval Reserve. He was quickly promoted to skipper and had taken command of *Drumtochty* ten days previously. Around 1100 his vessel hit a mine, which exploded under and abaft the engine room. She sank quickly, taking Carpenter and ten of her crew with her. One of the dead was John Forrest RNCVR, a Canadian volunteer who died a long way from his native land. Two survivors were picked up by the paddle minesweeper *Goodwood* and transferred ashore via the monitor *M-21*.

The massacre of the drifters

The 'light barrier' had a strong psychological effect on the Germans. It undoubtedly made transit on the surface more difficult, but it also served as a reproof and a taunting lure. As a result, the disaster which Bacon had feared was not long in coming.

On the night of 14/15 February, the Germans tried to put an end to their torment with a decisive attack on the Folkestone–Gris-Nez barrier. Two half-flotillas of destroyers were deployed in the attempt.

Along the length of the barrier were moored a series of buoys, which were used to assist the patrolling vessels to maintain their positions. About two and a half miles on either side of this line were stationed trawlers, paddlers and other small craft, to either burn flares or to use searchlights. On the night in question there were also fifty-eight drifters patrolling the barrage line.

At 0040, one half-flotilla of four destroyers started the attack from the northwest by firing on the paddle steamer *Newbury*, whose revolving searchlight made her an easy target. By some miracle she was undamaged. The destroyers then proceeded slowly down the drifter line and sank the drifters *W Elliot* and *Veracity*. The paddler *Lingfield* and a motor launch also came under fire, but made good their escape by extinguishing all lights and running for home.

The next wave of attackers came from the southeast and at the Gris-Nez end of the barrier. At 0045, three destroyers appeared out of the darkness and quickly fired at and set on fire the Admiralty-built trawler *James Pond*. Her crew endeavoured to extinguish the flames and beach her, but in the end had to abandon ship. Next to suffer was the drifter *Clover Bank II*. A destroyer, misjudging her distance in the dark, suddenly loomed alongside her and opened fire with her guns at maximum depression and firing on the roll. The top side of the little drifter was turned into matchwood and set on fire, her skipper and all bar one of her crew killed immediately. With the sort of madness which is later inexplicable, Seaman Gunner Frederick Plane ran through the smoke and fire to man the drifter's only gun, mounted forward and, finding it loaded, returned the fire at point-blank range, single-handed, half-blinded, stupefied by smoke and noise.

The destroyers then proceeded down the line of drifters, firing as they went. *Cosmos*, *Christina Craig* and *Jeannie Murray* were sunk, with only three survivors escaping from the hail of shells. All fourteen crew of the *Jeannie Murray* were lost, including her telegraphist, Frederick Seed RNVR, until October 1916 a teacher at South Moor, County Durham. *Golden Grain*, *Golden Rule*, *Violet May* and *Treasure* were all attacked and damaged. On board *Violet May,* enginemen James Ewing and Alexander Noble succeeded in launching their boat, and lowered into it the mate, mortally wounded, and an injured deckhand. The remainder of the crew lay dead on deck, scattered amongst the blazing wreckage. They paddled clear of the burning wreck, but when the enemy had passed by closed up to her again, despite the danger from fire forward, steam pouring from her wrecked engine room and ammunition exploding about her decks. Ewing and Noble assessed that they could save the ship, boarded her, put out the fires and sailed her back to Dover. The mate, Charles Barber, died.

The early morning of destruction was not yet finished. At about 0130 the German ships turned back along the barrier towards France and on the return journey met and sank the drifter *Silver Queen*, which had on board the unlucky survivors of *Cosmos*. Finally, after firing on two more drifters, the Germans headed back to their base at Zeebrugge.

In total, seven British drifters and a trawler were sunk, together with three drifters and a paddle steamer damaged. British dead numbered eighty-nine officers and men, every single one of them RNR or RNVR. It was not a triumph of arms for Keyes and his programme.

The Admiralty tried to put a brave face on it. In a press release they stated:

> The German destroyer raid on the English Channel on the night of 14/15 February had for its primary aim the destruction of the Auxiliary Patrol Forces on outpost duty. This much was evident from the deliberate and systematic manner in which, once touch was established in the inky darkness, the attack was carried out. A large force was chosen for the enterprise, comprising ten at least of Germany's largest and fastest destroyers. That these succeeded in sinking seven armed fishing vessels and returning to their base without being intercepted by the British patrols proper can be ascribed to accurate foreknowledge of the disposition of these forces (information readily supplied by aerial reconnaissance).

They also invented an unlikely sounding conversation, placed in the mouths of the two engineers from the *Violet May*:

> 'A doot she's sinkin',' said Ewing, stoutly. Noble said nothing. He was not given overmuch to speech, but he made the painter and proceeded to climb inboard again. Ewing followed, and between them they fought and overcame the fire. 'Dinna leave me, Jamie,' cried the mate piteously, 'dinna leave me in the little boat.' 'Na, na,' was the reply. 'We'll nae leave ye,' and presently they brought their wounded back on board, and took them below again. The mate was laid on his bunk, and Ewing fetched his shirts from his bag and tore them up into bandages. 'An' them his dress shirts,' murmured Noble. It was his first and last contribution to the narrative.[2]

No doubt the two brave engineers were suitably embarrassed.

And the *Dover Express* carried a report of the thoughts of a sailor present:

> 'This is not the first fight of a similar character in which I have taken part during this war,' he said, 'and yet, thank God, I am unhurt. But it was by far the worst of the four scraps which I have been engaged in. It was a terribly one-sided affair ... It was a fine, starlight night, and was so calm, there was not a breath of wind and only a very slight haze. The fleet of drifters to which I was

attached was on patrol duty. Being then off duty myself, I went down to my bunk, but before turning in I was reading a book.

'Suddenly at about one o'clock in the morning, I was startled by heavy and rapid firing, the noise of hurrying footsteps on the deck overhead, and the issuing of rapid orders. My first impression was that we had seen, and were firing at, a submarine. Picking up my lifebelt I hurried on deck. The noise of the cannonade at this time was almost deafening. The first thing I saw on reaching the deck was the blowing up of one of our drifters, which was not far away from our port quarter. She went up in the air enveloped in a great sheet of flame, in the midst of which I distinctly saw her two masts and funnel fall with a splash into the water, sending up spray in all directions.'[3]

Later in the morning, the rescued survivors and the recovered dead were landed at Dover. The injured were taken to hospital, whilst the dead were placed in motor lorries and taken to the town's Market Hall. Crowds watched on as the bodies, wrapped in blankets, were lifted on to stretchers and carried into the building. As the local newspaper had it, 'The injuries that the men had received were of a very terrible nature, and were due in almost all cases to shells and splinters. Altogether thirty-six bodies were landed'.[4]

Many of the dead were never recovered. Among these was the commanding officer of the drifter *Clover Bank II*, 31-year-old Richard Crafter. He was typical of the RNR men who enlisted from the merchant service. Son of the harbourmaster of Liverpool, Richard senior, he had entered the Leyland Line as an apprentice and by the outbreak of war had risen to the position of second officer on ss *Victorian*. He immediately volunteered for the RNR and was allocated to the Dover Patrol where he worked largely on minesweeping trawlers. His prowess was clearly marked and he was quickly promoted to lieutenant and command of some of the smaller craft.

Eighteen months earlier he had married Maggie Colquhoun. After the ceremony, the relatives of the newlyweds had assembled at the house of the bride's parents, whilst Richard and Maggie left for honeymoon in Richmond-on-Thames: their happiest day, no doubt. Captain Bird wrote to Maggie 'he was one of my best officers, and one whose service I shall greatly miss. The patrol were [sic] all out to hunt an enemy submarine. The officers and men behaved most gallantly, and foremost among them was Lieut. Crafter.'[5] Crafter was not forgotten in death, being awarded the DSC in the April. This may not have helped his wife; she was left with a young son, born in November 1917, and £295 in her late husband's will.[*]

It had been a fight which pitted a heavily outgunned force against fast and well-armed opponents. As one sailor put it, 'the only thing I can compare it to is a picture of a man armed, say, with a revolver or a pop-gun being expected to do battle in a small boat with an armed cruiser'.[6] The following day, 'there was considerable difficulty in getting the boats to go to sea ... the crews felt that the navy had let them down'.[7] And Signalman William James Wood of *Marksman* noted in his diary: 'it was a great pity and some great miscarriage on someone's part that they [the German destroyers] were not engaged by our patrols'.[8]

Keyes, perhaps in exculpation or in order to boost the self-image of the men manning the nets, recommended a large distribution of medals. Frederick Plane received the DSM, as did twelve other sailors. There were also awards of five DSCs, two bars to a DSC and three CGMs, two of which were awarded to James Ewing and Alexander Noble (gazetted 16 March 1918).

There was a more quotidian loss that night as well, one which would attract few headlines. On the 14th, ss *War Monarch*, a brand new American-built collier, was on a voyage from Hull to Italy with a cargo of coal. She was torpedoed by the German submarine *UB-57*, eleven miles east of the Royal Sovereign light vessel. On this occasion, there were no casualties – just another lost merchantman and a frightened crew.

Before the war, coal had been Britain's largest export and the shipment of coal throughout the war was an important political, as well as industrial, weapon. France was almost entirely dependent on Britain for its coal for home and factory (it had lost 68 per cent of its coal production owing to the German invasion) and Italy had been offered preferential amounts of coal as part of its decision to enter the war on the Allied side. Moreover, the Foreign Office used the ability to supply or restrict coal to neutral countries such as Holland, Sweden, Norway and Denmark as a negotiating tool to gain

---

[*] Crafter's father, Richard senior, had four sons altogether: two in the army, both of whom had been wounded, and his eldest son, a seagoing engineer, who was captured by the Germans when his ship was torpedoed and became a prisoner of war in Germany.

reciprocal guarantees that it and other key locally produced raw materials would not be (re-)exported to Germany. For example, in 1917 an agreement was made with Norway whereby Britain would deliver 250,000 tons of coal per month, in return for preferential access to Norwegian ores and other products, and the removal of Norway as a supplier to Germany. British high quality, especially Welsh, coal was an essential for steamships, and for many railway and other power applications.

Losses amongst the colliers sailing to France had become so severe that, after the declaration of unrestricted submarine warfare on 1 Feb 1917, the French requested that colliers be convoyed. They were escorted by armed trawlers and the first coal ship convoys sailed on 10 February to Brest, Cherbourg and Le Havre. Subsequently, only fifty-three ships were lost out of 39,352 sailings. Sailings to Italy were not so protected, as *War Monarch* proved.

HMS *Botha*, 21 March 1918

The Germans began a new and massive offensive in Picardy on 21 March, which broke through the Allied lines at St Quentin. It was accompanied by increased naval activity on the coast, in an attempt to disrupt lines of communication, the orders for which had been issued by the commodore of the German Flanders Flotilla on 18 March. It was an important operation for the German navy, for the German state was now primarily a military one, run by the army and under the fiat of Ludendorff and von Hindenburg. The navy needed to show that it could still make a contribution to the salvation of the Fatherland.

The naval plan ordered was for an attack against railway traffic east and south of Dunkirk, the line at Dunkirk-Bray Dunes and the railheads at La Panne and Dunkirk itself. In the early morning of 19 March, a motor launch on patrol located a group of four enemy destroyers near the light buoy at the northern end of Zuidcoote Pass (an access point through the mine barrage). The Germans were carrying out a preliminary reconnaissance. Thus alerted, Keyes put his forces at instant readiness with a mixed Anglo-French group of destroyers on the alert in the Dunkirk Roads.

These forces comprised *Botha*, the flotilla leader, accompanied by *Morris* and four French destroyers, *Capitaine Mehl*, *Bouclier*, *Oriflamme* and *Magon*. In Dunkirk harbour, and ready to provide assistance if necessary, were the monitors *Terror* and *General Craufurd*.

Botha was another destroyer intended originally for the Chilean navy, built in 1914 and armed with six 4in guns and two sets of twin torpedo tubes. Her captain was Commander Roger L'Estrange Murray Rede RN, born in Australia in 1878 to an army colonel, and a Royal Navy man since the age of fourteen. He had already been mentioned in despatches for an attack against an enemy submarine carried out on 7 August 1917.

The German forces deployed were significant, comprising nine destroyers, six large torpedo boats, and four small 'A'-class torpedo boats. They began their bombardment at 0345 on 21 March. Ten minutes later, *Botha* and her consorts slipped their cables and hared out in pursuit. They found their targets at 0435 and immediately opened fire. For once there seems to have been no recognition problems, for they received the wrong reply to their challenge and did not further equivocate.

Rede was leading the line in *Botha*. Ten minutes into the action she was hit in the no. 2 stokehold and a steam pipe was fractured, causing her speed to fall off. Seeing the enemy vessels were drawing ahead, Rede went hard a-port to attack them with torpedoes. He then closed the leading torpedo boat to ram and made clean contact with *A-19*, striking her amidships and cutting her in two pieces which immediately fell away and sank. The German destroyers started to lay a smokescreen which covered most of the force from view, and Rede could only see *A-7*, astern of his ramming victim, which he raked almost point blank with his after armament.

So far, so good, but the gods of war are capricious. One of the French destroyers, *Capitaine Mehl*, mistaking *Botha* for an enemy, fired a torpedo which hit amidships and exploded with terrific force, blowing a large hole in her port side. Rede gave orders to abandon the ship, but a few minutes later they were cancelled when it was assessed that she still had a chance of survival, despite having taken a lot of water on board and with her engines and boilers wrecked.

On board the ship it was chaos. Artificer Evan Edward Wellman was first to react when escaping steam made it impossible for the watchkeepers to get out of the affected boiler room. Wellman isolated the compartment by closing stop valves from the upper deck whilst the ship was under heavy fire at the time, saving the lives of the men and allowing their escape. Stoker First Class John Darrock also played a role in the escape of those trapped below. He entered the damaged boiler room of the ship, with red-hot steam escaping all around him, and assisted the watchkeepers to get on deck, again under heavy fire.

Under the cover of smoke and darkness, and with heavy shells from *Terror* falling amongst them, the remaining German vessels made good their escape. With the coming of daylight, the only sign of the enemy was the ship set on fire by *Botha*'s guns, *A-7*. She was finished off by *Morris*, which then took *Botha* in tow and, with a protective screen of the French destroyers, just managed to reach Dunkirk with her. The French navy later gave out that *Botha* had been fired on 'owing to her not answering challenge quickly enough',[9] although the fact that *Botha*'s fighting lights were no longer lit, as the electric circuit had been severed during the engagement, might have made that difficult.

Rede had shown the sort of courage and elan which Keyes lived for and the admiral became his greatest fan. Rede was awarded the DSO for his gallantry, the citation reading:

> He took his ship through a heavy barrage of gunfire, and, without waiting to ascertain that the rest of his division were following, proceeded to engage the enemy with ram, torpedo and gun fire. He rammed and cut in two an enemy torpedo boat. The success of the action was undoubtedly due to his gallant leadership and initiative.[10]

The captain of *Morris*, Lieutenant Commander Percy Ralph Passawer Percival, received a bar to his own DSO. Wellman received the DSC and Darrock the CGM. Keyes subsequently appointed Rede to the brand-new flotilla-leader *Douglas* and made it his temporary home when in Dunkirk, whilst pushing Rede forward for advancement to the rank of captain, an intention which was eventually fulfilled in December 1918, but not without some heavy lifting by Keyes with Wemyss. This short and, for the Germans, rather fruitless raid against the Flanders coast was seemingly the only attempt that the Imperial Navy carried out in the Patrol's area to support their great offensive on land, the Spring Offensive or *Kaiserschlacht*, Lundendorff's last throw of the dice to win the war.

On 1 April the RAF was founded, amalgamating the Royal Flying Corps (RFC) and the RNAS. Keyes was a proponent of air warfare, and especially patrols to keep the U-boats submerged (until their batteries ran out) and bombing of the U-boat pens. On taking over the Patrol he had under his orders the 5th Group of the RNAS, comprising five squadrons and approximately ninety aeroplanes, mainly based on airfields to the west of Dunkirk. These were all lost to him at the formation of the combined force and he subsequently received 'only a fraction of what he wanted and the British air attacks were neither sufficiently heavy nor sustained long enough for really effective results.'[11] Keyes believed that 'golden opportunities were lost for inflicting heavy losses on the enemy on the Flanders coast'.[12] This is perhaps a little unfair as 5 Group (now RAF) flew 1,127 anti-submarine missions between May and October 1918, together with seventy-two as escort. Airships in 5 Group also flew 657 anti-submarine missions.[13] But there is no doubt that a general neglect of naval aviation was to Britain's detriment throughout the post-war period.

Twisting the Dragon's Tail: The Zeebrugge and Ostend Raids, 1918

As previously described, the German occupation of Zeebrugge and Ostend and their subsequent deployment there of the Flanders Flotilla of destroyers and submarines was a constant thorn in the flesh of the Royal Navy. The Germans were able to threaten the cross-channel communications and supply chain, together with the Downs area of heavy commercial traffic into London and other southern ports, and gain shortened access to the Atlantic shipping concentration areas for trade interdiction. And as the U-boat predation on British trade gained in ferocity and tonnage, so proliferated the number of schemes for ending the menace.

Back in the early days of the war, Captain Herbert Richmond, serving in the Admiralty as assistant director of the Operations Division, had minuted on 13 October 1914 a recommendation that the ports of Zeebrugge and Ostend be blocked before the Germans took them (which they did two days later).

Then in 1916 Vice Admiral Lewis Bayly, commanding the Western Approaches from his base at Queenstown and thus in the thick of the anti-submarine effort, produced a detailed plan for landing troops in occupied Belgium to seize Ostend and Zeebrugge. Ambitious in scope and objective, it called for men and equipment that were both in short supply and was quietly shelved.

Shortly afterwards, the offensively minded Commodore Tyrwhitt at Harwich also produced a plan. This called for the destruction of the lock gates by an explosives-packed blockship protected by smoke and poison gas. The possibility that the poison gas would impact on the local populace was something he had overlooked, but the Admiralty didn't and rejected the idea. Undismayed, Tyrwhitt recast his thinking and now proposed an attack on Zeebrugge harbour mole and the capture of the town itself to effect operations against the German flank. Admiral Bacon was asked for his views on the plan and deprecated it, adding to the animosity between the two men. Bacon did not entirely reject the idea of an attack on the gates, but remained convinced that the best chance of success lay in long-range bombardment and, as has been described in Chapter 14, attempted to put such thoughts into practice.

Keyes's arrival at Whitehall in October 1917 coincided with both the continued high levels of shipping losses and the failure of the Third Battle of Ypres (see above), which had failed in an attempt to throw back the Germans and allow for the taking of the Belgian ports. German U-boats were destroying more than 500,000 tons of shipping each month, but were losing no more than two submarines per month in return. Keyes reasoned that the immediate tasks were to stop the transit of submarines through the Strait of Dover and, importantly, to nullify the problem at source, by denying the Germans the use of the Belgian ports.

Keyes passed his thoughts to First Sea Lord Jellicoe, and Jellicoe passed them on to Bacon, asking for a response. In reply, Bacon suggested that the long, curved harbour mole could be stormed by men landed by means of a forward-mounted ramp from a monitor and that they could then storm the lock gates and destroy them. To distract the Germans, he proposed a bombardment of the German heavy gun battery at Knokke, to convince them that the landing was intended for that location, not the harbour. In these ideas was sprung the genesis of the plan that became the Zeebrugge Raid.

Bacon presented his plan at the Admiralty on 18 December 1917: the idea of landing troops on the mole (a long barrier protecting the harbour from the sea and at the time the longest in the world) appealed to Keyes's aggressive temperament and he persuaded the Admiralty Board that the operation should proceed. Bacon was unofficially told that he was to command the attempt, to take place in February, but then Geddes and Wemyss conducted their putsch and Bacon was no longer in command. Now Keyes had free rein to run the Dover Patrol his way. And Zeebrugge and Ostend were firmly in his sights.

22 April 1918

A small armada of ships set sail towards the Belgian coast at 1700. Destroyers, monitors, MLs, CMBs, minesweepers, submarines; two ex-River Mersey ferries, *Iris* and *Daffodil*; and six very old cruisers, *Vindictive*, *Thetis*, *Intrepid*, *Iphigenia*, *Brilliant* and *Sirius*. The latter five vessels were packed with concrete; the former was heavily protected and carried all sorts of close-range firepower, including howitzers and a flame-thrower. There were also two old submarines, each crammed with explosives. Two hundred Royal Marines and a naval landing party were loaded on board the ferries and *Vindictive*. In command was Roger Keyes, flying his flag in the destroyer *Warwick*.

This unlikely looking force had originally sailed on 11 April but, in sight of the objective, unfavourable weather conditions had led to a turnaway and postponement. A planned air bombing raid in support was unable to be recalled and went ahead anyway. Now, on the eve of St George's Day, Keyes was finally to carry the attack to the enemy. As the force assembled at Swin Deep, Keyes signalled to Acting Captain Alfred Francis Blakeney Carpenter, commanding *Vindictive*, 'St George for England'. Perhaps feeling posterity's breath on his shoulder, Carpenter, a member of Keyes's 'magic circle' – having been his navigator on *Venus* and worked for him at the Admiralty, from whence Keyes had plucked him – replied, 'May we give the dragon's tail a good twist.'

The plan was straightforward in outline, but complex in execution. Under cover of smoke and bombardment, *Vindictive* and the ferries *Iris* and *Daffodil* were to land the marines on Zeebrugge harbour mole, from whence they would destroy German gun positions and prevent the enemy from interfering with the remainder of the operation. Explosive-packed submarines would position themselves under the viaduct which joined the mole to the mainland and blow themselves up, destroying the bridge and hence the enemy's pathway for resupply of men and equipment to the mole. And *Thetis*, *Intrepid*, *Iphigenia* would sail into the harbour and sink themselves in the Bruges canal entrance, thus blocking entry and exit for the foreseeable future. Meanwhile, *Sirius* and *Brilliant* would head for Ostend with their escort and under the command of Commodore Hubert Lynes[*] and sink themselves to block that canal link too.

---

[*] Lynes was senior naval officer at Dunkirk, as well as being a noted ornithologist.

It looked simple, but there were many 'moving parts' and inter-dependences. The harbour and its environs were heavily protected with guns of large and small calibre alike. The tides were difficult and there was only one dredged channel into Zeebrugge harbour proper. There were constantly shifting sandbanks in the immediate approaches, and there were bound to be hidden German minefields. To take advantage of the high tides, they would have to go in at around midnight. Navigation would be by dead-reckoning and a light onshore wind was essential to ensure the success of the smokescreen. It was a tough ask and one which Keyes's (and previously Bacon's) intelligence officer, Captain Grant, had argued strongly against, to no avail.

What is more, the Germans knew they were coming. During the abortive sailing of 11 April, *CMB-33* had managed to get itself captured by the Germans off Ostend. Against all instructions, the commander was carrying his secret orders and navigation charts on board; it did not take the Germans very long to work out that an assault on Zeebrugge was in the offing. Added precautions were taken, with more men and guns moved into the immediate area.

Keyes had long ago decided that he would not allow the army to take part; the navy's marines would fulfil that role as would naval landing parties. This was to be an all Royal Navy affair, to restore that body's prestige in the public eye after the disappointments of Jutland and the much lamented lack of a climactic sea battle and victory. After the 11 April failure, the Board of Admiralty instructed him to stand the men down. Losses to submarines were thought to be abating under the effect of convoy, and Room 40, Admiralty intelligence, had word that submarine commanders had been instructed not to risk the Dover Strait and the barrier. But Keyes persuaded Wemyss to intercede for him and promised early action. The glory and honour of the navy (and Roger Keyes) was at stake.

Every man on the blockships was a volunteer. Apart from the men already serving in the Dover Patrol, Admirals Beatty at Scapa, Sturdee at the Nore, and Colville at Portsmouth had all put out the call for officers and men to take part in a 'secret and dangerous mission'. Officers were sought who were unmarried or lacked dependants. At this distance, it may seem strange that men were still volunteering for hazardous duties from a sense of honour and patriotism so far into a brutal war, but the chivalric urge they followed had been deeply ingrained into them by the Victorian and

Edwardian eras in which they had grown up. The dominant moral codes of the Vicwardians were derived from their reverence for the chivalric, the lost Eden of Arthurian legend, Camelot, the Round Table and for their obsession with England as a new Rome. The educational system was founded on the classics. The ancient Greeks and Romans were seen as great exemplars to imitate, their legends and myths as modern moral codes to be followed. And of course there was a strong religious element to the chivalric – the Christian ethic of love and self-denial, of putting others before one's self.

Chivalry and self-sacrifice, unspoken love and yearning, the pursuit of ideals and good deeds, women as 'the Angel in the House', were the tropes of the age. H E Luxmore, a master at Eton, gave his favourite departing pupils copies of G F Watts's painting, *Sir Galahad*. John Percival, headmaster at Clifton College, christened his sons Arthur and Lancelot. In every boy's room at Eton there hung a copy of a painting of the disaster at Majuba Hill by Lady Butler. It depicts an officer with uplifted sword charging towards certain death with the cry *Floreat Etona* ('may Eton flourish').

The chivalric code also governed the Victorian approach to personal bravery. In schoolrooms all over the country the texts were Arthur and his knights, Prince Rupert, Moore at Corunna, Nelson at Trafalgar, Gordon and the Dervishes. Captain Lawrence Oates's self-sacrifice in Scott's attempt on the South Pole (beaten by the more professional Amundsen who rued that, with his death, Scott would be the one to be remembered) was held up in hundreds of books as an exemplar of chivalric and Christian courage. When, in January 1914, the trustees of the British Museum accepted from his widow the original of Scott's polar journal, the director, Sir Frederic Kenyon, was moved to write that the document would 'do much to enforce the lesson which was often in Captain Scott's mind during the latter days of his great march, the lesson that men of English race can face death without flinching for the honour of their nation'.[1]

Keyes had directed that only single officers and men could volunteer for the blockships. He interviewed each officer personally. The code of chivalry is evident in the comments he makes about these interviews in his memoirs.

It was very interesting to watch their reactions when I told them that the enterprise would be hazardous, and finally said to them that the best chance of escape I could offer them after it was a German prisoner of war camp ... with one exception only, they appeared simply delighted and most grateful for the honour I had done them in offering them such a wonderful prospect! Then I gave them the outline of the plan and said that although I would make every endeavour to save them after they sunk their ships, I felt that it was a very forlorn hope. They took everything for granted asked few, if any, questions and went away apparently full of joy and gratitude.[2]

Captain Carpenter's understated and stiff-upper-lip attitude may be seen as typical; on taking leave of his father he simply said, 'Well goodbye dad, sometimes we don't come back'.[3] Before the ships left harbour for the mission, Keyes had the signal 'Any man wishing to leave his vessel may do so' flown for thirty minutes. No one did so.[4]

And now these latter-day Galahads were sailing towards Zeebrugge, and some to Ostend, (Keyes had, with a remarkable lack of subtlety, given the raids the code name Operation ZO) with glory their intent, but quite possibly death in their minds. Thirty-one-year-old rating Percy Pointer in *ML-512* described how they felt. 'Our blood tingled and we laughed and jumped like schoolboys at a football match.'[5]

The first requirement was smoke: lots of it, thick and cloaking, to render the approaching vessels invisible to the enemy. This was primarily the job of the CMBs, acting as mobile smoke floats. They were using a new technology specifically invented for the occasion by Wing Commander Frank Arthur Brock RNAS, scion of the famous fireworks family. Amongst Brock's contribution to the war effort thus far were the Dover flare, used in the illumination of the barrage, the Brock colour filter and the Brock bullet (or Brock incendiary bullet or Brock anti-Zeppelin bullet – the first German airship to be shot down was destroyed by this projectile). Brock's new and improved smokescreen, or 'artificial fog' as he preferred to call it, was ingenious. A chemical mixture was injected directly under pressure into the hot exhausts of the motor torpedo boats and other small craft, or the hot interior surface of the funnels of destroyers.* The

---

* An unintended by-product of Brock's development of his new smokescreen chemical was that Britain ran out of artificial sweetener. Brock needed chlorosulphonic acid for his admixture and this was an important raw material for saccharine production. Saccharine was becoming useful as sugar was in short supply, but it was banned in the USA as unsafe, and questions were being asked in the House of Commons as to why it should be banned there and not in Britain. The War Cabinet thus found it very easy to decide to divert supply of the lachrymator to Brock; saccharine suddenly became scarce.

larger ships each had welded iron contraptions, in the region of 10ft in height, hastily assembled at Chatham. These were fed with solid cakes of calcium phosphide. Dropped into a bucket-like container full of water, the resulting smoke and flames roared up a chimney and were dispersed by a windmill arrangement. The smoke was as dangerous to the user as it was hindrance to the enemy. Signalman William Wood, now serving on *Warwick*, described it as 'hardly smoke, more like fog. The acid made it nip the eyes and sting the face so that it was necessary to smear one's exposed parts with Vaseline. The other ingredients of the gas choked when one tried to breathe, hence the use of respirators.'[6]

At 2320 the monitors laid down a covering fire on Zeebrugge and Ostend, trying to suppress the defences. There were nine of them, with guns from 15in to 7.5in in calibre. They were joined by the Royal Marine and Royal Navy siege artillery that Bacon had placed in the dunes in France. CMBs and MLs rushed ahead of the force and laid smoke around Zeebrugge harbour. Destroyers formed a screen on the seaward side of the advancing landing vessels and blockships. Despite the smoke, the defences were hitting home on *Vindictive*. Then, at 2356, the wind changed direction and *Vindictive* was exposed to view. Every German gun that could bore on her to disastrous effect. Half the men of the landing parties were killed or badly wounded. The commanding officers and their deputies of both the marine and naval landing parties were killed. Carpenter increased speed and ran for the protection of the seaward side of the mole. At 0001 on St George's Day he bumped into it, over 400yds from the intended landing place.

Vindictive had been fitted with narrow landing brows (gangplanks) for the men to run up to access the mole. Many had been smashed away by shellfire and others destroyed by the vessel's sudden banging against the concrete wall. Carpenter could not get his ship to lie still against the wall. Massive grappling hooks, which were meant to secure the ship, proved incapable of being deployed in the teeth of machine-gun fire. Finally, *Daffodil*, arriving three minutes after *Vindictive*, and commanded by a half-blinded Lieutenant Harold Campbell, took matters in hand by using her bow to push the old cruiser tight against the mole, and some purchase could be gained. After fifteen minutes under heavy gunfire, men began to inch up the gangplanks onto dry land – and into a hail of machine-gun fire. They could only arrive in penny packets due to the narrowness of the brows and their limited number. This was precisely what Bacon had warned against when he had recommended a broad ramp and front exit, allowing for a rush of men to overwhelm an enemy. Worse, the men on *Daffodil* could only get off her via her bow and a transit of *Vindictive*'s shell-swept decks. It was wholesale slaughter.

Lieutenant Commander Arthur Harrison on *Vindictive* was an England rugby union international, a back row forward. He had been taken for dead after the first German salvos and moved below deck with a shattered jaw. But he astonished both his doctors and his men by reappearing on deck to lead the naval landing party, in spite of his pain and blood loss. He mobilised the attack, before dying amid the ensuing carnage, along with all but two of his men, for which valour he was to receive the Victoria Cross.

Because of the delay from 11 April, the altered timings meant high tide was 4ft lower than planned and men on *Iris*, intended to disembark onto the mole alongside *Vindictive*, could not get off her and were quickly improvising ladders and ropes. *Iris* could not get her grapnels to seize on the mole, so two of her officers, Lieutenant Hawkins and Lieutenant Commander Bradford, climbed up on the parapet in full view of the enemy and tried to secure the grapnels. Both were shot and fell into the water between the ship and the wall. George Nicholson Bradford came from a valiant family. His brother had won the VC on the Western Front in 1916, only to die a brigadier general in November 1917. Another brother, James, died in France in May 1917, having been awarded the Military Cross only two months previously. And yet another, Thomas, survived the war, emerging as a colonel in the Durham Light Infantry and holding the DSO. And now George, born on St George's Day, died on it thirty-one years later and was awarded the VC for his gallantry, the second in his family.

Marines and naval ratings fought with bayonets, cutlasses, rifle and their fists. Wing Commander Brock, who had gone ashore to try to examine a new type of German rangefinder which was said to use sound waves, was cut down and killed. Commander Valentine Gibbs of *Iris* had both legs blown away and later died of his wounds.

Lieutenant Richard Douglas Sandford, son of the Archdeacon of Exeter, managed to drive his explosive-laden submarine into the harbour and up against the viaduct. The explosion achieved its objective and the viaduct was downed, but as the crew attempted escape in a skiff most were wounded. Eventually they were rescued by a picket boat commanded by Sandford's elder brother, and transferred to a destroyer.

Now the three old cruisers entered the harbour. *Thetis* was meant to ram the lock gates, but staggered under the weight of enemy fire and finally reached the timber breakwater just short of the objective where Commander Ralph Sneyd blew his charges and sank her. Half the ship's small crew were dead or wounded, but the living were rescued by an ML under Lieutenant Hugh Littleton RNVR, who braved a torrent of enemy fire to take the men off. *Intrepid*, commanded by Lieutenant Stuart Bonham-Carter, should logically have attempted the task which *Thetis* had failed to complete, but her commander followed his orders to the letter and instead sank his ship across the canal channel. An ML again took the men off. Bonham-Carter, who had taken to the water, grabbed a rope trailing a passing ML and was towed out of the harbour until his shoulders gave way and he let go. Fortunately for him, he was spotted at that very moment and pulled on board.

The MLs were everywhere. *ML-110* and *ML-424* were both sunk with the loss of five men. *ML-110*, commanded by 41-year-old Lieutenant Commander James Dawbarn Young RNVR, in peacetime a surveyor turned barrister whose father had been president of the Royal Institution of Chartered Surveyors, had preceded the blockships towards the harbour entrance. Young had volunteered to light the entrance with calcium flares. His vessel came under sustained enemy fire and he was hit three times, mortally wounding him. Despite his injuries, Young gave orders to abandon his crippled ship, was rescued and died on the way back to Dover. As for *ML-424*, she was disabled by heavy gunfire and her captain killed. Lieutenant John Robinson RNVR, second in command, took charge and managed to get the wounded away in the dinghy, then destroyed the vessel by setting fire to the engine room. Another launch, *ML-128*, had been detailed for rescue work in the harbour, but her engines broke down and she arrived too late; her commander, Lieutenant Raphael Saunders RNVR, now went into the maelstrom and took off *ML-424*'s remaining crewmen.

ML-282, under the command of Lieutenant Percy Thompson Dean RNVR, followed *Intrepid* and *Iphigenia* into the canal itself and loitered there under heavy fire to pick up the blockship crews. Dean eventually found himself with 109 men on board, so overloaded that she was almost under water and would not answer her helm for there were too many feet standing on the rudder cables. Going out of harbour, she was badly hit by enemy gunfire, killing her coxswain and wounding her second in command. Eventually she reached *Warwick* and transferred her huddled masses. *ML-512*, on smoke-laying duty, was attacked by a remotely controlled motorboat, directed from a Gotha bomber circling above. By dint of hiding in her own smoke, she managed to escape.

The screening destroyers also suffered. *North Star* was hit by land-based artillery and disabled. Her captain, Lieutenant Commander Kenneth C Helyar, stayed on the bridge of his ship under constant fire and, as naval tradition dictates, was the last man off the ship. Some of his eighty crewmen were rescued by *Phoebe*, who lost three of her own men in the process of trying to take the crippled ship in tow, but seventeen of Helyar's were killed and twenty-five made prisoners of war.

Somehow, *Vindictive* got men back on board and slipped the harbour. Carpenter was injured, but he conned the ship to the protection of the waiting destroyers and nursed her back to Dover. *Iris* and *Daffodil* too managed to get back to port, the former guided by her dying navigating officer, Lieutenant George Spencer RNR, gasping out the courses to steer. She had been badly hit as she pulled away from the mole and then hit amidships by a shell which killed or injured many Royal Marines on board, who probably thought they were sailing to safety. During her painful return, Keyes called out to *Iris* from his flagship *Warwick*. 'Do you want anything?' he shouted across. A tense voice, quivering with emotion, replied, 'For God's sake send us doctors and dressings, we are a boatload of wounded.' 'How many killed?' responded Keyes. 'Seventy killed and wounded,' came the answer.[7]

The intended and simultaneous raid on Ostend was a complete failure. By the simple expedient of moving the Stroombank navigation buoy one and a half miles to the east, and removing the Bell buoy altogether, the Germans ensured that Commander Godsal in *Brilliant* could not find the harbour entrance in the dark. Groping along the coast, he ran hard into a sandbank and *Sirius*, following close behind, ran into him. That was the end of that. They blew their charges and the crews were collected by the ever-attendant MLs, which were under the overall command of Captain Ion Hamilton Benn RNVR, braving heavy shore-based gunfire. Lieutenant

Roland Bourke RNVR came alongside the ships several times to take men off in *ML-532*.

Hamilton Benn is worthy of a moment's consideration. An RNVR officer, he served, like so many RNVR men, in the motor launches. Having already achieved distinction under Bacon and gained the DSO, he was now to be further recognised by Keyes for his part in the raids. A founder member of Charlton Athletic AFC, a pre-war honorary colonel of the 20th (Woolwich & Blackheath) Battalion of the London Regiment, Conservative MP for Greenwich 1910–22, three times mentioned in despatches, and a director of the Port of London Authority since its inception, he had joined up in October 1914 aged fifty-one, displaying the full *noblesse oblige* of an English gentleman.

Keyes immediately claimed a great success for the raids. He announced that the harbours were blocked, the scourge eradicated and the mission a complete victory. The press hailed a new Nelson. The truth was rather more prosaic.

The blockships were in the wrong position when sunk, and only managed to obstruct the canal for a few days. The Germans removed two piers in the western bank of the canal near the blockships and dredged a channel through the silt near the sterns of the blocking vessels, and were then able to move submarines along the channel past them at high water. Captain 'Teddy' Evans was emphatic that the canal was not blocked. He could, he noted, 'easily take the *Broke* past the blockships at high tide'.[8] The official historian recorded later that before the raid, two submarines entered or left the Flanders bases each day and continued at that rate during the week after the raid,[9] and the German official history recorded that the conduct of the war suffered 'only minor and temporary restrictions'.[10] What is more, the lives of 227 brave men had been squandered and another 356 men were badly wounded.

Keyes pressed for many decorations for his men (and hence reflected honour on himself). He asked Captain Carpenter of *Vindictive* and the most senior officer present, to recommend who deserved to be awarded Victoria Crosses. Carpenter found it impossible to choose, as he felt that all concerned had shown great courage. But Keyes was determined that several VCs should be awarded, and his solution was to invoke Clause 13 of the Victoria Cross Warrant of 28 January 1856. This allowed those present at an action to choose one of their number to be awarded the VC to represent them all.

Naval and marine officers each voted for their own candidates, while naval ratings and marines voted for candidates from the ranks. This produced four nominees, one of whom was Captain Carpenter! Then Keyes added four more, together with a request for twenty-one DSOs, twenty-nine DSCs, sixteen CGMs, 143 DSMs and 283 names to be mentioned in despatches. He also submitted fifty-six names for immediate promotion for service in action. His recommendations were sent to the Admiralty, but they balked at awarding eight VCs for one action. Eventually they rejected his recommendations, on the grounds that he had asked for too many awards for gallantry, and that the proportion of officers to men was too high. Keyes refused to accept their decision and eventually got his way by the simple expedient of refusing to attend his own investiture (he had been made a KCB the day after the raid), thus pressurising the King, and hence the Admiralty, into approving all the awards he had requested.

Eight Victoria Crosses were eventually awarded, two posthumously (see Appendix 4). Among those honoured were Lieutenants Richard Sandford and Percy Dean. It was an unheard of number of VCs for a small action, and many on the Western Front were outraged. When Keyes visited the Admiralty, Admirals May and Wilson (himself a VC) gave him a severe talking-to about the waste of men the mission had entailed. And Jacky Fisher's opinion of the raids was damning. He later wrote that 'no such folly was ever devised by fools as such an operation as that of Zeebrugge ... it's murder and it's criminal'.[11] But Britain needed a victory and Keyes provided one, albeit under false pretences. As the historian Richard Hough noted, 'Zeebrugge was a courageous and thrilling exploit deserving its place in history, not for its tangible results ... but for its inspiration'.[12] And example and inspiration were sorely needed in April 1918. After all, it was only eleven days after Field Marshal Haig had issued his 'special order of the day':

There is no other course open to us but to fight it out. Every position must be held to the last man: there must be no retirement. With our backs to the wall and believing in the justice of our cause each one of us must fight on to the end. The safety of our homes and the freedom of mankind alike depend upon the conduct of each one of us at this critical moment.

'The people of Britain had never really lost their faith and confidence in the Royal Navy, only repeatedly in its administration. Zeebrugge confirmed this faith in the most glorious manner,'[13] noted Hough, 'Zeebrugge … was an expensive British rebuff and defeat and was instantly hailed as a great victory, with St George slaying the dragon in accordance with tradition. It was put about that the nest of U-boats had been destroyed.'[14]

It is odd that the public and sailors believed that Jutland was somehow a loss to the navy and yet, in reality, it was a strategic gain. Zeebrugge was a complete failure and yet was heralded as a victory and restored pride in the service.

9 May 1918

But Keyes was not yet content. He now proposed a second raid on Ostend to finish the job. Lynes again volunteered to lead it and the old cruisers *Sappho* and the much knocked about *Vindictive* were pressed into service as blockships. Opinion at the Admiralty was against the operation, but Keyes again persuaded Wemyss to let him proceed. Captain Grant was disgusted, and argued so strongly against the plan that Keyes's chief of staff requested that he be transferred, as did Grant himself. Grant wrote that Keyes 'believed his own heroics', and requested Keyes not to mention him in his despatches.[15]

Once again it was a failure. The force sailed on 9 May, but *Sappho* broke down at the outset and so *Vindictive* had to go it alone. Commander Alfred Godsal (commanding *Vindictive* and who had commanded *Brilliant* in the Zeebrugge raid) and Lynes had carefully consulted charts of Ostend, following the previous operation's failure owing to the repositioning of navigation buoys. Their efforts were rendered worthless by a sudden fog which obliterated all sight of the shore. Steaming back and forth across the harbour entrance in the fog, as the covering monitors and German shore batteries engaged in a long-range artillery duel over them, Godsal tried to find the piers marking the entrance to the canal. During this period, the MLs lost track of the cruiser and it was only on the third pass that *Vindictive* found the entrance, accompanied by just one of the launches. Heading straight into the mouth of the canal, guided by a flare dropped by the ML, *Vindictive* became an instant target of the German batteries and was badly hit, the shellfire seriously damaging her propellers.

Commander Godsal intended to swing *Vindictive* broadside on into the channel mouth, but as he ordered the turn, the right screw broke down completely, preventing the cruiser from fully turning. At that moment the problem became irrelevant, for a heavy shell from on shore hit Godsal directly and blew up the bridge and most of the people on it, including First Lieutenant Victor Crutchley, a giant of a man, who staggered to the wheel and attempted to force the ship to make the full turn into the channel. It was to no avail, as she was stuck fast on a sandbank.

Crutchley ordered the charges blown and the ship abandoned, making a check of the ship himself by torchlight before leaping over the side into the only launch which had kept up with the ship, *ML-254*, commanded by Old Etonian Lieutenant Geoffrey Drummond RNVR. His vessel had suffered grievously at the hands of the onshore gunners, Drummond himself was wounded, and his executive officer dead. But Crutchley was 'a tower of strength. He reduced the fire [on board], bound up the wounded and put a tourniquet round my leg,' remembered Drummond.[16]

ML-254 then began slowly to leave the harbour mouth, carrying thirty-eight survivors from *Vindictive*'s fifty-five crewmen, huddled on deck where they remained exposed to machine-gun fire from the shore. As Drummond turned his boat seawards and proceeded back to the offshore squadron, one of the missing launches, *ML-276*, passed her. Drummond called to her commander, Lieutenant Rowland Bourke RNVR, that he believed there were still men in the water, and Bourke, a Canadian citizen who had previously been rejected by all three services by reason of poor eyesight and who wore owlish glasses, immediately headed to the harbour to search for them. Drummond meanwhile set course to rendezvous with *Warwick*, but collapsed and Crutchley took command, using his massive frame to bail, whilst standing up to his waist in water.

Hearing shouts for help, Bourke entered the harbour but could not find anyone. Despite heavy machine-gun and artillery fire, he went back to the old cruiser four times before they discovered a sailor and *Vindictive*'s badly wounded navigator Lieutenant Alleyne, previously navigating officer on the monitor *Lord Clive*, in the bottom of a boat. Bourke heaved them on board, to be joined by two more ratings who appeared from nowhere and jumped aboard, but as he did, two shells struck his launch, smashing the lifeboat and destroying the compressed air tanks. This stalled the engines and caused a wave of corrosive acid to wash over the deck, severely damaging the launch's hull and almost suffocating the unconscious

Alleyne. Under heavy fire, the boat staggered out of the harbour and was taken in tow by another late-coming ML. After the operation, Bourke's launch was discovered to have fifty-five bullet and shrapnel holes.

Lieutenant Sir John Meynall Alleyne, 4th Baronet Alleyne of Four Hills, Barbados, was a 29-year-old regular officer who had volunteered for *Vindictive* as he had three years' experience as a navigating officer off the Belgium coast. He had been wounded in the back when descending from the monkey island to the conning tower and it 'bowled me over and put one leg out of action'.[17] Alleyne was slumped on the floor when 'Abandon ship' was sounded and was unceremoniously hoisted onto the back of a chief quartermaster, carried out, and dropped into the water. Seeing a rope trailing from a ML, he grabbed it, but couldn't get on board, and then the boat took off at speed and he 'went down like a paravane'.[18] When he was able to surface, he saw another ML closing in on him and likely to use him as a fender, so he let go, and the two boats disappeared into the darkness. Alleyne swam back to *Vindictive*, where he found a ship's boat with one end in the water and one on the davit head, and a seaman in it. The rating pulled him in and Alleyne told him to climb up the rope and cut the boat free of the davit. Suddenly there was an intense outbreak of firing and an ML raced into view at full speed. As she came abreast of the shattered cruiser, a voice called out, 'Is anybody there?' and 'We holloa'd our best and she ran up alongside,'[19] and he was able to clamber aboard.

But Sir John's ordeal was not yet over:

> We lay on the upper deck while she steamed full speed out of the harbour. I was a bit amazed at the time by a rather heavy rating who insisted on lying on top of me as I was pretty sore, and it was not until sometime afterwards that I realised that the gallant fellow was making a splinter screen of himself.[20]

When finally ashore, Alleyne discovered that he had been hit by a machine-gun bullet, which had gone through a button of his monkey jacket and come out the back.

ML-254 transferred her survivors to *Warwick*, whose first officer, Lieutenant Frederick Trumble, had left the bridge to supervise the discharge of the wounded to his ship. As he leant over the side, his head was blown apart by a round from the launch's forward Lewis gun; although the magazine was off, one round had been left in the breech and was triggered by the violent motion of the vessel.[21]

Then *Warwick*, with Keyes on board and now carrying a deck-load of wounded men, hit a mine and began to sink. The destroyer *Velox* was lashed alongside and survivors from *Warwick*, *Vindictive* and *ML254* transferred across to her. Thus entwined, this sad combination reached Dover early the following morning. Sixteen British sailors died. And the canal was not blocked. It was another failure, but again Keyes could do no wrong and three more VCs were awarded, to Bourke, Drummond and (by election) Crutchley (see Appendix 4). Like Carpenter, Crutchley was another member of Keyes's 'magic circle', having been a lieutenant on *Centurion*, which Keyes captained in 1916, and had come favourably to his commanding officer's attention, not least because he played polo.

Still undeterred by the loss of life and the continued failure, Keyes planned a final throw of the dice, a third attempt on Ostend. He persuaded a reluctant Admiralty (once again working his way with Wemyss) to let him have the old battleship, *Swiftsure*, which he intended to use as a blockship, and recruited Commander Andrew B Cunningham[*] to command her. Once again, she was stripped out and fitted with extra protection and short-range weapons, while Cunningham rounded up another eager team of knights errant. Perhaps luckily for them, the operation was called off two days before it was meant to take place. First, the Germans had ceased to use the canal from Ostend as a means of getting to and from Bruges, and secondly, they had laid a big minefield off the port, which would make getting a big old battleship through very unlikely.

---

[*] Cunningham would become a famously aggressive admiral in the Second World War and, in October 1943, First Sea Lord.

The Long Watch Ends: The Loss of *Glatton* and the Armistice, 1918

Roger Keyes received the plaudits and the rewards for the Zeebrugge and Ostend raids. As noted above, he was appointed a Knight Commander of the Order of the Bath on 24 April 1918, the day after the Zeebrugge affair, becoming 'Sir Roger' (he was later advanced to Knight Commander of the Royal Victorian Order on 10 December 1918 and made a baronet on 29 December 1919). Meanwhile, there was a war to be fought.

In line with his strategy of using his destroyers in groups, Keyes formed a new division based at Dunkirk. For two to three weeks at a time, four destroyers would be based there, escorting the monitors who were bombarding the Belgian coast, patrolling the Zuydecote Pass and 'generally making a nuisance of themselves on the enemy's right flank. I don't suppose we did any damage,' commented Lieutenant R T Young, now serving in *Mastiff*, 'but it kept the enemy on his toes.'[1]

Young had a well-formed view of Keyes as commander. He wrote:

The Dover Patrol under Roger Keyes was a very different affair than it had been under Reginald Bacon, who was Vice Admiral when I was first there in *Lochinvar*. Keyes's tactical dispositions were much better, but despite the fact that he was bathed in the glory of the Zeebrugge raid, I don't think he had the confidence of his command to the same extent as Bacon had.[2]

Some of his men thought Keyes self-centred and a trophy hunter.

On 30 June there was an unfortunate 'blue on blue' incident when the British submarine *E-33* was attacked by two Dover Patrol destroyers, *Broke* and *Moorsom*. The commanding officer of *Broke* was Commander Bertram Ramsay, last met on *M-25*. Ramsay had taken command of *Broke* in October 1917, after 'Teddy' Evans's appointment to be Bacon's chief of staff, and he found it in a 'curious state', lacking discipline, dirty, sick bay a disgrace, no firing practice for a year, and leave-breaking rife.

Ramsay's attempts to remedy these perceived faults immediately got him into the bad books of Captain (D) Wilfred Tomkinson.* It is possible that Ramsay was in part to blame for this breakdown in relationship. He was a man of firm opinions and unafraid of expressing them. At the beginning of the war he was serving as flag lieutenant to Vice Admiral Douglas Gamble in the 4th Battle Squadron. Ramsay wrote of his admiral, 'I know ten times as much as him about his job,'[3] and was generally deeply critical of Gamble in his diaries. They had at least one stand-up row 'about my shortness of manner at times and the War College training which he resents very much, or rather the way in which I display it'.[4] Nonetheless, Tomkinson 'never lost a chance to find fault with [Ramsay]'.[5] And Tomkinson was part of Keyes's group of favourites, having served under him in the Boxer campaign. If Tomkinson hated one, then so did Keyes, who, wrote Ramsay's wife Helen, 'took a hard and unjust view of my husband'.[6]

Following the *E-33* incident, the subsequent court of inquiry cleared Ramsay of any fault, considering that in the circumstances the two Dover destroyers were justified in their actions, and that no blame attached to them. Keyes violently disagreed with the finding and wrote what Ramsay called a 'Hymn of Hate' to the Admiralty, rejecting the decision. The Admiralty sided with Keyes.

Ramsay's troubles did not end there. On 3 November *Broke* collided with HM Ambulance Transport *Princess Elizabeth*,** which she had been escorting as they entered Dover harbour. A court of inquiry was convened, but before it could meet Keyes was overheard saying to his staff that Commander Ramsay 'was to be

---

* Later, as an admiral, Tomkinson would be blamed and censured for his handling of the 1931 Invergordon mutiny.
** Ambulance transports, which were camouflaged and armed for their own defence, were introduced after the German declaration on 19 March 1917 that they would attack hospital ships.

found guilty for the collision'.[7] Unsurprisingly, Ramsay was subsequently censured and received an 'expression of Their Lordship's displeasure' as a result. Ramsay's wife also averred that Keyes prevented her husband being awarded the DSO (although he was mentioned in despatches for the second Ostend raid).

Ramsay believed the findings of the court to be most unfair and complained to Tomkinson, to no avail. He confided to his diary: 'feel they are waiting to have me at every turn and we risk mishaps everyday under [illegible] circumstances. It is a most uncomfortable feeling'.[8] The wrong side of Keyes was a bad place to be and not likely to produce the sort of risk-taking that he claimed he supported.

The Dover Patrol in 1918

Keyes still had considerable resources at his disposal. The 6th Destroyer Flotilla, which formed the core of the Dover Patrol, stood, on 6 July 1918, at forty-one vessels: the old protected cruiser *Arrogant* (depot and flagship), the flotilla leaders *Botha*, *Broke*, *Faulknor*, *Swift*, *Velox*, *Warwick* and *Whirlwind*, and the destroyers *Afridi*, *Amazon*, *Cossack*, *Crusader*, *Gipsy*, *Kangaroo*, *Leven*, *Manly*, *Mansfield*, *Mastiff*, *Matchless*, *Melpomene*, *Mentor*, *Meteor*, *Milne*, *Miranda*, *Moorsom*, *Morris*, *Murray*, *Myngs*, *Nugent*, *Panther*, *Phoebe*, *Racehorse*, *Saracen*, *Senator*, *Sikh*, *Syren*, *Termagant*, *Trident*, *Viking*, *Violet* and *Zubian*. With his fifteen monitors and five submarines, one aircraft carrier, thirty-one MLs and CMBs, his 131 net drifters, seventy trawlers, three yachts and nineteen trawler and paddle minesweepers, plus a further eight vessels in the Downs Boarding Flotilla, it was a considerable armada.

But the problem was there was no one to fight. The German destroyers did not come out again after the March 1918 engagement, but a steady stream of submarines continued to exit the Belgian ports and cause ongoing losses with minelaying and anti-commerce activity. The Patrol contented itself with bombardment, anti-submarine and minesweeping duties, which was difficult enough. Its last confirmed submarine 'kill' was *U-109*, which hit a mine in the barrage on 29 August and sank with the loss of twenty-eight men, eight surviving, although *UB-113* sailed from Zeebrugge on 14 September and went missing with all hands, presumed mined.

In September, Keyes was involved in an incident which nearly resulted in the destruction of the harbour at Dover and probably much of the town too. *Glatton* and her sister ship *Gorgon* were originally built as coastal defence ships for the Royal Norwegian Navy, as *Bjørgvin* and *Nidaros* respectively. *Glatton* had been requisitioned before being handed over to the Norwegian navy at the beginning of the war, but was not completed until 1918, although she had been launched over three years earlier.

After completion, *Glatton* sailed for Dover on 11 September to prepare for an offensive planned for later that month. She was captained by Commander Neston William Diggle, previously captain of the monitor *General Wolfe* and a friend of Keyes. The admiral had invited him for tea with his family and afterwards, when they were out walking together on the Dover cliffs, a tremendous explosion was heard from the harbour.

It was 1815 on 16 September. *Glatton*'s midships 6in magazine had suffered a low-order explosion that ignited the cordite stored there. Flames shot through the roof of 'Q' turret and started to spread aft. Burning fuel oil added to the conflagration. Keyes and Diggle jumped into the admiral's wife's car and sped to the harbour, where they found the ship in flames and many badly burned men needing treatment. Worse, they saw that next to the burning ship was moored the ammunition ship *Gransha* which, if she went up, would destroy much of Dover itself.

Diggle and a petty officer tried to flood the magazines and open the seacocks, but could not reach the after magazines because of the blaze. Worse, the cries of men trapped below could be heard. Many sailors from neighbouring vessels were on board trying to help: Lieutenant George Devereux Belben DSC, from *Trident*, together with three other men (Sub Lieutenant David Hywel Evans RNVR, Petty Officer Albert Ernest Stoker and Able Seaman Edward Nunn) fought tenaciously to rescue the injured and trapped, for which they were later awarded the Albert Medal. *Swift* sent all her boats for survivors, but was then ordered to leave harbour for her own safety.

Keyes determined to sink *Glatton* to put the fires out, but the first destroyer he boarded did not have steam up. The second, *Cossack*, fired a torpedo which struck the anti-torpedo bulge amidships, but failed to explode, because it had been fired too close to the burning ship. Her second torpedo blew a hole in *Glatton* at 1940, but the torpedo's warhead was too small to penetrate through her bulge, and the hull and the monitor remained afloat, still burning. In a frenzy of fury, Keyes transferred to the destroyer *Myngs* and ordered her to fire on *Glatton* with her 21in torpedoes at 2015. They were aimed at the hole blown in *Glatton*'s starboard side by *Cossack*'s second torpedo, in order to blast a hole through to her other side. *Myngs* succeeded in this objective, causing the blazing ship to sink, turning over on her starboard side until her masts and superstructure rested on the harbour bottom and the fire was extinguished by the inrushing water. Casualties were heavy. Ninety-four men and four officers were killed, including her second in command Lieutenant Commander Reginald J B Drew. But Dover was saved.

At the subsequent court of inquiry, Diggle was reprimanded with an expression of Their Lordships' displeasure for the 'negligent manner in which the Naval Magazine Regulations were carried out'.[9] This did not prevent him being belatedly awarded the CMG for 'service in command of the ships of the Dover Patrol since 1915' on 23 May 1919.[10] Was it the benefit of being in Keyes's clique again? And it was not until March 1930 that the fifty-seven men trapped below when *Glatton* sank were finally exhumed during salvage and breaking operations and buried in a single grave at Gillingham cemetery.*

August and September 1918 also saw the deployment of a weapon system which had sprung from Bacon's fertile mind, but came into being under Keyes's watch. The Admiralty had offered Bacon three huge 18in guns in 1917, each weighing 150 tons and, in Admiral Bacon's opinion, as a jest. But Bacon was a man to whom technical issues, such as how to employ such massive beasts, were meat and drink, and he proposed to mount them in the Palace Hotel, Westende, as soon as this had been captured as part of Operation Hush. When the necessary gains failed to come about and Hush was shelved, Bacon instead agreed with the Admiralty to have alternative gun mountings in three of the 12in monitors and mount a single gun on each, so as to be able to bombard the docks at Zeebrugge at a distance of twenty miles.

Bacon had long departed his post when these weapons finally came into use, one being mounted on the monitor *General Wolfe*, becoming operational in August 1918, and one in *Lord Clive* in September of the same year (the third had been intended for *Prince*

---

* There is a memorial for *Glatton*'s dead in the cemetery at Gillingham. It reads 'TO THE GLORY OF GOD AND THE HONOURED MEMORY OF FOUR OFFICERS AND NINETY-FOUR MEN WHO LOST THEIR LIVES THROUGH THE DISASTER TO HMS GLATTON ON THE 16TH SEPTEMBER 1918 ONE OFFICER AND FIFTY-SIX MEN ARE BURIED IN THIS GRAVE'.

Eugene but the war was over before she could be so fitted). They could fire a 3,320lb shell at a distance of 40,000yds but saw little action before the end of the war.

The dying kicks of war

As summer turned to autumn, it became clear that the German will to continue the war was failing, and during October they began to seek terms for an armistice. On 5 October the German Flanders Flotilla U-boats *UB-10*, *UB-40*, *UB-59* and *UC-4* all scuttled off the Flemish coast. On 14 October Keyes, flying his flag in the destroyer *Termagant* (a *Talisman*-class vessel originally designed for and ordered by the Ottoman navy), took *Gorgon* with him on a reconnaissance mission to see if the Germans were still holding the coast in strength. The fire of the Tirpitz and Raversyde batteries soon convinced them in the affirmative and *Gorgon* was forced to haul off at her maximum speed of 14 knots (which was actually faster than she had made in trials). The monitor was straddled and hit by splinters. The following day she returned to the Flanders coast and fired off thirty rounds from her two 9.2in guns in just twenty minutes, targeting the Middelkerke battery. To this strange Norwegian hybrid ship and her captain Commander Charles A Robertson-Scott, younger son of a major general, went the honour of firing the Dover Patrol's last shots of the war against the Germans on the occupied coast. Two days later, 17 October, the Germans evacuated Ostend; Zeebrugge followed on the 19th.

But the dying didn't stop. On 19 October the Racecourse-class paddle minesweeper *Plumpton* hit a mine, sank off Ostend and was beached; ten men were lost and one man subsequently died of wounds. The lost crewmen were a mixture of RNR, RNVR and two regular RN. On 20 October *M-21*, a 7.5in-gunned monitor (originally built with a 9.2in gun), struck a mine off Ostend. Five men were killed and an attempt was made to tow her to Dover, but she sank off West Pier. Her mining was watched by Keyes, who was in transit to inspect the newly German-free Zeebrugge on *Termagant*. And on 21 October *ML-561* was mined and sunk off the Belgian coast; Lieutenant John E Purvis RNVR, from Alnwick, Northumberland, one of three brothers who had served in the war, died with his vessel. Then *P-12* sank after a collision in the Channel on 4 November, with one rating dying of his injuries two days later.

Germany had started to seek an armistice under its new

government of Prince Max of Baden on 5 October and had asked President Woodrow Wilson of the USA to mediate between all parties. One of Wilson's preconditions for so doing was that Germany should end its submarine war. Riding over the objections of Admiral Scheer, the chief of the Imperial Navy staff, the German government made this concession on 20 October. The following day all U-boats at sea were recalled home. The English Channel was free of submarine predators for the first time in over four years.

At this point, the men of the Dover Patrol could perhaps have thought that their war was over. But it was nearly not so. An enraged Scheer ordered Admiral Hipper, commander of the German High Seas Fleet, to prepare for an attack on the British fleet, utilising the main battlefleet, reinforced by the newly available U-boats released from Flanders. According to orders on 24 October, this was to include an attack against the Flanders coast by the 2nd Torpedo-Boat Flotilla, supported by three light cruisers, and against the Thames Estuary by the 2nd Scouting Group with four light cruisers and the 2nd Torpedo-Boat Half-Flotilla. The raid on the Thames and the Flanders coast were scheduled for dawn on 31 October. It was expected that these raids would draw out the British Grand Fleet from Scapa and the encounter between that force and the High Seas Fleet was planned for the afternoon and evening of the same day. As a result, the Dover Patrol would have been plunged into a very nasty battle when the war was effectively over.

Fortunately, Scheer's plan did not come to pass. Revolution was in the air within the German fleet. Years of inactivity and poor officer–men relationships had led to the rise of Bolshevism amongst the crews. The evening of 29 October was marked by unrest, and serious acts of indiscipline within the German ships, with the men convinced their commanders were intent on sacrificing them in a deliberate attempt to sabotage the Armistice negotiations. Open revolt broke out in many of the battleships, and the men refused to follow orders, although it might be noted that the torpedo-boat and submarine crews remained loyal to their posts.

Hipper saw no alternative to cancelling the operation, which he did on 30 October, and ordered the fleet dispersed in the hope of quelling the insurrection. It was a narrow escape for all concerned, from what would have been a needless and bloody fight.

Thus unnecessary sacrifice was avoided. The most common cause of death now being noted in the Admiralty records was 'illness'. The great influenza outbreak of 1918/19 was beginning to take its terrible grip on war-weakened nations, a grip which would eventually kill as many as the war itself had. The Patrol suffered with the world and men who had survived the crushing duty of night patrols and anti-submarines actions now succumbed to a tiny virus. This included Able Seaman Albert McKenzie, who had survived Zeebrugge to be awarded the VC, only to then die of influenza on 3 November.

The Armistice finally came at 1100 on the eleventh day of the eleventh month. But nobody thought to tell some of the units of the Dover Patrol. *Amazon* was patrolling between Dungeness and Beachy Head when she met a French trawler decorated in flags, the crew cheering and waving. Asked (in French) why they were celebrating, they replied that the war was over. 'We knew nothing of it,' recalled Cook Evans, 'and ordered them to return to harbour.' When *Amazon* returned to Dover, the church bells were ringing and ship's sirens blowing. They then received a message that all shore leave was cancelled until further notice. 'Disappointing,' noted Evans, 'but on reflection very wise, the forces would have gone berserk'.[11]

Lieutenant R T Young was still serving in *Mastiff* when the Armistice was announced. The signal from the Admiralty ordered that 'submarines on the surface are not to be attacked.' Young related, 'my captain [George Atwood] directed that if a submarine was detected on the surface in a position from which a torpedo attack could be delivered, these orders were to be disregarded and [the submarine] was to be attacked at once.'[12] The days of trust between gentlemen at sea were long gone.

Bertram Ramsay in *Broke* had left Dover harbour at 0745 on the 11th for patrol duty. He received notice of the Armistice, an RT message at 1000 stating that the peace had been signed and to cease hostilities. As he approached Boulogne, he and his crew saw transports coming out of port, decked with flags and firing rockets.

First Sea Lord 'Rosy' Wemyss had been the British naval representative at the negotiation of the Armistice in the Forest of Compiègne. The Dover Patrol destroyer *Termagant* under Commander Andrew Cunningham was despatched from Boulogne to bring him back to England. At 0600 on the 12th Wemyss and his staff arrived on board and Cunningham set off for Dover at pace. About halfway there, it was discovered that Wemyss had left his copy of the Armistice document behind in Paris; much worse, he had also left his razor (Wemyss was fastidiously clean-shaven). His staff, under Captain J P R Marriott, spent the rest of the trip keeping out of his way and his temper.

After the Armistice, the Patrol remained active in the English Channel, although now a reduced quantity with the submarines and scout cruisers sent elsewhere, and a long list of ships under repair. Likewise, the Downs Flotilla was much decreased, to a handful of trawlers and the armed yacht *Sigismund* (see also Appendix 5). Keyes was not present often and day-to-day command was exercised by Rear Admiral Dampier, flying his flag in the 560-ton luxury steam yacht *Surf*, built by Hawthorne and Co in 1902 and hired by the Admiralty in February 1915. It was no doubt more salubrious than a destroyer.

But despite the peace, deaths continued. On 23 November 1918 *Nugent*, an 'M'-class destroyer recently arrived back from Lerwick, was out on patrol in relatively mild, drizzly weather. Despite this, Stoker Robert Smallbone from Newbury was lost overboard; his body was never recovered. A court of inquiry into his death determined that it was an accident. The last ship to be lost from the Patrol was the drifter *Glen Boyne*. She was engaged in clearing mines from the Dover Barrage on 4 January 1919 when she triggered one off. Two men, Engineman John Bissett RNR, aged thirty-two, and Stoker Second Class Edward Allen, eighteen, were killed in the blast.

Death was not always dealt out by the enemy's weapons or by the seas. Robert 'Robbie' Allen left the Royal Grammar School, Newcastle upon Tyne, in 1897. He was, by all accounts, a nice lad, kind, unaffected and honest. Robbie volunteered for war on its outbreak and was accepted into the RNVR as a sub lieutenant, initially on the Tyne Patrol. By 1918 he was with the Dover Patrol and had served in the Zeebrugge raid. Late in November, as the war was coming to a close and while on patrol, he contracted a severe chill which developed into pneumonia. He died on 23 November, in the RN Hospital, Chatham. And that same day, Lieutenant Richard Sandford VC, the submariner hero of Zeebrugge, died of typhoid fever at Cleveland hospital, Grangetown. The war had been over for twelve days, but it was still claiming lives.

There were victims of other kinds too. Many men found the experiences of the war so harrowing that they never really recovered from them. One such was Arthur George Watts RNVR, the son of an army doctor. Watts had been born in Chatham, Kent, and educated at Dulwich College. Encouraged to pursue a career in art by his mother, he attended Goldsmith's Institute in southeast London, the Slade School of Art and even furthered his studies at the Free Art School in Antwerp.

He was published in various journals in 1904, including *Pearson's*, *London Opinion*, *The Tatler*, *The Bystander* and, by 1912, *Punch*. A keen sailor and boat enthusiast, he purchased his first boat in 1910, and used his hobby to develop his career by writing and illustrating articles for *Yachting World*. In June 1913 he had taken his boat on a three-week tour of the Dutch and Belgian coast.

Unsurprisingly, the navy saw that this fitted him for service in the coastal motor boats and motor launches of the Dover Patrol as an RNVR officer. As a lieutenant commander, Watts led a smokescreen flotilla at the battles of Zeebrugge and Ostend in 1918, was awarded the DSO and mentioned in despatches. The citation of his medal said:

> Lieut.-Cdr. Arthur G. Watts, RNVR. This officer was in command of *ML-239* and leader of a smoke screen unit. He led his unit with skill and judgment in a very exposed position, and it was largely due to him that the screen was so extremely successful in his section.[13]

However, the experience of his service and the bedlam of the raids badly affected him and he suffered from shell-shock, being unable to work again at illustration until 1921, when he resumed his career with *Punch*. Subsequently, Watts illustrated E M Delafield's humorous novel *Diary of a Provincial Lady* and drew a number of amusing posters for London Transport during the mid 1920s. But the war never left him.[*]

Another who suffered from the experience was Lieutenant Commander Henry Boxer, who acted so bravely and skilfully in the rescue from *Anglia*. In 1911 he had been described by his commanding officer as 'zealous, good judgement, physically strong', and again in 1912 as 'good physique'. In January 1919 a sympathetic superior officer, Captain Godfrey, noted of the 33-year-old Boxer 'a

---

[*] Having survived the war to end all wars, he was tragically killed at the age of fifty-two in a plane crash on 20 July 1935, when returning from Italy.

good steady temperament, not very physically strong. The strain of service in destroyers in the war seems to have told on him.'[14] Boxer left the service at the end of the year, another man diminished by the effort of safeguarding the Narrow Sea.

And the advent of the peace did not bring about the end to losses in the Downs either. Alfred Henry Rickwood was a twenty-year-old telegraphist serving on board *Charm*, an armed boarding tug. On 28 June 1919 a large celebration of the peace was taking place in Ramsgate (to mark the signing of the Treaty of Versailles) and *Charm* was participating by firing signal rockets and other explosive 'fireworks'. Rickwood was at his post on the bridge of the vessel during the signalling display when some rockets caught fire and went off immediately beneath him. He was killed instantly.

PART FIVE
Life in the Patrol

The Downs Boarding Flotilla was part of the Dover Patrol, operating away from the limelight in the mundane but necessary duties of policing the ships passing through the Downs on their way to London or the North Sea. The towns of Dover and Ramsgate played an essential role in the duties of the Patrol. And the men of the Patrol, mostly volunteers, served in conditions which ranged from bad to indifferent. Here are their stories.

20

The Downs Boarding Flotilla

At the outbreak of war the main use of the Patrol in the Strait of Dover ... was to enforce the examination of merchant vessels for the discovery of contraband or enemy subjects trying to creep into Germany. Plans had been prepared before the opening of hostilities for a limited number of destroyers to carry out the examination service, boarding vessels at sea; only those vessels were to be sent to the Downs that objected to search, or were regarded as suspicious. Of course such examination in the fairway of traffic was found to be impossible, owing to sea conditions and the number of merchantmen involved. The Downs Boarding Flotilla grew therefore in size, and the Downs developed into a great anchorage for merchant ships.[1]

The Dover Patrol had the key responsibility of protecting the Channel and anti-submarine warfare. But the command also included the management of the Downs, a roadstead in the southern North Sea near the English Channel and off the east Kent coast, between the North and the South Foreland. An enormous amount of merchant shipping passed through this area, British and neutral, all of which had to be checked for 'contraband' – forbidden products of use to an enemy – and, if necessary, boarded for inspection.

The Downs had been selected as the examination ground for all vessels passing either up or down the Channel because of its strategic position. About 120 ships passed Dover daily in 1915 and 1916, and between eighty and a hundred per day in 1917. Most of these then anchored in the Downs. Had this Channel traffic been disrupted or reduced, London could have starved, and Bacon estimated that at least one-third of its population would have had to be removed immediately to the west coast of England where food could be landed. The Downs Flotilla thus had the twin duties of protecting the shipping anchored there and inspecting vessels for suspected 'illegal' trafficking in war goods.

In November 1914 Britain had declared a distant blockade of Germany and arrogated to herself the right to stop and search all ships, especially neutrals, to seek goods which might be of help to Germany and her allies in their war effort and confiscate them or otherwise prevent their delivery. To assist in this end she had mined the North Sea, requiring merchant shipping bound for German or neutral ports to use only safe channels, and submit to stop and search before receiving routeing guidance.

Goods that were not permitted to pass through a blockade were designated as contraband. The definition of contraband was established by the Declaration of London in 1909 (and which Britain, in fact, never ratified). Three definitions of contraband were established: one of 'absolute contraband', namely, articles which were clearly war materials; and another deemed 'conditional contraband', which comprised articles capable of use in either war or peace. This 'conditional' list included items such as ore, chemicals and rubber, all of which were becoming increasingly important to any modern war effort. The third category was a 'free list', containing articles that could never be deemed contraband.

Following the lead of the Hague Conference of 1907, the Declaration of London of 1909 considered food to be conditional contraband, that is, subject to interception and capture only when intended for the use of the enemy's military forces. Among the corollaries of this was that food not intended for military use could legitimately be transported to a neutral port, even if it ultimately found its way to the enemy's territory. The starvation of an enemy's populace was therefore meant to be outlawed as a weapon of war. The House of Lords had refused its consent to the declaration, which did not, consequently, ever come into full force. Many in Britain saw the starvation of their enemy as a legitimate weapon of war.

The day-to-day strategic control of the blockade came from the Foreign Office (FO), much to the irritation of the Admiralty who felt that the FO was too lenient in what was and wasn't permitted, and which nations should be considered suspect. An inefficient triumvirate of the Foreign Office, Board of Trade and Admiralty tried to manage the items on the contraband lists, which constantly shifted as the FO endeavoured to keep neutral nations, especially the Americans, on side, and many in the navy thought them more concerned to do this than to win the war by prevention of supply to Germany. This view was shared by many outside the navy too, such as Rudyard Kipling, who wrote 'nor is it any lie that, had we used the Navy's bare fist instead of its gloved hand from the beginning, we could in all likelihood have shortened the war'.[2]

The difficult task of executing these vague and changing instructions fell to the Downs Boarding Flotilla and the Dover Patrol (and their equivalents in the north, the 10th Cruiser Squadron).

The Downs outpost of the Dover Patrol's empire was based at Ramsgate and was under the overall command of the senior naval officer (SNO) for the port. From 21 January 1915 that officer was Captain George Napier Tomlin RN MVO, whose previous commands had included the Royal Yacht *Medina*. He was to serve as SNO until June 1917, being mentioned in despatches for his troubles.

The need for ships to undertake the duty, ships which were fast enough to overtake merchantmen, and large enough to accommodate sufficient men to form boarding parties and prize crews, led to the requisition or leasing of tugs and merchant ships, which, together with the occasional yacht and the odd detached destroyer, formed the Downs Boarding Flotilla. The size of the flotilla varied year by year, but seems to have been generally some eight to ten tugs (fifteen individual tugs served over the course of the war, the oldest built in 1889) and four to five armed boarding steamers. In June 1915, for example, there were eight tugs and four armed boarding steamers, but six months later, as the pressure of work constantly increased, there were ten tugs and five armed boarding steamers.

One of the latter was the Isle of Man packet SS *Peel Castle*, in peacetime owned by the Isle of Man Steam Packet Company and more usually plying the route between Douglas and Liverpool. She was hired into the navy in November 1914 and for the next three years, commanded by an ex-P&O officer Lieutenant Commander P E Haynes RNR, she fulfilled the duties of a patrol ship. These mainly consisted of regulating the traffic, examining neutral ships for enemies and contraband, and acting as a guard ship in the Downs, serving alternately ten days at sea and four days in port.

She had a varied career, being fired upon by a retreating merchantman and at least once by British shore batteries. She endured many air raids (Ramsgate suffered grievously from German air raids) and sent numerous boarding parties onto merchant ships.

Possibly the high spot of her career came in 1915. While searching a Holland America Line ship from New York, her boarding party captured two German prisoners, who were taken on board *Peel Castle* and examined by Tomlin. One of them proved to be the notorious Franz von Rinckler, one of Admiral Tirpitz's senior spies, who had organised a campaign in the United States against Great Britain, setting fire to factories and placing bombs in ships. The other man claimed to be a railway magnate from Mexico, but he turned out to be von Rinckler's chief assistant. They were promptly imprisoned and eventually deported to the United States for trial.

Another vessel employed in the Downs Boarding Flotilla was His Majesty's Yacht *Ceto*. She was a 185-ton steam-powered vessel, owned by Lord Iveagh, Edward Cecil Guinness, and lent to the war effort by him in 1914, whereupon she was fitted with two 3pdr guns. Her captain was Lieutenant Commander (later Commander) Francis Fitzgerald Tower RNVR, a 55-year-old gentleman of leisure and keen yachtsman, who owned properties in London and on the Isle of Wight and had volunteered for service at the beginning of the war. [*]

With some of the original crew and a smattering of fishermen, *Ceto* was used to stop and search merchantmen as well as escorting particularly valuable cargoes, such as oilers, through the Strait. They were often out at sea for ten days at a time, especially after the first of the Downs net barriers were laid, as she acted as guard ship for a period.

She was not in great condition, a patch on her boiler constantly giving problems, and on one occasion she lost a propeller whilst coaling and had to go out on patrol with only one screw. Frustrated at the bureaucracy involved in obtaining a new one through official channels, Tower telegraphed the supplier for one direct and paid for it from his own pocket. On another occasion *Ceto*'s steering gear broke down as she was entering Ramsgate harbour. It was a bit hairy and Tower recorded that 'thank one's stars grief didn't result'.[3]

Tower enjoyed his time in command. He regarded it as an 'adventure'. On 28 December 1914 SS *Montrose* (famous for being

---

[*] Of independent means, Tower had married the daughter of Sir Thomas Butler, 10th Baronet Cloughgrenan in 1884 and would in 1915 marry off his daughter Isolde to Fitzwalter George Probyn Butler, 17/27th Baron Dunboyne.

the ship on which Dr Crippen and his lover were captured in 1910), loaded up with concrete for blocking one of Dover harbour's entrances as protection against attack, broke adrift and drove right through Dover harbour from the western entrance to the eastern entrance without touching anything. It was blowing a gale that night and *Ceto* was ordered out to try to rescue the two men on board. Tower described it: 'as we opened out the South Foreland poor *Ceto* took it on board heavily and though we cruised about for hours, we did little good. [*Montrose*] drove ashore on the Goodwins, the crew being taken off by a tug.'[4]

One of the duties that Tower enjoyed most was when the first net defences were placed in position at the north end of the Downs and ships had to be taken through the gateway. The Admiralty had instructed Hood on 5 March 1915 that 'compulsory pilotage will come into effect at 6 a.m. March 10'.[5] However, there was a marked shortage of pilots and so Tower was ordered to do it himself. 'My method was to steam up alongside the waiting ship, hail her and ask her if she wanted to be taken through,' he wrote, 'and then steam ahead with "follow me" in international code flying at the masthead.'[6]

Once he was ordered to take an arrested trawler into harbour for inspection. The trawler was anchored near to *Ceto* and her anchor dragged, fouling *Ceto*'s cable, which made the ships fast to one another and 'driving about Deal in the dark'.[7] Eventually, the trawler winched the tangled mess on board and they were able to clear the chain.

Finally, this gentleman's adventure came to an end when the Admiralty instructed that all captains of such boats should have a Board of Trade certificate. Tower did not and stood down from command in April 1915. He had enjoyed it. 'What a pleasant and interesting time it all was and a good old ship,' he later noted.[8] And he thoroughly admired his admiral, Horace Hood. 'Admiral and Mrs Hood were kindness itself and I shall never forget the admiral. They used to say that *Harrier* and *Ceto* were his pet ships.'[9] When told he was losing Tower, Hood protested vigorously, but to no avail.

Another Downs Flotilla ship was the tug *Stanton*, originally based in Hartlepool and owned and operated by the North Eastern Railway Company. She was taken into the navy as an unarmed boarding vessel, again in November 1914, and renamed *Char*. Her original eight-man crew volunteered to stay with their ship and were enrolled in the MMR (Mercantile Marine Reserve). Royal Navy

Reserve men made up the rest of the crew, with two RNR acting lieutenants providing the command structure.

However, her life in the Patrol, and indeed those of her crew, were destined to be very short. In the early morning of 16 January 1915 and while on patrol in the Downs in very stormy weather, she approached a ship seemingly in distress, the Belgian oiler *Frivan*. While standing off to assess the situation, a large sea drove her against *Frivan*'s bow and holed her below the waterline. Mortally wounded and in gale force winds with huge seas, *Char* drifted away in the dark. The Belgian ship sent up distress rockets and the Deal lifeboat was launched but it was to no avail. Neither the tug nor her eighteen-man crew were ever seen again. Amongst the dead was Clement Powell, an officer's steward third class. Even on a tugboat, officers had to be properly looked after.

Ceto had been called out to search for the missing tug but, as Tower put it, 'nothing was found of her, a sad thing. I knew some of them well, one a Lieutenant RNR, a particularly nice fellow.'[10]

Accident also caused the loss of the yacht *Marcella*, an old 127-ton steam vessel built in 1887 and once owned (as *Marchesa*) by the Earl of Dudley. She had been taken into the Downs flotilla in July 1915 as an armed boarding vessel, but on 24 March 1916 she sank after a collision in the Downs. Fortunately, there was no loss of life.

The United States of America finally declared war on 6 April 1917, and with that act substantially changed the Downs Boarding Flotilla's activities. The USA and the northern neutrals had been the major source of contraband. Trade with Germany by the latter had by then largely been controlled by diplomatic means and treaties; now the former was an ally and any ship departing the USA was inspected at source. The duties of the flotilla now focused much more on anti-submarine activity and the provision of escorts for ships entering the Port of London, and it slowly passed into history. On 2 January 1918 it comprised two armed boarding steamers (one detached), a yacht, five tugs (one detached), and four trawlers. By the war's end there were no permanently assigned vessels.

Life in the Dover Patrol

The Dover Patrol was the longest continuous operation of the Royal Navy in the First World War. It was an arduous and difficult billet and called for skills and behaviours which had not been an essential part of the navy's expectation up to the start of the conflict. Life and service in the Dover Patrol was very different from the pre-war navy experience. It is important to consider this contrast to fully understand the key role played by the Patrol in relation to the change in behaviour that they had to manage.

In the years which led up to 1914, the Royal Navy was essentially a battleship navy. Service on board battleships, battlecruisers and armoured cruisers was seen as the ultimate posting and was generally necessary for further promotion.

The key position on a big ship was that of commander, effectively a chief operating officer whose task it was to present the ship to the captain as a fighting concern – although in the pre-war navy much attention was also devoted to a 'smart ship' and rather less to the fighting element. Gleaming paint- and brasswork, well-dressed crewmen and efficient drill were all prized rather more highly than fighting ability by many admirals and their captains. Gunnery was not necessarily of the highest priority. Target practice might be resisted and practice shells thrown overboard instead of being fired, as the discharge could damage the brightwork of the ship.

Dress code was a matter of great importance. Officers in the Royal Navy of the late 1890s had no fewer than seven different dress codes to follow, depending on the occasion. The garments and their usages were all listed in Admiralty Regulations. Just buying the clothing necessary would put a strain on many bank balances and to be inappropriately dressed would lead to a reprimand at best, and punishment or restriction of privileges at worst.

Fisher's drive and practical changes began to modify these attitudes but after his departure from the Admiralty in 1910 the pressure was not necessarily maintained. Submarines were not considered a fit role for an aspiring officer (see above) and many commanders would have preferred to be the number two on a big ship than command a destroyer.

Commanding a ship or a fleet was a well-rewarded position. Admirals received a good salary, when on active duty, and an entertainment allowance. In 1911 a rear admiral might receive a salary of £1,095 per annum. That equates to over £100,000 in today's money. If not required for service, an officer could be placed on half-pay, but this was an occupational risk worth taking, given the other joys of the role, for in addition to pay, flag officers received 'table money'. When travelling to their appointment they would, in 1913 for example, receive 30 shillings a day. On hoisting their flag, this was increased to £1,642 per annum (around £152,000 today). From this, a flag officer had to provide for the messing arrangements of his staff. Captains and admirals aboard the big ships enjoyed a standard of living which was second to none, waited on hand and foot.

This well-ordered and comfortable life was changed on the outbreak of war – not so much for the big ships, which spent much of their time in harbour – but certainly for the men of the Dover Patrol. An influx of Royal Naval Reserve (RNR) sailors, mostly merchant seamen and fishermen, and Royal Naval Volunteer Reserve (RNVR) men, mainly keen amateur sailors or adventurers, immediately diluted the carefully protected mores of the Royal Navy with civilian behaviour. This is an important point, for the Dover Patrol was essentially an amateur's navy. Fishermen, yachtsmen, clerks, merchant sailors, paddleboat crewmen: all played a significant part, and immediately after the war, if they had survived their experiences, slipped back into everyday, non-naval life, though often deeply marked by the campaigns they had fought.

Three reserve naval forces were increasingly critical to the manning of the Patrol. The Royal Naval Reserve and the Royal Fleet Reserve (RFR) were naval reserve forces drawn from professional officers and ratings of the mercantile marine, and ex-naval ratings. Membership of the former was voluntary, but many major mail steamer companies encouraged their employees to join. After basic training, further periodic training with the fleet was undertaken. As the war went on, whole crews of contracted or conscripted vessels were taken into the RNR, such as the trawlers and drifter crews of the Dover Patrol. The RFR was a force formed from former naval ratings who, after completing their contractual service with the Royal Navy, were liable to recall during times of emergency. The liability lasted for a specified numbers of years after leaving active service.

The empire, too, provided reservists. In Newfoundland, for example, an RNR service had been formed in 1903. Acceptance required that candidates be seamen or fishermen between the ages of eighteen and thirty. All men enrolled for five years and completed twenty-eight days' drill annually.

The Royal Naval Volunteer Reserve was another naval reserve force of men drawn from civilian occupations ashore. They were enthusiastic volunteers and not professional seafarers, somewhat similar to the Territorial Army. The volunteers carried out training in the evenings, at weekends and two weeks' annual training aboard naval ships or at naval establishments. All officers were promoted from the lower deck. They came from many walks of life and professions and were looked down upon by the professional navy (who gave them the soubriquet 'wavy navy' after the design of their stripes of rank). But during the course of the war, they progressively replaced regular RN and RNR men in smaller ships, including in the Dover Patrol, freeing the more experienced sailors for the larger vessels.

Finally, there was the Mercantile Marine Reserve (MMR). This encompassed Mercantile Fleet Auxiliaries (MFAs), ie, merchantmen on government service, and was divided into two parts. There were those vessels which were non-commissioned, which meant that they were on time-charter to the government and their crews remained subject to the usual civilian legislation of the Board of Trade, the Merchant Shipping Acts. Secondly, there were the commissioned MFAs. They were operated in a different manner, their owners having little to do with them and were classed as naval auxiliaries, flying the white ensign. Instead of commercial articles, officers and men of these vessels signed T124 forms, binding them to the Naval Discipline Act.

It was not just the change in personnel, but also the demands of constant patrol in small ships which quickly rendered the expected pre-war behaviours obsolete. Hood and Bacon both quickly adapted to the change. Hood had a low tolerance for routine, unusually for his rank. He bounced from ship to ship in the early days of his command, and was always energetically in the heart of the action. Bacon, too, went to sea, but worked more usually from an onshore office, in which he slept when operations were in progress.

But when Hood went to the Battle Cruiser Force under Beatty, he soon conformed to more traditional behaviour, so typical of the 'big navy'. Hood leased North Queensferry House on the shore of the Firth of Forth for himself and his family. It was a large house which, amongst other attractions, had strawberry beds and a tennis court. And onboard ship, Hood lived in some style too. There was an admiral's day cabin on the port side at the foot of the bridge and behind the forward gun turret, which was connected to the admiral's dining cabin on the starboard side, above the band's instrument room. To the rear of the bridge was an admiral's galley (ie, his private kitchen) and above it a shelter for his personal use. His steward would wait on him, his personal coxswain, Chief Petty Officer Best, would be on hand for odd jobs or transportation needs, and his secretary, Harold Rollo Gore Browne, ready to turn his wishes into actions. Browne, whose father was the Rector of Leckhampton and mother the daughter of the 10th Lord Rollo of Duncrub, played cricket, as did his brother Eric, who had played for Oundle 1st XI and for the Europeans against the Parsees at Poona (Pune) in 1912. Hood did like to get his cricketers around him.

In contrast, for the Dover Patrol the standard of the onboard accommodation was generally poor. The Brazilian monitors were comfortably built, but the other monitor classes, which were hastily thrown together for the war, were spartan in the extreme (one can still be seen at Portsmouth Historic Dockyard, the restored *M-33*). Destroyers were cramped and uncomfortable. Submarines were even worse, an experience shared equally by both British and German crews.

Early British and German submarines had been designed to protect ports and harbours, but by the start of the First World War they could spend around five days on war patrol, but only had seventy-two hours' air supply. What's more, they could only be submerged for around two hours at a time because they had to switch from diesel engines to an electric battery-powered system.

Because of the limitations of range of their electric batteries, U-boats tended to leave port on the surface at night and only submerged when spotted by the enemy, or after conducting an attack. Once submerged, the electric batteries posed a real threat to the crew. The storage battery cells, located under the living spaces, generated gas, and a ventilation failure risked explosion, a catastrophic event which occurred in several U-boats. If seawater got into the battery cells, poisonous chlorine gas was generated which choked, incapacitated and often killed the crew.

German and British submarine sailors suffered from the inability to fulfil basic hygiene requirements, and both they and the vessels stank. Officers would douse themselves in cologne to mask their own body odour and that of their men.

Once at sea, the big fleet battleships were still generally comfortable vessels. Not so the smaller craft of the Dover Patrol. Destroyer and submarine crews developed a dress code all of their own, and the sea conditions they enjoyed were difficult even in calm weather, and especially at night. As a contemporary writer had it, 'the commanding officer, who came aboard in immaculate gold lace and spick and span uniform climbs the bridge, sea-booted and with a thick muffler round his throat, wearing a cap and jacket in which he would in no circumstances be seen ashore'.[1] All the rest of the crew followed their skipper's example, both to protect their expensive naval uniforms, but also because 'destroyer work tells heavily upon clothes as well as upon the men who wear them'.[2]

The destroyer's bridge was reached by steep iron ladders, leading to a high perched, circular, canvas-screened structure in which were crowded several ratings, a gun, a chart table, wheel, helmsman and navigating officer. In any sort of sea, the ship rocked giddily to and fro such that descending the bridge ladders became fraught with danger. Progress along the decks was risky and hanging on to the lifelines essential. Spray and waves regularly soaked everybody on deck, including the occupants of the bridge.

Lieutenant Robert Travers Young joined *Lochinvar* in January 1917:

> it was pretty hard going escorting troop ships and hospital ships all day, patrolling the Channel all night; and it was a very hard winter ... during the first month of my time in destroyers I wondered why I had been so stupid as to abandon the solid comforts of a battleship for a life where I was usually cold, wet and seasick.[3]

For Sub Lieutenant V J Robinson on board *Laertes*, like *Lochinvar*, another 'L'-class destroyer (built in 1913, three 4in, 29 knots), it was a demanding routine, with frequent patrols of the cross-channel barrage, and escort and other duties. Dover, he thought, was 'a fairly rotten spot ... especially in bad weather'.[4]

The monitors suffered likewise. Slow and of shallow draught, they were not good sailers. In a heavy sea, waves broke over their decks and forward motion was difficult. Moored up and firing, the whole ship shook with every gunshot. The recoil frequently buckled the plates of the ship itself. The counter battery fire of the German guns dropped shells all around them, any one of which could put an end to many shipboard lives. Submarine or torpedo-boat attack whilst moored to fire was a constant menace.

For the coastal motor boats, being at sea meant being constantly wet. Known as 'scooters' or 'skimmers', and generally commanded by reserve officers, they relied on speed for their protection. They carried a crew of no more than four men, a commanding officer, a second in command, who also functioned as observer, and two engineers who sat crouched under the deck in front of the two officers. This position was particularly exposed and uncomfortable, perched beside their machinery whilst all the water breaking over the bows fell on them; they had to sit chin on toes, doubled up, managing the temperamental petrol engines.

The motor launches too endured harsh conditions. As one of their officers later described a typical mission:

there is a certain liveliness in the North Sea on this morning, quite a high sea is running, and soon the boat is feeling this, no boat sooner than an ML, and before long she is 'shipping it green.' Patrol may be a bit monotonous at times, but it can never be called dry work, anyhow in the winter. There are days when, however much you may wrap yourself up in oilskins, you will still get soaked, and your sea boots act as involuntary foot baths of ice-cold water. But this is a thing you have to grin (or curse) and bear on an ML on a rough day. Nor is the general wetness confined to the deck, as clothes, and boots testify if not worn for a few days, and a calm day is as bad as a rough one for this form of dampness.

Towards midday the wind abates a little, but not so the cold, and oilskins give place to duffel coats – thick wool, yellowy-brown coats with hoods, and which, if worn with these up and baggy trousers of the same material, give the appearance of a ship manned by giant teddy bears. Meals on an ML are 'movable feasts,' where the right hand never knows what the left hand may be doing, for while the latter is conveying food to the mouth the former is probably chasing the plate across the table or picking up a chop from the seat. No meal on patrol is ever dull.[5]

Even in the fleet auxiliaries all was not sweetness and light. On 28 April 1917, for example, there was a mutiny on the oiler *Oilfield*, 'an Arab having knocked a man's eye out'.[6] *Swift* sent an armed guard aboard to quell the disturbance.

There was little glamour in the operations of the Dover Patrol. It was hard, enduring and abrasive work and the Patrol took a sadistic pride in the fact that the duty was arduous and constant, unlike the units of the Grand Fleet, who spent much of their time at anchor in Scapa Flow or Rosyth. Officer's Cook W G Evans joined *Amazon* one Sunday in October 1916. He was met on the gangway by the coxswain and then made his way forward where he was intercepted by the first lieutenant who greeted him with, 'You are the new cook, I take it.' Evans replied in the affirmative. 'Do you know where your action station is?' continued the officer. 'No sir, I have only just arrived on board.' The first lieutenant fixed him with a glare. 'You have been on board this ship for nearly ten minutes. That is sufficient time for you to have found out where your action station is. Where have you come from, the Grand Fleet?' Again Evans replied, 'Yes, sir.' 'Well, let me inform you that this is the 6th Flotilla and we may be in action tonight. Go back to the Coxswain and find out where your action station is and come back and report to me.'[7] Whilst admiring their pride, it is interesting to note that a ship which only carried four, or at most five, officers needed a designated officers' cook!

And, of course, traditional British values and insouciance were exhibited by the Patrol's officers at all times. On 24 September 1917 at 0320 a damaged German submarine was reported by an air patrol to be near no. 6 buoy and making for Zeebrugge and safety. Two Dover destroyers were despatched with the signal 'Destroyers follow aircraft'. *Marksman*'s captain (Commander Lionel John Garfit Anderson), the senior officer present, sent a signal to the effect that 'if the submarine was sighted there was to be no poaching. The usual sportsman's rule as to whose bird it was would apply'.[8] From the grouse moor to the Channel was but a short step. But they didn't find the U-boat.

Lieutenant Reggie Ramsbotham was navigating officer on *Kempenfelt* when she was ordered to join the Patrol in September

1917. He welcomed it. 'I was rather pleased as Scapa got a bit boring,' he recorded, adding that in the Dover Patrol there was a 'hell of a lot of night patrolling and a lot of operational work against German destroyers on the Belgian coast'.[9]

There was, in fact, a well-established Dover destroyer routine by which each ship spent twenty-four hours at sea and twenty-four hours in harbour, but during the spell in port, full steam was kept on the engines and the ship had to be ready to respond instantly to any sudden orders. Every seventeen days there was a three-day boiler cleaning period and once every four months the ship was meant to spend twenty days in dockyard hands.

The continuous nature of the duty called for much dull, but also dangerous, patrol work. To take two weeks in 1917 as an example, *Swift* spent between 18 and 30 March at sea, first on barrage patrol and then patrolling the Downs. And losses were daily: in a four day period noted by *Swift*'s signalman, on 23 March SS *Mexico* was mined and sunk, likewise the destroyer *Laforey*. Next day the trawler *King Guy* was lost to mines. On the 25th HMS *Fawn* ran aground. And on the 26th *Myrmidon* was sunk after a collision with the merchant ship SS *Hamborn* off Dungeness.

And this contrast between the humdrum and the fearful was always present. On 1 October 1917 *Marksman* left Dunkirk at 0545 with *Terror* and some destroyers and paddle minesweepers. According to signalman William Wood:

[it was] a very quiet afternoon, watched drifters and small monitors laying nets and examining buoys. That forenoon no less than twelve mines were destroyed by gunfire. [I was] rudely awakened from an afternoon nap by the alarm bell. At action stations for three-quarters of an hour. Nothing seen.[10]

Lieutenant John Brooke was the last commanding officer of *Zulu* before she was sunk. He was proud of the 'incomparable 6th flotilla'[11] and their versatility. 'It is hard to explain in a short space the multifarious duties that fell to the lot of the Dover Patrol,' he later wrote:

No case was ever recorded of a destroyer asking to shelter in bad weather and there was a constant sea-keeping force (an arduous life for all concerned). Thirty days and nights at sea except for refuelling sometimes fell to our lot when casualties reduced the number of destroyers available. Constant patrolling, day and night, whether in support of the drifters watching the mine and net barrage ... or escorting transports to and from France ... and VIPs across the Channel.[12]

Brooke took a perverse delight in observing the discomfort of his highly placed passengers who all seemed to succumb to seasickness, even First Lord of the Admiralty (and former prime minister) A J Balfour, who spent one miserable voyage in the captain's cabin with his head between his knees and holding a large bucket.

Some found this sort of work dull. Young of the *Lochinvar* wrote: 'personally I found the Dover Patrol at this time a rather dreary affair; there were plenty of alarums and excursions but nothing ever came our way'.[13] And Commander Andrew Cunningham much preferred to be based at Dunkirk: 'I much preferred [Dunkirk] to Dover. There was more chance of action and one was relieved of the rather monotonous duty of escorting troop transports from Dover and Folkestone to Calais and Boulogne'.[14] But Dover also offered compensations. On HM Yacht *Ceto*, despite the vessel being 'pretty duff and crowded', the crew would fish for whiting whenever they could, and these were 'an excellent supplement to stores'.[15]

Ted Sproule was a Canadian RNVR who had volunteered for service in 1915 and joined the Dover Patrol in 1915 as a mechanic on the coastal motor boats (he later joined the RNAS and ended the war as a flight lieutenant). He was not enamoured of Dover, writing home that 'so far Dover hasn't held any charm for me, but providing I stay here long enough I may meet some nice people'.[16] But there were also some benefits: in July 1917 Sproule received forty-eight hours' leave and went up to London to the Hippodrome to see George Robey in *Zig-Zag*. He loved it, noting:

> there are simply marvellous and marvellously pretty stage settings for the different acts and dances. Of course the Hipp has a narrow, shall I say raised, aisle running from the stage direct right through the centre of the theatre, upon which the leading artists from time to time come out under spot light giving the audience a closer view.[17]

He also loved the leading lady, Lillian Major.

And it should never be forgotten that these men were human

beings with human failings, with the ordinary desires and behaviours of humankind. The armed trawler *Lord Minto*, in harbour at Dover, recorded in in its log book for 25 June 1915:

> R Lewis, cook, left ship by Skipper's orders to fetch provisions; failed to return on board till 5.00am Saturday morning; spent night in guard ship; reported to base, and ordered by Commander Rigg RN to refund £1.15 from his wages to crew, which he had spent and wasted from crew's money with which he had been entrusted to buy provisions.[18]

Another sort of human weakness was shown by two deckhands on the drifter *Girl Annie*, fishermen temporarily enlisted as RNR. Tiring of an evening's entertainment at the Dover Hippodrome they saw, through the window of the gallery, a cask of beer sitting temptingly below them. Scrambling out and sliding down the drainpipe, they opened the door of the yard and were able to roll the barrel towards the harbour and their vessel. This proved thirsty work and so about half way there they tapped the cask and, in the absence of glasses, drank up from an old paint tin. Their pleasure was attenuated by the arrival of the local constabulary and the evening ended in the police station cells.

In the magistrate's court the following day, they were arraigned before a strict teetotaller and regular navy man, Captain Cay RN, who inquired of the officer representing the Patrol, Commander George Venn RNR (second in command of the drifter division), as to the men's character. 'Your worship, they are two very good men at sea. I hope that you will fine them and not imprison them, as their services are valuable to the Patrol, and I am sure Chief Constable Fox will vouch for the general good behaviour of the Drifter Patrol.' Fox did so, and the men were subjected to a long lecture on temperance before Cay dismissed them, saying, 'These men will be punished by naval authorities, of course?' Venn replied, 'Oh yes, certainly,' and the erring sailors were acquitted.

Now they had to face naval discipline and the next morning appeared before Captain M A A Case. Case, who had a habit of shutting one eye when looking at anybody brought up before him, said, 'Well, commander, what have you got to say about these men?' Venn replied, 'Exceptionally good at sea, but seem to play the fool on shore, sir.' 'Yes, so I should imagine. Well, this time, as the Commander says you work well and are valuable to the Patrol, and as people are such damn fools that they cannot lock up their beer, you can go. Dismissed.'[19]

Dover and Ramsgate

No narrative about the Dover Patrol can be complete without considering the role of the towns that supported it, Dover itself, the so-called 'lock and key of the kingdom', and also Ramsgate.

Ramsgate

As has been noted, Ramsgate was home to both the Downs Boarding Flotilla and a part of the drifter contingent. The community suffered for its hosting of the Patrol. By the war's end, Ramsgate had gained the unwanted distinction of being England's most bombed town. Zeppelins and Gothas dropped 396 bombs on the town and she was hit by 343 shells. The hospital was attacked and on 31 October 1917 the gas works was completely destroyed in a bombing raid which also exploded all the gas mains in the town; the resultant damage was considerable. On another occasion, an ammunition dump at the harbour was bombed and went up with a blaze which could be seen from Calais. In Ramsgate, 200,000 windows were broken by the force of the blast and £38,000 (approximately £2.9 million at today's values) worth of damage to property later identified.

Ships in the harbour were frequently attacked. The *East Kent Times* of 19 April 1917 gave a vivid account of one such operation:

At 7.30 a.m. an enemy seaplane was observed by a patrol boat near the Goodwin Sands to be approaching Ramsgate, flying unusually low. Fire from the patrol boat's anti-aircraft gun was opened, but owing to the density of the mist, which overhung the water, visibility was very poor and the raider passed out of its sight. Few people were about at the time, but those on the West cliff soon afterwards saw a dark coloured seaplane come into view over Pegwell Bay at an altitude of not more than 500 feet.

The first impression, as it was seen to circle HM Monitor *Marshal Ney*, was that it was a British machine, but that idea was soon dispelled when, swooping down still lower on the landward side of the ship, the occupants released a ship's torpedo which had been carried slung between the floats of the machine.

The deadly missile was evidently intended for and directed at the monitor, but fortunately it failed to reach its objective, for, travelling in a semi-circle, it entered the mouth of Ramsgate Harbour and buried its warhead in the mud below a mud-hopper which was operating there. After releasing the torpedo, the pilot swung his machine round in the direction of the harbour and, passing over the western pier, appeared to develop engine trouble. He narrowly avoided collision with the structures on the East Pier and alighted on the water opposite the Royal Pavilion, only a short distance from the shore. The momentum after the engine had ceased took him to within a hundred yards of the sands. To put his engine into working order again occupied the pilot barely a minute, and, restarting, he rose slowly to the height of the cliffs, dropping two small bombs into the water as he did so. Before any of the patrol boats or cutters from the harbour could reach the spot, the machine was flying parallel to the east cliffs from where a handful of spectators could see both the pilot and the observer.

Danger to the denizens of Ramsgate was not confined to enemy action. On Saturday, 26 May 1917 at 0815, and as the town was just beginning to stir into life, there was a huge explosion in the harbour. Nearly all of the windows of nearby Nelson Crescent, Sion Hill and York Terrace were smashed and the shock wave brought down some tramway wires. HM Torpedo Boat No. 4 had blown up. Built in 1906, she had two years earlier taken part in the rescue of the survivors from *Anglia*. Now she lay broken in Ramsgate harbour and all over the town. Part of the boat came down in Albert Street, with another part in Queen Street. Smaller pieces hit roofs in Alpha Road and Clarendon Gardens. Altogether some four hundred houses were damaged, and many townsfolk narrowly escaped being hit by flying pieces of metal. Virtually every town-centre shop was damaged.

The vessel itself was utterly wrecked, and all but three of the seventeen men on board were killed. The blast had been caused by the accidental discharge of a torpedo whilst it was being cleaned. The men near the torpedo had been literally blown to bits, those below died in the resultant fire.

There was a real danger that when the flames reached the ammunition store, the consequent explosion would destroy large parts of the town, but brave and willing volunteers, sailors and firemen alike managed to remove most of the ammunition to the fish market on the harbour crosswall. Many houses and shops along the seafront had already been damaged, but without the courage of the men who moved the ammunition, the impact on the town would have been much worse.

Ramsgate gave the victims an impressive funeral. Their coffins were carried through the town to the cemetery on the flatbeds of motor lorries, draped in Union Jacks. And the funerals were attended by thousands of townspeople, who afterwards subscribed to the erection of a white marble cross with the dedication: 'In memory of those of His Majesty's Naval forces at Ramsgate who have given their lives in the service of their country during the war.'

At least forty-five Ramsgate citizens were killed during the war and another ninety-three injured, and the population halved from pre-war levels as people fled into the interior. Those that remained took cover in the myriad tunnels underground. But the town never stopped, and neither did the Downs Flotilla and the Ramsgate drifters.

Dover

At the outbreak of war, Dover harbour became a major port of embarkation and landing, as well as home to the Dover Patrol. Members of the Belgian royal family arrived at the harbour with the Belgian gold reserves and, during October 1914, 15,000 Belgian refugees came. A total of 1,260,000 wounded men would pass through Dover on their way back from the Western Front to meet daily hospital trains at the military-only Dover Admiralty Pier railway station, where a full Royal Navy captain presided over disembarkation and transport arrangements.

From July 1917, all overseas leave men came and went through Dover; 2,094 troop transports sailed from Dover carrying four million British, Commonwealth and American troops and 11,938 vessels were despatched from Dover to the continent. One eyewitness asserts that, in total, ten million man-movements were dealt with by Transport Command at Dover through the course of the war.[1]

The outbreak of war had brought an instant change to the community of Dover. The town was immediately declared an armed camp and the borough of Dover, under the Defence of the Realm Act, became part of Dover fortress. This meant that the military were in charge but, although public elections were suspended, councillors continued in office. Mayor Edwin Farley was re-elected by his colleagues in November 1914, 1915, 1916, 1917 and 1918! Unlike some Dover citizens, Farley never left the town during the war. An army garrison of 10,000 men was maintained, with its HQ at the castle and from 1916 the municipal borough of Dover and much of the rural district of Dover was designated a Special Military Area: residents were required to show an identity card/pass to enter the town and armed checkpoints were established at all routes of entry and exit.

Residents' lives changed immediately and completely. Many private and public buildings were taken over by the armed forces for the duration. The navy co-opted the waterfront. The beautiful Georgian and Regency villas off Marine Parade became offices for the three successive Dover Patrol admirals (no. 42), Admiralty offices (nos. 40 and 18) and paymaster's department (no. 16). Sidney Terrace, equally architecturally distinguished, housed the 6th Destroyer Flotilla's HQ and officers' quarters, whilst East Cliff gave shelter to HM Naval Depot (no. 23), the office of the harbour super-intendent (no. 22), the supply office and the RNAS officers' quarters (nos. 9 and 10). Likewise the rowing club and the Admiralty, Prince of Wales and Promenade piers became exclusive naval properties. Ratings were put into Oil Mill Barracks (a 1914 conversion). All the elementary schools in the town were taken up for military use. A central messing area was created in the sports grounds of Dover College and the isolation and smallpox hospitals became military only. Dover resembled nothing less than a gigantic armed forces depot.

On the establishment of the military regime in 1914, public entertainment and public houses were severely curtailed. Pubs closed at 2100 and servicemen were not allowed to enter them before 1700. Theatres and shows had to end by 2200. Nonetheless, the cinemas and theatres of Dover provided much needed entertainment for the men of the Dover Patrol, despite the curtailed opening hours. Probably the best of the theatres was the Royal Hippodrome in Snargate Street, which seated 600 people. But there were also a plethora of cinemas and the Connaught Room, which put on amateur dramatics throughout the war. In the face of the influenza epidemic of 1918, all cinemas in Dover were ordered to close on 18 November and thenceforward. Such a prohibition was not, however, applied to the more upmarket Hippodrome and Connaught facilities.

As a result of the naval presence and military activities, Dover gained the dubious distinction of becoming the first place in Britain to be bombed by a German aircraft. On a bright, sunny Christmas Eve 1914 at around midday, a Friedrichshafen FF29 German seaplane flew over the town. Pilot Lieutenant von Prondzynski leaned over the side of his plane and saw Dover Castle and the naval harbour below him. He lifted his bomb in both hands, controlling the plane with his knees and heaved the bomb over the side of the plane. He missed any target of military significance. But the explosion broke some windows in St James's rectory and knocked the gardener, James Banks, out of a tree he was pruning. This raid was the precursor to a total of 370 bombs and eighty-five shells which fell on the town during the war. In Dover, 207 bombs and shells were dropped on an area of less than three square miles, giving a density of over sixty-nine impacts per square mile. For comparison, London received 800, but spread over 144 square miles, a density of 5.5 impacts per square mile.

Dover's caves were opened to provide air-raid shelters. The town was ordered to be 'dark' at night, and special constables patrolled the streets with constant demands for the covering up of light-emitting crevices and keyholes. Despite this, approximately twenty-six inhabitants of the town were killed and seventy-five injured in the bomb and shell attacks, but the support for the servicemen by most of the citizens never faltered. They turned out to respect the coming home of the dead from the First Battle of the Dover Strait and they took to the streets again to honour the victory of the second. They welcomed back the *Vindictive* with loud cheering from an enthusiastic crowd.

Virtually the whole town was there the week before Christmas 1918 to greet Field Marshal Sir Douglas Haig and his senior commanders when they returned to England on the hospital ship *Jan Breydel* with an escort of the Dover Patrol's ships. All the craft in the harbour 'manned ship' along the two-mile route to the mooring. As Haig stepped onto the dockside, he was met by Vice Admiral Sir Roger Keyes. Behind Keyes, a man with a royal mace stood representing the King. A Royal Navy guard of honour and naval band in white helmets played music as Keyes and Haig walked together to their waiting transport. Both men were in their element as they acknowledged the adulation.

And after the Armistice, Dover welcomed home the prisoners of war. The first 800 were given a tumultuous reception by crowds and were greeted by the Prince of Wales. In total 55,398 POWs came home via Dover, meeting 130 trains at Admiralty Pier. And on 10 November 1920 the body of the Unknown Soldier was landed at Dover with full military honours from *Verdun*, a modern 'V'-class destroyer, for transport by train to Victoria Station and thence to Westminster Abbey for interment.

Over and above such moral support, Dover helped the war effort, and particularly the Dover Patrol, in more practical ways too. The Dover Engineering Works was a major employer in the town before the war and was famous for the manufacture of steam isolating valves, iron fittings and waterproof, airtight inspection covers. Situated in the middle of the town, employing and housing hundreds of workers, it had been owned since 1909 by the theatre architect Walter Emden (a quondam mayor of Dover) and managed by his nephew Vivian Elkington. The works became the reserve base workshop for the Dover Patrol, and played a key role in the maintenance and repair of all sorts of different vessels.

At the start of the war, the only naval engineering facility at Dover had been a small submarine base. When the 6th Destroyer Flotilla arrived, an engineering and dockyard facility was necessary and the workshops of the Dover Engineering Company were engaged for these tasks on a cost plus percentage basis. Another arrangement was made with the South East and Chatham Railway workshops, while Messrs Palmers, a firm of sheet metal workers, also of Dover, were later taken on as well.

By the end of 1917 there were over four hundred vessels operating under the auspices of the Dover Patrol and the volume of work generated necessitated a new and tiered arrangement. Repair work was done at the 6th Flotilla workshops, the first overflow being to the superintending civil engineers' workshop which employed about thirty civilian mechanics. Beyond this, repairs went to the Dover Engineering Co. under the 'very willing direction of Mr V Elkington, the managing director'.[2] Other more trivial defects were attended to by the South East and Chatham Railway workshops.

Thus Dover industry, railways and ordinary civilians contributed to the work of the Patrol. The womenfolk of Kent tried to do their bit too. Nine miles up the road in Deal, the mayor and ladies of the town set up a canteen for the Patrol's sailors; the Baptist minister's daughter was, however, obliged to resign her position after being caught sitting on a matelot's knee.[3]

Dover also provided for the wives and families of the naval officers who ran the Patrol. This was counter to established naval thinking, which feared the presence of wives would be a distraction. However, Admiral Bacon, at least, disagreed with accepted wisdom. He noted that:

> the work of the Patrol was so dangerous, so hard and so incessant that I sincerely desired that whenever the officers and men had a day or two off, those days should be as pleasant as possible, and therefore the more wives and families accumulated at Dover the better I was pleased.[4]

His encouragement of the practice drew criticism but he was adamant. Later he wrote:

> There is a silly and small-minded sect in the Navy which objected to the wives of naval officers and men being in the ports which their husbands frequent. In all my experience I have never known a case of duty being neglected for the sake of a wife or family. Generally the complaint is from the other quarter, that duty occupies so much of the husband's time that too little time is spent ashore.[5]

The drifter crews, too, were encouraged to bring their families to Dover and its environs. Commander Venn thought it might make the men better behaved. There was some initial resistance from the crews, but after the raids on the east coast by Hipper's battlecruisers, they came round to the idea.

Death was a frequent companion to the activities of the Patrol, but the womenfolk of Dover joined the naval wives in doing their best to help the widows and orphans left behind. Bacon was acutely conscious of this, a task which he felt himself and his colleagues unable to undertake through reasons of time and temperament: 'such work of mercy can be dealt with best by women,' he noted.[6]

And so Dover was inextricably linked to the successes and disappointments of the Patrol. As Admiral Bacon said:

> The Dover Patrol owes a considerable debt of gratitude to the Mayor of Dover, Mr Farley, the Corporation, and many inhabitants for their kindly help and generosity. No occasion for helping the Patrol was ever neglected. It is impossible to mention all who so kindly assisted the men and their wives. They are too numerous, and I hope the omission to do so will be forgiven.[7]

2 3

Envoi: Analysis and Conclusions

Keyes hauled down his flag at Dover on 20 March 1919 and was moved to the command of the Battle Cruiser Force at Rosyth, handing over to Rear Admiral Cecil Dampier who, from June 1917, had acted as admiral superintendent of Dover dockyard, officer in charge of shore establishments and King's Harbourmaster at Dover. His role was to run down and wind up the Patrol (now renamed the Dover Patrol Force) and by May it had lost the destroyers and submarines to leave only a collection of minesweepers and P-boats.

Most of the ships mentioned in this story failed to survive the 'Geddes Axe' of 1921/2 when defence spending was slashed overnight. As a result of these cuts, expenditure on the navy fell from £344 million in 1918/19 to £76 million in 1920/21. *Amazon* was scrapped in 1919, as was the patched-together *Zubian*, and *Broke* and *Botha* were resold to Chile in 1920. *Attentive* and *Foresight* went for scrap in 1920, and so did *Crusader* and *Leven*. *Swift*, *Lochinvar*, *Mastiff* and *Laertes* were all scrapped in 1921, as were most of their sisters. The majority of the monitors had their big guns taken out and were laid up ahead of scrapping (although *Erebus* and *Terror* would survive to fight in the next war).

There was no money and the hard-won lessons of the First World War had been quickly forgotten. The focus returned to big ships; everyone ignored the imperative of protecting the supply chain. At no time during 1914–18 was Britain ever to face the starvation that afflicted Germany and her allies, although it was only the belated adoption of convoy tactics during 1917, in the face of the German unrestricted submarine campaign, that prevented such an eventuality. The necessity for convoy escorts to be an important part of the fleet was immediately overlooked, as was the danger posed by

U-boats and the need to control the Channel with small, agile and fast ships – ships which, like the Dover Patrol, no longer existed.

But what were the achievements of the Patrol and its admirals in the years from its formation in October 1914 to the end of the war? In answering that question, it is first necessary to try to identify the criteria for success. The initial objectives set were to maintain a safe passage for men and supplies from England to France; to lay and clear mines from the Channel; and to check the cargoes of merchant ships passing through the Dover Strait as part of the blockade of Germany. But these objectives were soon incorporated into others. Bacon recognised this truth, with the benefit of hindsight, when he wrote:

> my three predominating preoccupations in 1916, therefore, were, first, the protection of the shipping in the Downs ... the preparation of plans for turning the enemy out of his Belgian bases; and, thirdly, the protection of the left flank of the Allied Army against a landing in rear. These were the essential responsibilities of the Patrol.

He dismissed submarine hunting as impossible: 'hunting submarines was almost useless and hopeless',[1] thus demonstrating another cause of the eventual rift between him and the Admiralty in late 1917.

In reality, the Patrol became a jack-of-all-trades: escort duty, contraband management, minesweeping, shore bombardment and anti-submarine work. These were all very different in tactical design, in execution and in degree of achievement. But the Patrol can boast one obvious success without cavil. The German navy never managed to disrupt the supply chain between Britain and France, nor the transport of arms and men to the Western Front. From beginning to end, Dover harbour remained inviolate from enemy disruption and not a single soldier was lost in the movement of men to France. And the Germans never gained even a semblance of control of the Narrow Sea.

A total of 101,872 special trains carried over twelve million soldier-movements and associated supplies to cross the Channel and converted ferries brought back one million wounded. There were up to twenty hospital trains a day. The Dover Patrol used Dover and Ramsgate harbours as bases to protect this traffic, and of the 125,000 merchant ships that used the Strait during 1914–18, only seventy-three were lost. A total of 2,094 troopship and 3,875 hospital ship movements were also protected. These are no small achievements and made a telling contribution towards winning the war.

Protection of trade and the Channel increasingly called for minesweeping activity. Between 1915 and 1917, Bacon estimated that his minesweepers had swept a distance equal to twelve times round the earth. Without them, and given the scale of German mining (they laid around forty-five thousand during the war), the British losses to mines would have been much more substantial than they were.

The Germans lost 178 of their 360 submarines during the First World War. The historian Dr Innes McCartney estimates that between twenty and twenty-two were sunk in the vicinity of the Dover Strait;[2] the Patrol can certainly make a claim on these. But perhaps more importantly, when the barrage and Patrol's deterrent effect was working (which, as we have seen, was not all the time), U-boats were forced to proceed via the northern passage, which doubled the distance that they had to travel to their patrol areas, largely the Atlantic Ocean and Irish Sea. This also exposed them to British forces based all along the east coast and with the Grand Fleet. Instead of a 700-mile round trip, it was 1,400; and this meant that they had only four days to operate in their designated target areas, considerably reducing the threat they posed. Moreover, Britain's largest port, London, was utterly denied to them.

But there were also several areas of failure. Most obviously, the barrage system was not always a deterrent and the transit of a significant number of U-boats through it in the latter part of 1917, for example, was unhelpful to the Allied cause. However, after the full implementation of the mine barrage (Bacon's December 1917 version), together with Keyes's improvements, it was clear that by the summer of 1918 the minefield had become a near impenetrable barrier to U-boats. Between December 1917 and November 1918, ten U-boats were sunk by mines within the barrage (see Appendix 6). If it is not clear which admiral should take the credit for that, the combination of ideas certainly proved effective.

Bombardments in support of the army, generally helpful in October and early November 1914, soon became exercises in futility. The constant bombardment of Zeebrugge and Ostend produced no obvious detrimental effects and the raids of St George's Day 1918, and 8 May were a complete failure, not to say shambles, in which many brave men were sacrificed for no strategic or tactical achievement except the (admittedly important) one of raising public morale, and the less important one of the glorification of Roger Keyes.

Overall, a total of eighty-four different destroyers served at Dover, of which eight were lost. More importantly, 2,000 men of the Dover Patrol died in the forty-nine months of its existence. The Royal Navy lost 34,654 men at sea during the conflict. The Patrol thus represents nearly 6 per cent of sea losses. These numbers are small compared to the staggering losses on the Western Front, but every dead sailor was a father, brother, son; everyone a painful loss to someone; everyone a death for the defence of their nation and its people. And many of the ones who survived were never the same again, like Lieutenant Commander Arthur Watts.

The duty was hard and demanding; compared to the Grand Fleet, the workload was punishing. It was undertaken largely by amateur sailors, fishermen and merchant seamen, mainly volunteers. It was officered increasingly by the same. In many respects, the Dover Patrol became a citizen's navy, harking back to the days of Drake and Raleigh. One may suspect that pleased Keyes.

And what of the Germans? The German strategy in the Channel seems in retrospect to have suffered from a want of aggression, at least as far as surface forces went. Admiral Bacon certainly thought so. 'The German Navy, however, appeared to have no sea instincts', he later wrote:

Really, naval operations are to a great degree governed by instinct, and instinct is a matter of heredity. Nothing was more clearly shown by Germany's general attitude than that her ideas were military rather than naval. Ashore, war is a science, and a great deal more of an exact science than at sea – reconnaissance, intelligence, information, and other hard facts can govern dispositions and attacks on land. At sea, conditions are always in a state of flux. Speed of movement, difficulties of obtaining accurate knowledge, varying weather and sea conditions, make it essential to act merely on surmise, always ready to find that the conditions have changed from those which were expected.[3]

In his opinion: 'She [Germany] wavered and failed lamentably, always trying to believe that, by using her submarines illegitimately, she could avoid a clear strategical decision as to the use of her major armaments.'[4]

Whatever the reason, be it the Kaiser's reluctance to commit his ships or a desire by the German army to have the British army in France, where they could destroy them, rather than confined to their own shores, there was no attempt made to interfere with the transhipment of the British Expeditionary Force in August. Subsequently, the German navy constrained itself by tying the bulk of its destroyers to the High Seas Fleet for the early part of the war. It was only after Jutland, and the post-battle reluctance to venture out with the full fleet again, that significant destroyer resources were shifted to Flanders.

Hood and Bacon were concerned that they simply did not have enough destroyers to undertake the tasks appointed. A considerable number of available British destroyers were with the Grand Fleet* and Jellicoe was extremely reluctant to let them go. But Hood had to defend against submarine attacks on merchant ships after late October 1914, as well as protect his bombardment forces, drifters and trawlers, hunt U-boats and escort ships across the channel. Bacon inherited these tasks and more.

Had the Germans realised how thin the Dover Patrol's resources were stretched, it is possible they would have been more positive in 1914 and 1915. Bacon noted that:

> for purely defensive work as distinct from such vessels as might have been lent for offensive operations against the enemy's coast, we had during the whole of 1915, and the greater part of 1916, only twenty-four destroyers, six only of which mounted 4in guns, the remainder being armed with 12pdrs. What with refits, not more than three-quarters of these were present at any one time in the Patrol, so that, allowing for the necessary rest of the officers and crews, only three 4in gunned destroyers and six

---

* For example, on 20 June 1915, Jellicoe had directly under his control 1 Destroyer Flotilla at Rosyth (23 vessels), 2 DF at Cromarty (23), 3 DF at Harwich (23), 4 DF at Scapa (23), 7 DF at Humber (12), 8 DF (9 plus 12 TBs) at Rosyth and Scapa Patrol (11). Additionally, 10 DF (15) was on convoy duty. By comparison 6 DF at Dover had 24 plus 4 TBs. Thus the Dover Patrol had only 15 per cent of the available destroyers and more than half of these were of an obsolete type; 76 per cent were under the control of the Grand Fleet.

12pdr vessels were available at any one time on patrol; and, taking breakdowns and losses into account, even that number was rarely available.[5]

At one point the entire force of 4in gunned destroyers available was precisely one – *Amazon*. Bacon had to arrange for dummy signals to be sent from auxiliary craft at sea to pretend that there were patrols out.

This lack of small boats was a direct result of the navy's obsession with big ships, the descendants of the ships of the line which won Trafalgar and the like. The problem was not new. Nelson lamented a lack of frigates in his time. In the spring of 1804, Pitt the younger, dying and recalled to the role of prime minister from Walmer Castle and Wallett's Court where he was trying to pass away in peace, criticised Earl St Vincent, in charge of the navy, for his building programme during the height of the Napoleonic wars. The navy had done what it had always done, constructing big ships to fight fleet engagements out at sea. Pitt thought this wrong. He said the navy required smaller ships that were easier to manoeuvre in the narrow confines of the Channel and the Dover Strait. Small vessels such as gunboats were needed to harass and disperse an enemy force. *Plus ça change*, as they say in Dunkirk.

Some authorities have argued that the German surface forces available for the Channel were inferior to their British opponents and thus a German strategy of caution was justified. For example, one modern historian argues: 'the [German] torpedo boats were deficient in offensive armament. German units were too small and with their lighter gun armament and lower speed, vulnerable. British destroyers were half as large again and threw, albeit not accurately, three times the weight of broadside'.[6]

This statement may be true for the most modern British vessels, but the Dover Patrol had its collection of '30-knotters' at the start of the conflict for which this statement cannot be supported. Their 12pdr (3in guns), often only one of them, supported by up to five 6pdrs (2.25in), were under-gunned compared to the German torpedo boats, which were frequently equipped with three 3.4in, or 4in weapons, dependent on build date (for example, the German destroyers *G-85* and *G-42*, sunk in the encounter with *Swift* and *Broke*, carried three 4.1in and three 3.5in guns respectively. The 'A'-class torpedo boats fought by *Botha* mounted two 3.4in guns. Other German destroyer types such as the 1915 'V' class carried three

237

3.4in weapons and the 'S' class, three 4.1in). But as the war wore on, it is certainly true that new British destroyers became more heavily and appropriately armed, and by the time Keyes took command, the quality and the quantity of the Dover Patrol destroyers was much superior to that of 1914/15.

Bacon probably made too much of his scarcity of resource in his recollections. But, as a different commander in a different war once said, 'it has been a damned nice thing – the nearest run thing you ever saw in your life',[7] at least during the period 1914–16. A more determined effort by the Imperial German Navy in the Channel might have caused great difficulties in both allocation of materiel and maintaining the essential flow of men and arms to the Western Front.

Three admirals

What of the leaders of the Dover Patrol, Hood, Bacon and Keyes? What successes can be claimed for them?

Hood is probably the most attractive individual of the three. More the model of a modern officer than many of his contemporaries, he threw himself into the job with keen enthusiasm, using his high intelligence to swiftly transform the forces he had inherited and turn them into a weapon which could be used for the task he was set, namely bombardment in support of the army (which was not the reason the Dover Patrol had been established). His men responded to him and he proved a popular and charismatic leader. Commander F F Tower RNVR wrote of Hood: 'from my knowledge of him I can feel the loss to the service of that most gallant and able man who I like to remember'.[8]

Hood was a natural leader of men with a light touch, well demonstrated in an anecdote of his time as captain of the cruiser *Berwick* in 1907. *Berwick* had returned to Portsmouth from a cruise, and the crew were allowed leave. It was lovely summer weather and there was a plague of leave-breakers who did not return to the ship when their shore-leave time was up. By way of excuse, many leave-breakers produced doctors' sickness certificates proving that they had been too ill to return to duty. These notes were available in the dockside inns and taverns for the sum of one shilling. Hood would have nothing to do with them. 'If you had returned to your ship and you were found to be ill, you would not have been made to work,' he told each culprit. 'You would have been put on the sick list and provided with proper medical attention. The only doctor's certificate I will accept is one stating that you are unfit to travel'. Each leave-breaker then received the appropriate punishment.[9]

But leave-breaking still continued, as did the sunny weather, although the price of fake certificates rose as a function of demand to half a crown. Hood accepted these new certificates, but had their owners put on a list entitled 'the likely to go sick on shore' list. The next time a man whose name was on the list requested to go on shore, he was sent for examination by the fleet surgeon, who told him that he was quite ill and not fit to go on leave. That stopped the leave-breaking sharpish.

Such behaviour endeared him to his men and the Dover Patrol came together as a fighting force under his watch. All were sad to see him go when he was removed from his command by Churchill.

Bacon, an altogether different personality, is difficult to assess, if only because he was his own worst enemy. His engineering bent made his input invaluable in the advancement of questions of materiel, such as Operation Huff and spotting tripods. And his engineer's understanding of the operational problems of establishing a cross-channel barrage was undoubtedly superior to Hood's: on those grounds his appointment can be comprehended. But his self-belief and arrogance ensured that he was, unlike Hood, unable to accept ideas other than his own and was incapable of changing his mind once it was made up. And he was a poor delegator, secretive and protective of his plans, even with his chief of staff.

But he too could show the human touch on occasion and certainly does not seem as unbending as some authorities have painted him. His men genuinely liked him and he was capable of a fatherly kindness. On one occasion, Lieutenant Brooke, commanding *Zulu* on a VIP trip, was bringing Lord Kitchener back from France into Dover harbour. It was pitch black, the harbour was crowded with shipping and Brooke was finding it quite difficult to get alongside. His discomfort was not helped by 'hails and unnecessary advice from a voice ashore ... finally the same voice directed me where to put the brow'. 'I will put the *?**!** brow where I want to and I have had quite enough of your infernal interference,' he exploded.[10] It was then that he discovered that his interlocutor was no one other than Admiral Bacon, come to welcome Kitchener.

'Do you usually address a Vice-Admiral in those terms?' a stony-faced Bacon demanded. Brooke was crestfallen and, somewhat shattered, retired on board. Then, on an impulse, he ran back on shore and apologised again to the admiral. 'That's all right, my boy,' said Bacon and drove off; and Brooke noted that 'Curiously, after that, I never seemed to be able to put a foot wrong'.[11]

On another occasion, one of Bacon's destroyer captains was in serious financial difficulties and close to bankruptcy. Without telling anyone, including the officer concerned, Bacon sent him £200 through an intermediary, and the potential bankrupt was saved from disaster.

And what of the man who conspired to replace Bacon, Roger Keyes? It can be argued that Bacon had to go anyway, because of his inability to recognise that he was wrong-headed in his claim that U-boats were not transiting his barrage in 1917. But undoubtedly Keyes pushed him out. And having gained the levers of power, his innovation was strictly limited: more destroyer patrols and the questionably useful addition of constant night-time illumination. Many thought he also had an eye to posterity when he gained control at Dover. Captain A C Dewar described him as 'a very limited man, absolutely obsessed with doing something striking and brilliant'.[12]

In the first part of this ambition, at least, he was successful, for Keyes will forever be remembered for the Zeebrugge and Ostend raids, glorious failures which he and the government propaganda machine spun into the fine gold of a victory. Personally, he was as brave, single-minded and charismatic as a lion. The future Admiral of the Fleet Andrew Cunningham described Keyes as 'a great fighter and fearing nothing. He had outstanding qualities as a leader; above all that asset which counts so much in war – the burning desire to get at the enemy'.[13]

But he was also a poor planner and a not much liked leader, outside of a charmed cabal. In this, he did not change with age. Robert Young served under Keyes in the rank of commander when the latter was CinC Mediterranean Fleet (1925–28): 'the tempo of the fleet was much too fast and artificially fast at that; from a service point of view you never had time to analyse an exercise and try to learn from it before you were halfway through the next one.'[14] And the closed shop seemed even worse to Young: 'those who didn't play polo knew their CinC as a remote figure in a frock coat and sword and I knew only too well that he was completely out of touch with his fleet.'[15]

For Keyes, Zeebrugge showed British pluck at its best. Failure, accompanied by glorious courage, was transmuted from a hopeless act to a demonstration of British character that would electrify the world. This was Grenville and *Revenge*, Hawkins, Drake, Frobisher and the Armada, Nelson and *Victory*. But no gallantry, valour or noble deed can hide the fact that Keyes's one claim to fame was a fraud.

The respective careers of the Dover Patrol's admirals after their command undoubtedly shows Keyes ascendant, but Hood would perhaps have overshadowed him, given the chance. This was not to be. Horace Hood died bravely on 31 May 1916 at the Battle of Jutland when his flagship *Invincible* blew up during a glorious charge at the enemy to rescue some smaller ships. Hood's actions drew much praise from his friend David Beatty. Writing to Evan-Thomas, commanding the 5th Battle Squadron, Beatty stated 'poor Bertie Hood's magnificent handling of his squadron will remain in my mind for ever'.[16] And in his official despatch after the battle, Beatty wrote:

> Admiral Hood, without an instant's hesitation, and in a manner that excited the highest admiration of all who were privileged to witness it, placed his ships in line ahead of Admiral Beatty's squadron. No admiral ever crowned an all too short career more devotedly or in a manner more worthy of the name he bore.[17]

Writing to Second Sea Sir Lord Frederick Hamilton, Beatty stated 'you should have seen him bring his squadron into action, it would have done your heart good, no one could have died a more glorious death'.[18] No doubt Keyes would have approved.[*]

Bacon, supplanted by Keyes, left his post with undisguised bad grace. But some in the navy deemed him too valuable to lose and he was too much a patriot to refuse Churchill, now Minister of Munitions, who asked him to become Controller of the Ministry's

---

[*] Hood would have appreciated Beatty's tributes, but perhaps might have been pleased more by receiving an obituary in the *Wisden Cricketer's Almanac* of 1917, a publication he undoubtedly read but never dreamt of being featured in. *Wisden* noted that Horace 'was a keen, if not very distinguished, cricketer. When in command of a battleship he always endeavoured to secure good cricketers as the officers of the ward and gun rooms. When in command of *Hyacinth* he was captain of the officers' team.'

Inventions Department. He was advanced to the rank of admiral in September 1918 and his name finally went onto the retired list on 31 March 1919. Bacon moved to Hampshire and devoted himself to shooting and to chairing the Romsey bench, spending his summers at his house near Lerici, on the Italian Riviera. He was also a prolific writer, producing biographies of Jellicoe and Fisher, both men he admired, and a portfolio of technical tomes. He died in 1947.

In the aftermath of the war, the South African millionaire Sir Abraham (Abe) Bailey commissioned in 1919 a set of three paintings to feature the British statesmen, military and naval commanders of the conflict. In 1921 Sir Arthur Stockdale Cope, under this commission, completed the painting *Naval Officers of World War One* (now at the National Portrait Gallery) which depicted twenty-two admirals in the Admiralty Board Room. Keyes is almost centre stage and ceding precedence only to Beatty. There is no Fisher, no Jackson, no Bacon. Jellicoe is sidelined, slumped in a chair off to the viewer's right. As an exercise in demonstrating the manner in which Keyes and Beatty were seen as the real naval heroes of the conflict, a position which they unflinchingly arrogated to themselves, it is unmatched. Tucked away in the background, under a portrait of Nelson, are the only three admirals in the war to die on active service, Cradock, Arbuthnot and Horace Hood, already fading away from memory.

Keyes benefited most from his time at Dover, not least financially. On 7 August 1919 the King, by Act of Parliament, granted him £10,000 (about £500,000 today) in recognition of his 'eminent service during the late war'. After commanding the Battle Cruiser Force, he was promoted to vice admiral on 16 May 1921 and then became Deputy Chief of the Naval Staff in November 1921, followed by Commander-in-Chief of the Mediterranean Fleet in June 1925, with promotion to full admiral on 1 March 1926. He very much wanted to be First Sea Lord after Beatty and Madden, but Madden believed (almost certainly rightly) that he would have been 'a political liability at a time of financial economy',[19] and Keyes ended his service as CinC Portsmouth between 1929–31.

On retirement from the navy, Keyes became a Member of Parliament (for Portsmouth North) in 1934. When the Second War broke out, he became liaison officer to King Leopold of the Belgians, with whom he had a personal relationship, and was then made the first Director of Combined Operations in June 1940 by Churchill, purely on the basis of Zeebrugge. In this post Keyes was not a success, and his plans did not meet with the favour of the chiefs of staff, leading to his removal from the post sixteen months later.

Keyes's eldest son, Geoffrey Charles Tasker, died a war hero in 1941. Born 18 May 1917 (after three daughters) he did not follow his father into the navy, but attended Sandhurst and was then commissioned into the Royal Scots Greys. On the outbreak of war he swiftly transferred to 11 Commando and in 1941 won the Military Cross for his actions with them in the Lebanon, fighting the Vichy French, during which time he became the youngest acting lieutenant colonel in the British army.

In October/November 1941 a plan was formulated at 8th Army headquarters to attack various targets behind enemy lines, including headquarters, base installations and communications facilities. One of the objectives was the assassination of Erwin Rommel, the commander of the Axis forces in North Africa, by a commando team.

Geoffrey Keyes planned the raid himself and chose the most hazardous task as his own: the assault on the headquarters of Rommel's Afrika Korps, established in a house near Beda Littoria. But like his father's plans, it didn't quite come together. The submarine landing went wrong and only some of the raiding party and their equipment actually gained the shore; the remainder of the team then had to brave very heavy rain in a difficult and tiring approach to their target. As he tried to enter the house, Keyes was challenged by a sentry. As they struggled in the doorway, his second in command shot the German and surprise was lost. Keyes charged in, fired his revolver into the first room, followed by the other officer who threw a grenade. Keyes then entered a second room on the ground floor, but was shot as he opened the door. He died a few minutes after being carried out by his comrades. This is the official account, although some authorities state that he had been shot in the back by his second in command.* The mission was a failure, the house was not Rommel's HQ, but a logistics centre that he seldom, if ever, visited, the men retreated, and later most of the team were taken prisoner.

It was a complete, if foolishly brave, cock-up, not dissimilar to Zeebrugge and Ostend. But eager for a hero, the authorities

---

* See M Asher, *Get Rommel, The Secret British Mission to Kill Hitler's Greatest General* (Cassell, 2004).

posthumously awarded 24-year-old Geoffrey Keyes the Victoria Cross. In this, at least, he outdid the father to whom he had been constantly trying to prove himself.

In January 1943 Roger Keyes was elevated to the peerage as Baron Keyes, of Zeebrugge and of Dover in the county of Kent, and died two years later. Perhaps unsurprisingly, given the role Zeebrugge had played in forming his later career, Keyes was buried at the Zeebrugge corner of St James's Cemetery in Dover, alongside the men who had died in the eponymous raid.

In Memoriam

> That which in the instance kept the German forces from breaking disastrously on any dark night into the Channel and jeopardising the very foundations of our resisting power, were not the wonderfully planned and executed defences of nets and mines, but the inimitable hearts of the men of the Dover Patrol.
>
> Joseph Conrad, *The Dover Patrol, A Tribute*

Two thousand men died serving with the Dover Patrol between 1914 and 1918. Some died heroically, some tragically, some screaming and fighting against the waves that overcame them, some just sinking from sight. Those that were left behind were determined to remember them. Memorials large and small were to flow from that desire for cathartic remembrance.

The first memorial to be enacted was a simple wooden roll of honour tablet, placed in November 1918 inside Holy Trinity Church by the families of the trawlermen who had been lost manning the minesweeping patrols. In the next war the church was bombed and destroyed, and the memorial was adopted by the Dover Sea Cadets at Archcliffe Fort. When they moved base in the 1970s, the memorial was given into the custody of the town council and by 2006 was being stored in a shed in Deal. There it remains to this day: out of sight, out of mind.

Dover's perpetual mayor, Edwin Farley, also decided on a monument to the sacrifices in the English Channel and in December 1918 launched an appeal for funds, backed by Lord Northcliffe (who made a personal donation of £1,000 – £62,000 today) through his newspaper, *The Times*. As part of the publicity drive, on 13 December Farley created Keyes a Freeman of Dover

Town. The fund was a considerable success, with more than £45,000 (perhaps £2.8 million today) being raised and by 19 January 1919 the foundation stone had been laid for a memorial at Leathercote Point, to the north of Dover at the northern end of St Margaret's Bay, a bleak, windswept headland overlooking the Channel waters. Sir Aston Webb, the architect of, among other things, Admiralty Arch, the facade to Buckingham Palace, the Victoria Memorial outside the palace and (in 1905) the Britannia Naval College, had been engaged to design the monument, which was dedicated by the Prince of Wales on 27 July 1921. It is a stylised Egyptian granite pillar, 82ft high with a pyramidal top; to the front (south side) a plaque carries the inscription: 'To the Glory of God and in Everlasting Remembrance of the Dover Patrol 1914–1918. They died that we may live. May we be worthy of their sacrifice.'

An identical pillar was erected on the opposite side of the Channel on the cliffs of Cap Blanc-Nez, near Sangatte, to honour the 'glorious co-operation and frank comradeship of the French and British navies during the Great War' in 1922; and in 1931 another smaller version was placed in John Paul Jones Park in Brooklyn, New York, as a tribute to the 'comradeship and service of the American naval forces in Europe during the World War'. There was still money left over to provide for a centre for naval men at Dover – the Dover Patrol Hostel – opened by Lady Keyes in 1923 (and later destroyed by enemy action in 1940).

The burnishing of Roger Keyes's reputation continued in November 1924 when he was asked to unveil Dover's town war memorial. After the ceremony, the assembled great and good went to the town hall where Keyes presented the now ennobled Sir Edwin Farley with the *Dover Patrol Golden Book* – a book containing all the names of the men who died in the Patrol. In beautiful gold-blocked gothic lettering this 'contains a record of all those who died in the service of their King and Country whilst serving in or attached to, the Dover Patrol'.

The village of St Margaret's-at-Cliffe is reckoned to be the nearest village in England to the coast of France, standing half a mile inland from the steep chalk cliffs of St Margaret's Bay. The parish church of St Margaret of Antioch, built in the twelfth century with wondrously preserved Norman architectural detailing and blind arcading, sits off the High Street, almost completely secluded by trees. On 27 December 1928 the sleepy village found itself the focus of great attention. The ubiquitous Keyes was there; Farley too; and the Bishop of Dover, John Victor McMillan. Here the *Golden Book* was 'given into the care of the Vicar and Church Council of St Margaret's-at-Cliffe by Admiral Sir Roger Keyes ... and dedicated by the Rt Rev the Lord Bishop of Dover'.[1]

Today the book sits under a glass frame, open at the title page, on the south wall of the church. It is unlit and dominated by the villagers' roll of honour, which includes their own VC, Lieutenant Colonel Christopher Bushell, who won his award on the Western Front in March 1918 and was killed in action the following August. And the road to the nearby monument at Leathercote demonstrates the same benign neglect. It is rutted and pitted, nearly impassable without a four-by-four vehicle.

There are other, smaller memorials to the Patrol. Hanging on the side of the town hall is a warning bell taken from the mole at Zeebrugge and presented to the town by the King of the Belgians through the good offices of (who else?) Roger Keyes. It is still rung each St George's Day in tribute to the Zeebrugge and Ostend raids. Next door to the town hall, in the small garden of remembrance which surrounds the town war memorial outside the Maison Dieu, there is a portion of one of the grapnels used on *Vindictive*. It was originally mounted near the entrance gate to Leney's Brewery, until that much loved edifice was demolished. And a casket made from the *Vindictive*'s timbers was presented to Lady Farley on 22 June 1920.

Nor was Zeebrugge forgotten in Europe. On St George's Day 1925, the Anglo-Belgian Union erected a memorial, paid for by subscription, at the shore end of the Zeebrugge mole. It took the form of a figure of St George and the Dragon on the top of a tall column. It was unveiled by King Albert and Queen Elizabeth of Belgium and amongst those attending the ceremony were many survivors of the Zeebrugge raid who had been ferried over by a Royal Navy cruiser.[*]

Lord Northcliffe's support for the Patrol has already been noted above. In 1921 he asked his friend the novelist Joseph Conrad to write a tract about their activities to coincide with the dedication ceremony of the Leathercote Point monument and to be published that same day in *The Times*.

---

[*] This memorial was destroyed by the occupying Germans in World War II, but a new, smaller memorial has been built in its place.

Conrad had served nineteen years as a merchant sailor, obtaining a master mariner's certificate in 1892, two years before ill health forced his retirement from the sea. For fifteen of those nineteen years he had sailed under the red ensign. For him, to write in praise of the Patrol now was a pleasure; so much so that the following year he published a limited edition of his words as a fourteen-page book, *The Dover Patrol, a Tribute*. With pale blue printed wrappers, it was published for private circulation by H J Goulden of Canterbury in an edition of seventy-five copies.

And there was more trivial recognition in 1919, when the firm of H P Gibson produced a board game 'The Dover Patrol or Naval Tactics', which closely resembled the schoolboy pastime of 'Battleships'.

However, in the years immediately following the war not everyone thought that sufficient honour had been done to the exploits of the Patrol. On 9 May 1923 Sir Bernard Falle MP (for Portsmouth) asked a question in the House of Commons of the Parliamentary Secretary to the Admiralty. Was he aware, Falle intoned, 'that, in answer to a question, 16 August, 1916, regarding recognition of the arduous duties and admirable work of the Dover patrol flotillas, the Financial Secretary promised that this arduous service would be fully considered with a view to suitable recognition; and if he can say when such recognition will be granted?'

Commander Bolton Eyres-Monsell responded for the government:

The names of officers and men of the Dover Patrol figure largely in the lists of honours published after the 16th August, 1916, and the Admiralty see no reason for supposing that a fair measure of recognition has not been accorded them. I might mention, in particular, the *London Gazettes* of the 10th May, 1917, the 23rd May, 1917, the 16th March, 1918, the 23rd July, 1918, the 28th August, 1918, the 20th September, 1918, the 19th February, 1919, and the 20th February, 1919, in which a number of these names appear.[2]

In other words, enough was enough.

And so the Dover Patrol faded from sight. With the passing years, those who remembered it grew fewer. Their memorials became less cared for; their memories less clear. The lessons they had so painfully learned were also forgotten. First Sea Lords Wemyss,

Beatty and Madden returned the focus of the navy to big ships. The successes of convoy were forgotten. The need for small ships to hold the ring around Britain's coasts was again largely ignored. This proved regrettable and nearly fatal to the country when the Second World War came round. And after that war, a ruined and nearly bankrupted Britain began the long haul towards a new mission in the world and the acceptance of loss of prestige, status and empire.

By the end of World War One, people and politicians had, to an extent, lost their faith in the navy; there had been no sweeping from the sea of the enemy's navy, and the anti-U-boat campaign had been a long struggle. Few people understood the navy's achievements in the enforcement of blockade and the keeping free of major trade and supply arteries such as the English Channel. The horrific slaughter, the shells, gas and mud of the Western Front dominated much of the public thinking about the war. The naval sacrifices of the past were increasingly forgotten and so was the Dover Patrol and its men. Those who did think about matters naval, academics and naval historians for example, expended millions of words on Jutland, Beatty and Jellicoe; but the Dover Patrol and its quotidian duties were much less vaunted. Hough and Bennett, for example, in their histories of the war at sea, do not even index it. The exploits and the men of the Patrol drifted into oblivion.

But not quite. In 1998 the minor American composer Douglas E Wagner (born in Chicago in 1952) wrote and published a new march for concert band beginners. He called it 'The Dover Patrol'.

Author's Notes

The two most difficult things about writing a book are to start and to finish. A book never seems to end, there is always more detail, more dates, more 'stuff' that an author can put in. But at some point the story must close. A tale has a natural rhythm and conclusion and I feel I have come to the end of this one. There are bound to be omissions but none, I hope, which spoil the intention to recount a history through the people and actions of the Patrol.

Writing a book is a labour of love but it is not a solo occupation. Many people lend help and support, moral or otherwise. This is my chance to say 'thank you'.

It is a fact that the historical writer in the UK is blessed that the country possesses some of the best archives (and archivists) in the world. My gratitude is due to the trustees and staff of those organisations whose resources make the writing job both easier and more interesting. Primary sources consulted for this volume include those held at the following institutions: The National Archives, Kew; the Imperial War Museum, London; Churchill Archive Centre, Churchill College, Cambridge; the National Maritime Museum, Greenwich; the National Museum of the Royal Navy, Portsmouth; and the Dover Museum and Bronze Age Boat Gallery. I should also thank the people behind the marvellous website Naval-history.net which is an incomparable resource for any naval writer.

Jon Iveson at Dover Museum was generous with his time and his knowledge and was able to provide a rare glimpse of Dover in the war through the museum's photography collection. Likewise Heather Johnson at the National Museum of the Royal Navy discovered some marvellous photographs of the aftermath of the Zeebrugge raid. Sue Cameron made the chart of the minefields.

My thanks are especially due to Julian Mannering for commissioning the book and for advice and encouragement throughout the process of writing it. And to Vivienne, I can only say 'thank you'; her help with, and enthusiasm for, my writing projects has been invaluable. My friends, both in the UK and France, have suffered my enthusiasms with patience. I appreciate it.

Most books contain errors of commission and omission. If there are errors or solecisms the fault is mine and I should like to hear of them: to err is human.

In the course of writing a book, I find that I form a sympathy for one or more of the characters. In this narrative, the driven, mercurial and likeable Hood, forced to learn the game *and* the rules as he went along in a new command, excites compassion. But it is among the minor characters in the book that I find the one I like best. Francis Fitzpatrick Tower was an Edwardian gentleman of leisure, pottering with his boats on the Isle of Wight and at his houses round the country. At fifty-five years old, well into middle age, he responded unhesitatingly to his country's call and found it all great fun too. When told he could no longer command on the water, he became a staff officer at various southern ports, made three cruises on a Q-ship, and then helped run the base at Kingstown as part of the Coast of Ireland Station (Western Approaches) where he served till the war's end. A grateful nation awarded him the OBE.

I'm sure he took great pride in his sons. Tower's eldest son, Francis Thomas Butler joined the navy in 1902, captained HMS *Hood* between 1933–35 and rose to a knighthood and the rank of vice admiral in 1939. And his third son, Ion Beauchamp Butler, also served in the navy in the Great War, won the DSC in 1915 and later rose to the rank of rear admiral and naval ADC to the King. He predeceased his father, killed in an air raid on London in 1940.

F F Tower himself lived to see the futility of the so-called 'war to end all wars', dying aged eighty-four at his home in Cowes in 1944; he was cremated and his ashes interred at Northwood Cemetery on the little island he loved so much. Surely he was a true, and immortal, 'Unicorn'.

Composition of the Dover Patrol on 1 November 1914

The following list outlines the vessels (excluding trawlers, drifters and other auxiliary craft) assigned to the Dover Patrol shortly after its formation. It is based on Admiralty 'pink lists'.[1] It demonstrates well the varied nature of the Patrol's composition even at this early stage in the war.

Scout cruisers
Attentive (Captain D)   *Adventure*   *Foresight*

Destroyers (T = Tribal class)
Afridi (T)   *Cossack* (T)   *Crane*   *Crusader* (T)   *Fawn*   *Flirt*
Ghurka (T)   *Syren*   *Leven* (Downs Flotilla)   *Maori* (T)
Mermaid   *Myrmidon*   *Nubian* (T)   *Racehorse*   *Zulu* (T)
Viking (T)   *Mohawk* (T)

Destroyers repairing
Greyhound   *Kangaroo*   *Saracen* (T)   *Tartar* (T)   *Gipsy*
Amazon (T)   *Falcon*

Operating with monitors off the Belgian coast
Three monitors, *Severn, Mersey, Humber*
Sirius (old cruiser)
Rinaldo (old sloop)
Wildfire (old sloop)
Vestal (old sloop)
Bustard (old gunboat)

Excellent (old gunboat)
Brilliant (old cruiser)
Venerable (old battleship)
Revenge (old battleship)
Hermes (seaplane carrier)

Submarines
Flotilla III:
Forth (depot ship)   *B-3*   *B-4*   *B-5*   *C-14*   *C-15*   *C-16*

Flotilla IV:
Arrogant, Hazard (depot ships)
C-17   *C-18*   *C-31*   *C-32*   *C-33*   *C-34*   *C-35*   *S-1* under repair

APPENDIX 2

Hood's Ships

The vessels that comprised the Dover Patrol in 1914 were an eclectic and inchoate collection plucked from all three navy fleets, and often served and commanded by volunteers. At the heart of the Patrol were the ships of the 6th Destroyer Flotilla.

This comprised the scout (or patrol) cruisers (destroyer leaders) *Attentive*, *Adventure Foresight* and *Sapphire* with twenty-four destroyers, Tribal class (also known as 'F' class), the so-called 'C' class (30-knotters) and the 'B' class.

The first three cruisers were *Sentinel*- or *Adventure*-class vessels, mounting 4in guns (with two 6in for *Adventure*) built in 1904. As a breed, the scout cruiser was hampered by short range owing to its limited fuel capacity. The destroyers generally mounted 4in, 12pdr and 6pdr weapons. All twelve Tribals (or thirteen if one counts *Zubian*) served in the Dover Patrol.

The three monitors just completed at Barrow for the Brazilian government had been purchased in the first days of the war. They were the direct descendants of the bomb ketches used by Horace Hood's ancestors in the eighteenth and nineteenth centuries, essentially designed for coastal operations, especially in shallow seas, but now out of date and, until this acquisition, unrepresented in the Royal Navy. Such craft were at the time poorly regarded and were treated as no more than floating batteries for coastal defence, as they were unfitted for any sort of seaway, and hence fleet action. Indeed, their three and a half day journey from Vickers at Barrow to Dover was almost their last. A heavy swell and gale in the Irish Sea washed right over their upper decks and hatches and penetrated the crew accommodation. The messes soon flooded and the crew had to evacuate to the wardroom at the aft of the ship. In any sort of wind, their shallow draught made them pretty well unmanageable.

However, all this rather ignored their utility for coastal attack, something Hood had immediately spotted. They were each armed with twin 6in guns in a forward turret and two 4.7in howitzers to the rear. However, the constant usage soon wore out their Vickers 6in guns, and *Severn* and *Mersey* had replacement weapons fitted; two single 6in gun turrets were mounted and the 4.7in weapons were moved to the boat deck to accommodate the second turret.

The remaining bombardment vessels came straight from the Third Fleet and were crewed almost entirely by volunteers. These were ships which had been laid up pre-war as no longer wanted by the service, and had been kept 'warm' by a care and maintenance party prior to their intended scrapping. With the declaration of war, they were re-crewed from the naval reserve and hastily pushed into action.

Brilliant was an *Apollo*-class protected cruiser launched in 1891. Obsolete by 1914, she had, to Hood, the inestimable benefit of carrying two 6in guns and six 4.7in. Many of her sisters had already been broken up, but she served the Dover Patrol well.

Rinaldo and *Vestal* were *Condor*-class sloops, originally fitted with barque-rigged sails and launched at the end of the nineteenth century. They carried four 4in guns and four 3pdrs. By 1914, *Rinaldo* had become the tender and training ship to HMS *Vivid*, Devonport Royal Naval Reserve and *Vestal* training ship and tender to HMS *Excellent*, Portsmouth. They were thoroughly out of date.

Wildfire was a composite sloop of the *Nymph* class, launched in 1888 and used as a shore training ship and then general depot ship at Sheerness. Armed with four 4in and four 3pdr guns, she too had originally been equipped with a full sailing rig. She was renamed *Gannet* in 1916.

Bustard was a third-class gunboat launched in 1871 and thus some forty-three years old at the time of war. She was a flatiron coastal gunboat, of usefully shallow draught, armed with one 6in and one 4.7in gun.

Hazard was a *Dryad*-class gunboat launched in 1894 and mounting two 4.7in guns. In 1901 she had been converted into the world's first submarine depot ship and her first captain in this role was, coincidentally, Reginald Bacon.

Hood was also assigned, at various times, many antiquated

battleships, although he always seemed to be ambivalent about having them.

Revenge (later renamed *Redoubtable*) was a *Royal Sovereign*-class vessel, launched in 1892. In their day, these ships were considered an excellent weapon, armed with four 13.5in guns, but were made obsolete by the advent of *Dreadnought*-type ships. From 1905 she had been placed in the reserve and then the Second Fleet, manned by a much reduced 'nucleus crew'. Unlike her sister ships, *Revenge* was given a reprieve from the scrapyard by the outbreak of World War I, and in August 1914 it was decided to bring her back into service for use in coastal bombardment duties. In September and October 1914 she was refitted at Portsmouth for Hood's use, a refit which included the relining of her worn-out 13.5in guns to 12in.

Majestic was launched in 1895 as the name-ship of her class and mounted four 12in and twelve 6in guns. In 1912 she was laid up into the Third Fleet, from which she was recommissioned into the Channel Fleet at the outbreak of war.

Venerable was another pre-dreadnought battleship, launched in 1899 and armed similarly to *Majestic.* In 1912 she had been transferred to the Second Fleet, in reserve.

Russell and *Exmouth* were *Duncan*-class pre-dreadnoughts, launched in 1901 and armed with four 12in and twelve 6in guns. Both were part of the Second Fleet by 1913 with a nucleus crew. Hood also had the brief use of *Implacable*, a *Formidable*-class battleship also mounting four 12in guns in two turrets and launched in 1899; and even more briefly of *Mars*, an 1896-vintage battleship, previously acting as guard ship at the mouth of the Humber, and which was then attached to the Patrol from 9 December through to the 11th. She was later sent to Belfast for decommissioning and disarmament.

Hood also had submarines attached to his forces. Submarines *C-32* and *C-33* were typical of the vessels used, built in 1909, armed with two torpedo tubes and home to sixteen men.

APPENDIX 3

Bacon's Monitors

The Dover Patrol was the beneficiary of the new monitors which came into service between June and October 1915. They had been built at breakneck speed, the orders for them having been placed only in December the previous year.

At one time or another, *Lord Clive, Prince Rupert, Sir John Moore, General Craufurd* and *Prince Eugene* all served in the Patrol. For speed of building, they were all armed with a twin turret of 12in guns, obtained by decommissioning battleships of the obsolete *Majestic* class, dating from 1893. They were coal- and steam-powered, but could make less than 7.5 knots (their best speed on trails was only 8 knots), which was extremely slow for tidal waters and left them easily open to attack by faster ships and submarines as well.

However, they were able to pack a powerful punch. Their big guns could fire a shell weighing 850lbs over a range of some 21,000yds. For comparison, the famous French artillery piece, the 'Seventy-Five', fired a shell of about 12lbs; a destroyer's 4in gun, one of 25–30lbs; and the 6in monitors, ex-Brazil, of Admiral Hood's fleet, 100lbs. They were thus comparatively highly destructive as artillery weapons.

Once in service, they were quickly found to require modification: 6in guns were fitted for defence against destroyer attack and Maxims to protect against fast motor launches; anti-aircraft weapons were added too, all of which made them even slower. Towards the end of the war, two of them were fitted with an additional 18in gun, which made them, if possible, even less speedy.

Bacon also benefited from *Marshal Soult*. She was the second *Marshal Ney*-class monitor (a class of two), commissioned in

August 1915, armed with a brace of 15in guns and, after a 1917 refit, two 6in as well. Both ships were diesel-powered, which meant that they had no need of boiler rooms, which suited their low draught, nor did they need large funnels, which reduced the amount of superstructure. The engines provided were originally designed for much smaller freighters and proved particularly troublesome; *Soult's* Vickers-built engines never achieved her design speed of 9 knots, finding 6 knots difficult enough, which meant that in any sort of seaway she had to be towed into position.*

The seagoing qualities of the monitors, or rather their lack of them, gave constant problems. On 20 September 1917 *Marshal Soult* was on bombardment duty off the Flanders coast when a big storm blew up against which she could make no headway at all. She asked *Marksman* for a tow, but the shore batteries got the range and a 15in shell parted the tow rope. Now under fire and helpless, she radioed for a cruiser and destroyer escort. *Attentive, Miranda* and *Mastiff* all put out from Dunkirk and, with great difficulty, towed the recalcitrant monitor back to harbour in the teeth of a howling gale.

Sometimes the weather was so bad that the monitors could not be deployed at all. On 2, 3, 4, 5 and 6 October 1917, for example, bombardment plans were cancelled. The ships just couldn't go out.

Marshal Ney also served with the Patrol, but she was a terrible sailer and her MAN diesel engines were a constant source of trouble. Launched in June 1915, she was dubbed 'practically a failure' by *Jane's Fighting Ships*, and in 1916 her 15in barbette was stripped off and given to *Erebus*, which was launched that year. *Marshal Ney* was then rearmed with a single 9.2in gun and four 6in guns for service as a guard ship for the Downs. When first arriving at her new station, she met an easterly gale off Dungeness and signalled that she was helpless and in danger of grounding. Bacon recognised that the tide would take her clear and signalled her new captain that 'the *Marshal Ney* usually navigated the waters of the Patrol sideways!' [1]

Erebus and *Terror*, by far the most effective of the Dover Patrol's monitors, have been described in the text. Bacon thought them the two best assets of the Patrol for bombardment purposes as their maximum speed of 14 knots, or 12 when steaming comfortably, was an absolute luxury compared to the rest of his monitors.

---

* *Marshal Soult* ended her war as an accommodation ship at Chatham and Sheerness.

Bacon was also provided with up to six *M-15* class monitors, *M-23*, *M-24*, *M-25*, *M-26*, *M-27* (and later, *M-28*), which were operational from mid-1915 onwards. They originally mounted two 9.2in guns, removed from old cruisers. However, Bacon divined that the 9.2in guns of the 'M'-class ships were useless to these vessels for bombardment work on the coast, slow in loading, and short in range (only 11,000yds, inside the range of the German defensive batteries). Their only possible value was when used at close quarters, but this entailed them being within the reach of, and likely to be sunk by, enemy shore-based artillery. In early 1917 he approached the Admiralty to ask to be allowed to substitute 6in or 7.5in guns in lieu. Bacon proposed to install the larger weapons thus freed up ashore near Nieuwpoort, in addition to the naval guns already emplaced there, again for counter-battery work. The 'M'-class vessels operated with a mixed array of power plants, usually diesel, although *M-24* had four paraffin engines.

The monitor's modus operandi was to sortie, usually under cover of darkness, to gain position at dawn. A host of smaller boats accompanied them, some of which were used to lay a protective smokescreen, behind which the monitors anchored and began their firing, often assisted by spotting from an aeroplane in the latter years of the patrol. A contemporary writer described them thus: 'monitors move like snails and fight like bulldogs'.[2]

The Zeebrugge and Ostend Victoria Crosses

Quoted from the *London Gazette*; punctuation, spelling and ship's names in quotation marks as per the original newspaper.

Zeebrugge and First Ostend

Commander (Acting Captain) Alfred Francis Blakeney Carpenter, R.N. For most conspicuous gallantry.

This officer was in command of "Vindictive." He set a magnificent example to all those under his command by his calm composure when navigating mined waters, bringing his ship alongside the mole in darkness. When "Vindictive" was within a few yards of the mole the enemy started and maintained a heavy fire from batteries, machine guns and rifles on to the bridge. He showed most conspicuous bravery, and did much to encourage similar behaviour on the part of the crew, supervising the landing from the "Vindictive" on to the mole, and walking round the decks directing operations and encouraging the men in the most dangerous and exposed positions. By his encouragement to those under him, his power of command and personal bearing, he undoubtedly contributed greatly to the success of the operation. Capt. Carpenter was selected by the officers of the "Vindictive," "Iris II.," and "Daffodil," and of the naval assaulting force to receive the Victoria Cross under Rule 13 of the Royal Warrant, dated the 29th January, 1866.

Lieutenant Richard Douglas Sandford, R.N, For most conspicuous gallantry.

This officer was in command of Submarine C.3, and most skilfully placed that vessel in between the piles of the viaduct before lighting his fuse and abandoning her. He eagerly undertook this hazardous enterprise, although, well aware (as were all his crew) that if the means of rescue failed and he or any of his crew were in the water at the moment of the explosion, they would be killed outright by the force of such explosion. Yet Lieutenant Sandford disdained to use the gyro steering, which would have enabled him and his crew to abandon the submarine at a safe distance, and preferred to make sure, as far as was humanly possible, of the accomplishment of his duty.

Lieutenant Percy Thompson Dean, R.N.V.R. (Motor Launch 282). For most conspicuous gallantry.
Lieutenant Dean handled his boat in a most magnificent and heroic manner when embarking the officers and men from the blockships at Zeebrugge. He followed the blockships in and closed "Intrepid" and "Iphigenia" under a constant and deadly fire from machine and heavy guns at point blank range, embarking over 100 officers and men. This completed, he was proceeding out of the canal, when he heard that an officer was in the water. He returned, rescued him, and then proceeded, handling his boat throughout as calmly as if engaged in a practice manoeuvre. Three men were shot down at his side whilst he conned his ship. On clearing the entrance to the canal the steering gear broke down. He manoeuvred his boat by the engines, and avoided complete destruction by steering so close in under the mole that the guns in the batteries could not depress sufficiently to fire on the boat. The whole of this operation was carried out under a constant machine-gun fire at a few yards range. It was solely due to this officer's courage and daring that M.L.282 succeeded in saving so many valuable lives.

Captain Edward Bamford, D.S.O., R.M.L.I. For most conspicuous gallantry.
This officer landed on the mole from "Vindictive" with numbers 5, 7 and 8 platoons of the marine storming force, in the face of great difficulties. When on the mole and under heavy fire, he displayed the greatest initiative in the command of his company, and by his total disregard of danger showed a magnificent example to his men. He first established a strong point on the right of the disembarkation, and, when satisfied that that was safe, led an assault on a battery to the left with the utmost coolness and valour. Captain Bamford was

selected by the officers of the R.M.A. and R.M.L.I. detachments to receive the Victoria Cross under Rule 13 of the Royal Warrant, dated the 29th January, 1856.

Serjeant Norman Augustus Finch, R.M.A., No. R.M.A./12150. For most conspicuous gallantry.
Serjeant Finch was second in command of the pompoms and Lewis guns in the foretop of "Vindictive," under Lieutenant Charles N. B. Rigby, R.M.A. At one period the "Vindictive" was being hit every few seconds, chiefly in the upper works, from which splinters caused many casualties. It was difficult to locate the guns which were doing the most damage, but Lieutenant Rigby, Serjeant Finch and the Marines in the foretop, kept up a continuous fire with pompoms and Lewis guns, changing rapidly from one target to another, and thus keeping the enemy's fire down to some considerable extent. Unfortunately two heavy shells made direct hits on the foretop, which was completely exposed to enemy concentration of fire. All in the top were killed or disabled except Serjeant Finch, who was, however, severely wounded; nevertheless he showed consummate bravery, remaining in his battered and exposed position. He once more got a Lewis gun into action, and kept up a continuous fire, harassing the enemy on the mole, until the foretop received another direct hit, the remainder of the armament being then completely put out of action. Before the top was destroyed Serjeant Finch had done invaluable work, and by his bravery undoubtedly saved many lives. This very gallant serjeant of the Royal Marine Artillery was selected by the 4th Battalion of Royal Marines, who were mostly Royal Marine Light Infantry, to receive the Victoria Cross under Rule 13 of the Royal Warrant dated 29th January, 1856.

Able Seaman Albert Edward McKenzie, O.N. J31736 (Ch.). For most conspicuous gallantry.
This rating belonged to B Company of seaman storming party. On the night of the operation he landed on the mole with his machine-gun in the face of great difficulties and did very good work, using his gun to the utmost advantage. He advanced down the mole with Lieutenant-Commander Harrison, who with most of his party was killed, and accounted for several of the enemy running from a shelter to a destroyer alongside the mole. This very gallant seaman

was severely wounded whilst working his gun in an exposed position. Able Seaman McKenzie was selected by the men of the "Vindictive," "Iris II," and "Daffodil'" and of the naval assaulting force to receive the Victoria Cross under Rule 13 of the Royal Warrant dated the 29th January 1856.

(London Gazette, 19 July 1918)

Posthumous award of the Victoria Cross

Lieutenant-Commander George Nicholson Bradford, R.N. For most conspicuous gallantry at Zeebrugge on the night of the 22nd–23rd April, 1918.

This officer was in command of the Naval Storming Parties embarked in "Iris II." When "Iris II." proceeded alongside the Mole great difficulty was experienced in placing the parapet anchors owing to the motion of the ship. An attempt was made to land by the scaling ladders before the ship was secured. Lieutenant Claude E. K. Hawkings (late "Erin") managed to get one ladder in position and actually reached the parapet, the ladder being crashed to pieces just as he stepped off it. This very gallant young officer was last seen defending himself with his revolver. He was killed on the parapet. Though securing the ship was not part of his duties, Lieut.-Commander Bradford climbed up the derrick, which carried a large parapet anchor and was rigged out over the port side; during this climb the ship was surging up and down and the derrick crashing on the Mole; waiting his opportunity he jumped with the parapet anchor on to the Mole and placed it in position. Immediately after hooking on the parapet anchor Lieut.-Commander Bradford was riddled with bullets from machine guns and fell into the sea between the Mole and the ship. Attempts to recover his body failed. Lieut.-Commander Bradford's action was one of absolute self-sacrifice; without a moment's hesitation he went to certain death, recognising that in such action lay the only possible chance of securing "Iris II" and enabling her storming parties to land.

Lieutenant-Commander Arthur Leyland Harrison, R.N. For most conspicuous gallantry at Zeebrugge on the night of the 22nd–23rd April, 1918.

This officer was in immediate command of the Naval Storming Parties embarked in "Vindictive." Immediately before coming alongside the Mole Lieut.-Commander Harrison was struck on the head by a fragment of a shell which broke his jaw and knocked him senseless. Recovering consciousness he proceeded on to the Mole and took over command of his party, who were attacking the seaward end of the Mole. The silencing of the guns on the Mole head was of the first importance, and though in a position fully exposed to the enemy's machine-gun fire Lieut.-Commander Harrison gathered his men together and led them to the attack. He was killed at the head of his men, all of whom were either killed or wounded. Lieut.-Commander Harrison, though already severely wounded and undoubtedly in great pain, displayed indomitable resolution and courage of the highest order in pressing his attack, knowing as he did that any delay in silencing the guns might jeopardise the main object of the expedition, i.e., the blocking of the Zeebrugge-Bruges Canal.

(*London Gazette*, 14 March 1919)

Second Ostend

Lieut. Geoffrey H. Drummond, R.N.V.R.
Volunteered for rescue work in command of M.L. 254. Following "Vindictive" to Ostend, when off the piers a shell burst on board, killing Lieutenant Gordon Ross and Deckhand J. Thomas, wounding the coxswain, and also severely wounding Lieutenant Drummond in three places. Notwithstanding his wounds he remained on the bridge, navigated his vessel, which was already seriously damaged by shell fire, into Ostend harbour, placed her alongside "Vindictive," and took off two officers and thirty-eight men – some of whom were killed and many wounded while embarking. When informed that there was no one alive left on board he backed his vessel out clear of the piers before sinking exhausted from his wounds. When H.M.S. "Warwick" fell in with M.L. 254 off Ostend half an hour later the latter was in a sinking condition. It was due to the indomitable courage of this very gallant officer that the majority of the crew of the "Vindictive" were rescued.

Lieut. Roland Bourke, D.S.O., R.N.V.R.
Volunteered for rescue work in command of M.L. 276, and followed "Vindictive" into Ostend, engaging the enemy's machine guns on both piers with Lewis guns. After M.L. 254 had backed out Lieutenant Bourke laid his vessel alongside "Vindictive" to make further search. Finding no one he withdrew, but hearing cries in the water he again entered the harbour, and after a prolonged search

eventually found Lieutenant Sir John Alleyne and two ratings, all badly wounded, in the water, clinging to an upended skiff, and rescued them. During all this time the motor launch was under a very heavy fire at close range, being hit in fifty-five places, once by a 6 in. shell – two of her small crew being killed and others wounded. The vessel was seriously damaged and speed greatly reduced. Lieutenant Bourke, however, managed to bring her out and carry on until he fell in with a Monitor, which took him in tow. This episode displayed daring and skill of a very high order, and Lieutenant Bourke's bravery and perseverance undoubtedly saved the lives of Lieutenant Alleyne and two of the "Vindictive's" crew.

Lieut. Victor A. C. Crutchley, D.S.C., R.N.
This officer was in "Brilliant" in the unsuccessful attempt to block Ostend on the night of 22nd/23rd April, and at once volunteered for a further effort. He acted as 1st Lieut. of "Vindictive," and worked with untiring energy fitting out that ship for further service. On the night of 9th/10th May, after his commanding officer had been killed and the second in command severely wounded, Lieut. Crutchley took command of "Vindictive" and did his utmost by manoeuvring the engines to place that ship in an effective position. He displayed great bravery both in the "Vindictive" and in M.L. 254, which rescued the crew after the charges had been blown and the former vessel sunk between the piers of Ostend harbour, and did not himself leave the "Vindictive" until he had made a thorough search with an electric torch for survivors under a very heavy fire. Lieut, Crutchley took command of M.L. 254 when the commanding officer sank exhausted from his wounds, the second in command having been killed. The vessel was full of wounded and very seriously damaged by shell fire, the fore part being flooded. With indomitable energy and by dint of baling with buckets and shifting weight aft, Lieut. Crutchley and the unwounded kept her afloat, but the leaks could not be kept under, and she was in a sinking condition, with her forecastle nearly awash when picked up by H.M.S. "Warwick." The bearing of this very gallant officer and fine seaman throughout these operations off the Belgian coast was altogether admirable and an inspiring example to all thrown in contact with him.

(*London Gazette*, 27 August 1918)

Composition of the Dover Patrol on Armistice Day 1918

Excludes trawlers, drifters and other auxiliary craft; based on Admiralty 'pink lists'.[1]

Monitors
Erebus Terror Gorgon Marshal Ney Sir John Moore
M-21 M-24 M-26 M-27

Destroyers
Broke Manly Mastiff Meteor Morris Termagant Trident
Afridi Amazon Cossack Crusader Viking Zubian Leven
Gipsy Racehorse Violet

Destroyers under repair
Mentor Myngs Matchless Faulknor Saracen Syren
Kangaroo Panther

Torpedo boat
TB-4

P-boats
P-17 P-21 P-24 P-47 P-48 P-50 P-57 P-58 P-64
Under repair: *P-11, P-49, P-52*

Minesweepers (10th Minesweeper Flotilla)
Chelmsford Lingfield Newbury

Survey vessels

Esther (a trawler purchased off the stocks)
Daisy

Other

Surf (hired yacht, flagship Rear Admiral Dover))
Alert (1894 screw steel sloop)
Sigismund (armed yacht, Downs Flotilla)

APPENDIX 6

U-boats Sunk in the Areas Covered by the Dover Patrol

When	U-boat	Fate	Where
9 Dec 1914	U-11	Mined	Off Belgian coast
18 Dec	U-5	Mined	Off Belgian coast
4 Mar 1915	U-8	Attacked by Dover Patrol vessels	Dover Barrage
30 Apr	U-37	Mined	Off Sandettie Bank
29 Nov	UB-13	Mine net	Off Belgian coast
5 Jul 1916	UC-7	Mined	North of Zeebrugge
7 Dec	UC-46	Rammed	HMS *Liberty* (Harwich Force) near Goodwin sands
8 Feb 1917	UB-39	Mined	Off Sandettie Bank
8 May	UC-26	Rammed	HMS *Milne* (Harwich, detached to Dover Patrol) off Calais
21 May	UB-36	Mined	Off Flanders
19 Jul	UC-1	Mined	Off Nieuwpoort
28 Jul	UB-20	Mined	Off Zeebrugge
24 Aug	UC-72	Mined	Dover Strait
27 Sept	UC-6	Mine net	Off North Foreland
3 Oct	UC-14	Mined	Off Zeebrugge
4 Oct	UC-16	Mined	Off Zeebrugge
14 Oct	UC-62	Mined	Off Zeebrugge
1 Nov	UC-63	Torpedoed	HMS *E-52* (Harwich Force) off Goodwin Sands
24 Nov	U-48	Attacked by Dover Patrol vessels	Goodwin Sands

19 Dec	*UB-56*	Mined	Dover Strait
26 Jan 1918	*U-109*	Mined	Dover Strait
26 Jan	*UB-35*	Depth charged	HMS *Leven* (Dover Patrol)
8 Feb	*UB-38*	Mined	Dover Strait
10 Mar	*UB-58*	Mined	Dover Barrage
5 Apr	*UC-79*	Mined	Off Cap Gris Nez
11Apr	*UB-33*	Mined	The Varne
19 Apr	*UB-78*	Mined	Off Dover
22 Apr	*UB-55*	Mined	Dover Strait
2 May	*UB-31*	Mined	Dover Strait
17 Jun	*UC-64*	Mined	The Varne
26 Jun	*UC-11*	Mined	Dover Strait
2 July	*UB-108*	Mined	Off Flanders
14 July	*UC-77*	Mined	Off Flanders
14 Aug	*UB-103*	Mined	Off Flanders
14 Aug	*UB-57*	Mined	Off Flanders
22 Aug	*UB-109*	Mined	Dover Barrage

(This list is culled from various sources and should not be read as the definitive statement).

Out of thirty-six U-boats sunk and identified here, over 83 per cent were sunk by mines or nine nets.

Bibliography and Primary Sources

Unpublished primary sources

Private papers of G E Haigh, Imperial War Museum, Documents 7431

Private papers of W G Evans, Imperial War Museum, Documents 10964

Private papers of Commander R T Young OBE RN, Imperial War Museum, Documents 11487

Private papers of Captain W B Forbes RN, Imperial War Museum, Documents 10977

Private papers of Commander F F Tower OBE RNVR, Imperial War Museum, Documents 11440

Private papers of Captain Sir J M Alleyne RN, Imperial War Museum, Documents 3631

Private papers of Captain J Brooke RN, Imperial War Museum, Documents 10823

Private Papers of Captain R R Ramsbotham RN, Imperial War Museum, Documents 11493

Private papers of Commander V J Robinson RN, Imperial War Museum, Documents 11336

Logbook of Captain Albert James Enstone, RNAS, National Maritime Museum, MSS/72/094

Private Papers of Admiral Sir Frederick Hamilton, National Maritime Museum, HTN/101-29

Private Papers of Captain H Grant, National Museum of the Royal Navy, MSS 217

Diary of William James Wood, National Museum of the Royal Navy, 2008.7

Percy Pointer MSS, National Museum of the Royal Navy, 2005.75

Hood MSS, Churchill Archives Centre, GBR/0014/Hood

Churchill Papers, Churchill Archives Centre, CHAR13

Ramsay MSS, Churchill Archive Centre, RMSY

The Papers of Admiral of the Fleet Lord Wester Wemyss, Churchill Archive Centre, WMYS

Memoirs of Admiral Sir Henry F Oliver, 2 vols, 1946 (unpublished), National Maritime Museum, OLV/12

Admiralty publications
Naval Staff Monograph, vol VI, The Dover Command, vol I (March 1922)

Other publications
HMSO, *British Vessel Losses 1914–1918* (1919)

Newspapers and periodicals
Bootle Times
Daily Sketch
Daily Telegraph
Dover Express
East Kent Times
Flight
Hansard
Marlborough Express (NZ)
Melbourne Argus (Aus)
Preston Leader (Aus)
Spectator
The Penny Illustrated Paper and Illustrated Times
The Times

Bibliography
The following books are referenced in the text and notes. The place of publication is London unless otherwise given.

Abbatiello, J, *Anti-Submarine Warfare in World War 1* (Routledge, 2006)
Bacon, R, *The Dover Patrol*, 2 vols (George Doran Company, New York, 1919)
Bayly, L, *Pull Together* (George G Harrap and Co, 1939)
Bennett, G, *Charlie B* (Peter Dawnay, 1968)
Bostridge, M, *The Fateful Year* (Viking, 2014)
Brock, M, and E Brock (ed), *Margot Asquith's Great War Diary 1914–1916* (OUP, Oxford, 2014)
Bywater, H, and H Ferraby, *Strange Intelligence* (Constable, 1931; republished Biteback, 2015)
Callo, J, and A Wilson, *Who's Who in Naval History: From 1550 to the Present* (Routledge, Abingdon, 2004)
Cannadine, D, *The Decline and Fall of the British Aristocracy* (Papermac, 1996)
Churchill, A J, *Blood and Thunder* (History Press, Stroud, 2014)
Churchill, W S, *Thoughts and Adventures* (Thornton Butterworth, 1932)
————, *The World Crisis*, vol 2 (Thornton Butterworth, 1923)
Corbett, J, and H Newbolt, *Naval Operations, The History of the Great War based on Official Documents*, vols I–V (republished Naval and Military Press and Imperial War Museum, 2014)
Coxon, S ('Dug Out'), *Dover during the Dark Days* (John Lane, The Bodley Head, 1919)
Cunningham, A B, *A Sailor's Odyssey* (Hutchinson, 1951)
De Chair, D, *The Sea is Strong* (George G Harrap and Co, 1961)

Dunn, S R, *Formidable* (Book Guild, Sussex, 2015)

————, *The Scapegoat* (Book Guild, Sussex, 2014)

Egremont, M, *Some Desperate Glory* (Pan MacMillan, 2014)

Evans, E, *Keeping the Seas* (Sampson, Low, Marston and Co, 1920)

Fisher, J, *Memories* (Hodder and Stroughton, 1919)

Friedman, N, *Naval Weapons of World War 1* (Seaforth Publishing, 2011)

Fuller, J, *Memoirs of an Unconventional Soldier* (Nicholson and Watson, 1936)

Gibbons, F, *And They Thought We Wouldn't Fight* (George Doran Company, New York, 1918)

Goldrick, J, *Before Jutland* (Naval Institute Press, Annapolis, 2015)

Halpern, P, *A Naval History of World War 1* (UCL Press, 1994)

————, *The Keyes Papers* (Navy Records Society, 1973)

Hamilton-Paterson, J, *Marked for Death* (Head of Zeus, 2015)

Horne, C, *Records of the Great War*, vol II (National Alumni, 1923)

Hough, R, *The Great War at Sea* (OUP, Oxford,1983, 1986)

'Jackstaff', *The Dover Patrol* (Grant Richards, 1919)

Jellicoe, J, *Jellicoe Papers*, 2 vols (Navy Records Society, 1968)

————, *The Crisis of the Naval War* (Cassell, 1920)

Keyes, R, *Naval Memoirs*, 2 vols (Thornton Butterworth 1934–35)

Kipling, R, *Twenty Poems by Rudyard Kipling* (Methuen, 1918)

————, *Sea Warfare* (Macmillan, 1916)

Lake, D, *The Zeebrugge and Ostend Raids 1918* (Pen and Sword Military, Barnsley, 2015)

Lambert, N, *Planning Armageddon* (Harvard University Press, Cambridge, Mass, 2012)

McCartney, I, *Lost Patrols* (Periscope Publishing, Penzance, 2003)

Marder, A J, *Portrait of an Admiral; the life and papers of Sir Herbert Richmond* (Harvard University Press, Cambridge, Mass, 1952)

————, *From the Dreadnought to Scapa Flow*, vols I–V (OUP, Oxford, 1965; republished Seaforth Publishing, 2014)

Philpott, W, *Attrition* (Abacus, 2014)

Roskill, S, *Earl Beatty* (Collins, 1980)

————, *Churchill and the Admirals* (Collins, 1977)

Smith, H H, *A Yellow Admiral Remembers* (Arnold, 1932)

Smith, P, *Into the Minefields* (Pen and Sword Maritime, Barnsley, 2005)

Thompson, J, *The Imperial War Museum Book of the War at Sea* (Sidgewick and Jackson, 2005)

Tuchman, B, *The Proud Tower* (Hamish Hamilton, 1966, republished Papermac 1980)

Unwin, P, *The Narrow Sea* (Headline, 2003)

Winton, J, *The Victoria Cross at Sea* (Michael Joseph, 1978)

Young, R, and P Armstrong, *Silent Warriors, Submarine Wrecks of the United Kingdom*, vol 2 (History Press, Stroud, 2009)

Online resources
Dreadnoughtproject.org
Maxwell, G, *The Motor Launch Patrol*
(www.motorlaunchpatrol.net/written_accounts/histories/motor_launch_patrol
)
Naval-history.net
Sproule R, *The War Letters of Robert Edwin Sproule* (www.europeana1914-1918.eu)

Further reading
The reader who wishes to learn more about the subjects addressed in this book may be interested in the following suggested further reading.

Buxton, I, *Big Gun Monitors* (Seaforth Publishing, 1978, 2008)
Crossley, J, *Monitors of the Royal Navy* (Pen and Sword Maritime, Barnsley, 2013)
Fayle, C E, *Seaborne Trade* (John Murray, 1920)
Karau, M, *The Naval Flank of the Western Front* (Seaforth Publishing, 2015)
Kendall, P, *The Zeebrugge Raid 1918* (History Press, Stroud, 2009)
Pitt, B, *Zeebrugge. 11 VCs Before Breakfast* (Cassell, 2002)
Woodman, R, *More Days, More Dollars: The History of the British Merchant Navy*, vol IV (History Press, Stroud, 2010)

Notes

The following abbreviations will be used for brevity.

Institutions

IWM: Imperial War Museum, London

TNA: The National Archives, Kew

NMM: National Maritime Museum, Greenwich

CAC: Churchill Archive, Churchill College, Cambridge

NMRN: National Museum of the Royal Navy, Portsmouth

Books (see Bibliography for full details)

NavOp: *Naval Operations, The History of the Great War based on Official Documents*

FDTSF: *From Dreadnought to Scapa Flow*

It is the convention that page numbers be given for citations. This is not always possible in the modern world. Some digitised documents lack page numbering and some archives hold unnumbered single or multiple sheets in bundles under one reference. Thus, page numbers will be given where possible but the reader will understand that they are not always available or, indeed, necessary.

Preface

1. 'Jackstaff', *The Dover Patrol*, p24.
2. Unwin, *The Narrow Sea*, p9.
3. Philpott, *Attrition*, p338.

Chapter 1

1. Shakespeare, *Richard II*, act 2 scene 1.
2. Hamilton-Paterson, *Marked for Death*, p71.
3. Dunn, *Formidable*, p39.
4. GBR/0014/Hood, 6-6, CAC.

Chapter 2

1. Bayly, *Pull Together*, p121.
2. Cunningham, *A Sailor's Odyssey*, p97.
3. Evans, *Keeping the Seas*, p35.

Chapter 3

1. Lambert, *Planning Armageddon*, p53.
2. Goldrick, *Before Jutland*, p60.
3. Bywater, *Strange Intelligence*, p41.
4. Smith, *Into the Minefields*, p7.
5. CHAR 13/41/152. 1 October 1914, CAC.
6. Goldrick, *Before Jutland*, p181.
7. CHAR 13/42/149, CAC.
8. Bywater, *Strange Intelligence*, p108.
9. The numbers given are estimated from http://www.navweaps.com/Weapons/WAMBR_Mines.htm; http://h100.tv/timeline/world-war-1/1914/10/03; http://www.theodora.com/encyclopedia/m2/minesweeping_and_minelaying.html; Smith, *Into the Minefields*, p95; Friedman, *Naval Weapons of World*

War One, p363; HMSO, *British Vessels Lost at Sea*, 1919.
10. Kipling, *Twenty Poems from Rudyard Kipling*, 'Minesweepers'.
11. Docs 7451, IWM.
12. Docs 10823 p1, IWM.
13. Jellicoe, *The Crisis of the Naval War*, Ch3 ff.

Chapter 4
1. Tuchman, *The Proud Tower*, p380.
2. Arthur Conan Doyle, *The Siege of Antwerp*, October 1914; Horne, *Records of the Great War*, vol II.
3. Ibid.
4. Roskill, *Earl Beatty*, p86.
5. Marder, *Portrait of an Admiral*, p112.
6. Egremont, *The First World War the Poets Knew*, p46

Chapter 5
1. GBR/0014/Hood, 3-2, CAC.
2. Churchill A, *Blood and Thunder*, Ch 21 ff.
3. Smith, *A Yellow Admiral Remembers*, p210.
4. Marder, *FDTSF*, vol 2 (1965), p8.
5. Hough, *The Great War at Sea*, p209.
6. Fisher, *Memories*, p104.
7. Marder, *FDTSF*, vol 2 (1965), p9.
8. Dunn, *The Scapegoat*, p72.

Chapter 6
1. 'Jackstaff', *The Dover Patrol*, p19.
2. Docs 10823 p1, IWM.
3. CHAR 13/40/28, CAC.
4. CHAR 13/40/31, CAC.
5. *London Gazette* 13 April 1915, Hood's dispatch 11 November 1914.
6. GBR/0014/Hood, 5-1, 20 October 1914.
7. Ibid, 20 October 1914.
8. Corbett, Newbold, *NavOp*, vol 1, p222.
9. Evans, *Keeping the Seas*, p23.
10. GBR/0014/Hood, 6-2, Fisher to

Ellen Hood, undated October 1914, CAC.
11. Halpern, *A Naval History of World War* 1, p35.
12. GBR/0014/Hood, 6-2, Bridges to Hood, 28 October 1914, CAC.
13. Lambert, *Planning Armageddon*, p280.
14. Roskill, *Churchill and the Admirals*, p37.
15. CHAR 13/40/62, 23 October 1914, 0340, CAC.
16. GBR/0014/Hood, 5-1, 24 October 1914, CAC.
17. CHAR 13/40/77, CAC.
18. GBR/0014/Hood, 5-1, 29 October 1914, 2300, CAC.
19. Ibid, 27 October 1914.
20. Ibid.
21. Ibid.
22. Ibid, 28 October 1914.

Chapter 7
1. GBR/0014/Hood, 5-1, 30 October 1914, CAC.
2. Ibid.
3. Ibid.
4. Ibid, 2 November 1914.
5. Ibid, 3 November 1914.
6. Ibid, 4 November 1914.
7. Ibid.
8. Ibid, 5 November 1914.
9. Ibid.
10. CHAR 13/42/40, CAC.
11. GBR/0014/Hood, 3-20, CAC.
12. GBR/0014/Hood, 6-2, 23 October 1914, CAC.
13. Bacon, *The Dover Patrol*, vol 1, p50.
14. GBR/0014/Hood, 6-6, letter to 'Nelson' 23 March 1915, CAC.

Chapter 8
1. Bacon, *The Dover Patrol*, vol 1, p86.
2. GBR/0014/Hood, 6-2, CAC.
3. CHAR 13/42/97, CAC.
4. CHAR 13/42/98, CAC.

5. CHAR 13/42/146, CAC.
6. Ibid.
7. *Naval Staff Monograph*, vol 6, p17.
8. CHAR 13/60/9, CAC.
9. CHAR 13/60/30, CAC.
10. Ibid.
11. Ibid.
12. Ibid.
13. *Naval Staff Monograph*, vol 6, p20.
14. Bennett, *Charlie B*, p346, quoting De Robeck MSS letter 30.4.17.
15. ADM 196/51/263, NA.
16. GBR/0014/Hood, 3-20, CAC.
17. GBR/0014/Hood, 6-3, Fisher to Hood 9 April 1915, CAC.
18. Ibid, Jellicoe to Hood, 1 May 1915.
19. Ibid, undated handwritten note.
20. Bacon, *The Dover Patrol*, vol 1, Preface, xviii.
21. Roskill, *Earl Beatty*, p126.
22. GBR/0014/Hood, 6-3, 15 May 1915, CAC.
23. Marder, *FDTSF*, vol 2 (1965), p288.
24. Ibid.
25. GBR/0014/Hood, 3-20, CAC.

Chapter 9
1. Bacon, *The Dover Patrol*, vol 1, p52.
2. *The Penny Illustrated Paper and Illustrated Times* (London), 20 October 1906.
3. Marder, *FDTSF*, vol 2 (1965), p353.
4. ADM 116/3108, unnumbered folio.
5. *Dictionary of National Biography*, entry by AB Sainsbury, 2004, http://www.oxforddnb.com/index/10 1030516/Reginald-Bacon.
6. Churchill W, *Thoughts and Adventures*, p102.
7. Halpern, *The Keyes Papers*, vol 1, p376.

Chapter 10
1. *London Gazette*, 11 January 1916,

publishing Bacon's dispatch of 3 December 1915.
2. Coxon, *Dover in the Dark Days*, p126.
3. CHAR 13/53/41, CAC.
4. *London Gazette*, 11 January 1916, publishing Bacon's dispatch of 3 December 1915.
5. Ibid.
6. Ibid.
7. www.greatwarnurses.blogspot.fr; 'This Intrepid Band'.

Chapter 11
1. Bacon, *The Dover Patrol*, vol 2, p393.
2. GBR/0014/Hood, 6-3, Perkins to Hood, 20 May 1915, CAC.
3. GBR/0014/Hood, 6-6, letter to 'Lulu C', 15 May 1915, CAC.
4. Ibid.
5. Ibid, letter from *Invincible* to a family friend, 14 August 1915, CAC.
6. Ibid.
7. Ibid.
8. Docs 10977, p42, IWM.
9. *Daily Telegraph*, 3 August 1915.
10. Churchill, World Crisis vol 2, p1238.
11. Bacon, *The Dover Patrol*, vol 2, p396.

Chapter 12
1. *The Times*, 1 February 1916.
2. *Melbourne Argus*, 29 February 1916.
3. *London Gazette*, 25 July 1916, publishing Bacon's dispatch of 29 May 1916.
4. Brock and Brock, *Margot Asquith's Great War Diary*, p280.
5. Oliver, *Memoires*, vol 2, pp125–6.
6. Docs 10964, IWM.
7. Ibid.
8. Ibid.
9. Ibid.
10. Ibid.
11. *London Gazette*, 8 May 1917.

Chapter 13
1. *London Gazette*, 23 May 1917.
2. Evans, *Keeping the Seas*, p187.
3. Docs 11493, IWM.
4. Lake, *The Zeebrugge and Ostend Raids 1918*, p2.
5. Bacon, *The Dover Patrol*, vol 2, p400.
6. Ibid, p401.

Chapter 14
1. Docs 7431, 17 March 1917, IWM.
2. *London Gazette*, 12 May 1917.
3. Docs 7431, 21 April, IWM.
4. Docs 10964, IWM.
5. Ibid.
6. Coxon, *Dover in the Dark Days*, p74.
7. *Marlborough Express*, 26 July 1917.
8. Marder, *Portrait of an Admiral*, p248.
9. Docs 7431, 29 July 1917, IWM.
10. Ibid.
11. ADM 196/143/493, NA.
12. MSS/72/094, NMM.
13. *Flight* magazine 19 July 1917.
14. Abbatiello, *Anti-Submarine Warfare*, p66.
15. Marder, *Portrait of an Admiral*, p245.
16. Gibbons, *And They Thought We Wouldn't Fight*, p45.
17. Philpott, *Attrition*, p277.
18. Fuller, *Memoirs of an Unconventional Soldier*, p117.
19. Bacon, *The Dover Patrol*, vol 1, p304.

Chapter 15
1. *Spectator*, 1 November 1919, p18.
2. WMYS 6/4/19 p11, CAC.
3. Ibid, p13.
4. Ibid, p13.
5. Ibid, p11.
6. Ibid, p11.
7. Ibid, p15.
8. Ibid, p15.

9. Ibid, p15.
10. Churchill W, *The World Crisis*, vol 2, p1239.
11. WMYS 6/4/19 p16, CAC.
12. Keyes, *Naval Memoirs*, vol 2, p115 and 137.
13. Corbett and Newbolt, *NO*, vol 5, p181.
14. Bacon, *The Dover Patrol*, vol 2, p410.
15. Marder, *FDTSF*, vol 4 (2014), p319.
16. WMYS 6/4/19 p16, CAC.
17. Marder, *FDTSF*, vol 4 (2014), p319.
18. Ibid.
19. WMYS 6/4/19 p17, CAC.
20. De Chair, *The Sea is Strong*, p238.
21. Cannadine, *Decline and Fall of the British Aristocracy*, p277.
22. Lake, *The Zeebrugge and Ostend Raids 1918*, p20.
23. Ibid, p31.
24. Marder, *Portrait of an Admiral*, p293.
25. Oliver, *Memoirs*, vol 2, pp170–1.
26. Bacon, *The Dover Patrol*, vol 1, Preface, xv.
27. Ibid, Preface, xix.
28. *Spectator*, 1 November 1919, p18.

Chapter 16
1. MS 217, p20, NMRN.
2. Hough, *The Great War at Sea* (1986), p156.
3. Ibid, p177.
4. Marder, *FDTSF*, vol 5 (2104), pp39–40.
5. Ibid, vol3 (2014), p105.
6. CHAR 13/28/93-95, Jan 1914, CAC.
7. Docs 11497, p108, IWM.

Chapter 17
1. MSS 217, p14, NMRN.
2. *Dover Express*, 22 February 1918.
3. Ibid.
4. Ibid.

5. *Bootle Times*, 22 February 1918.
6. *Dover Express*, 22 February 1918.
7. MSS 217, undated letter Grant to Bacon.
8. 2008.7, p28, NMRN.
9. Docs 7431, 21 March 1918, IWM.
10. *London Gazette*, 18 June 1918.
11. Halpern, *A Naval History of World War One*, p415.
12. Keyes, *Naval Memoirs*, vol 2, p341.
13. Abbatiello, *Anti-Submarine Warfare*, p126/7.

Chapter 18
1. Bostridge, *The Fateful Year*, Preface, xxvi.
2. Lake, *The Zeebrugge and Ostend Raids 1918*, p69.
3. *Preston Leader*, 20 July 1918.
4. 2005.75, letter to family, NMRN.
5. Ibid.
6. 2008.7, p33, NMRN.
7. 2008.7, 23 April 1918, NMRN.
8. MSS 217, NMRN.
9. Corbett and Newbolt, *NO*, vol 5, p265.
10. Halpern, *A Naval History of World War One*, p416.
11. Fisher, *Memories*, pp50–1.
12. Hough, *The Great War at Sea* (1986), p316.
13. Ibid.
14. Ibid.
15. MSS 217, NMRN.
16. Winton, *The Victoria Cross at Sea*, p169.
17. Docs 3631, p3, IWM.
18. Ibid, p4.
19. Ibid, p6.
20. Ibid.
21. 2008.7, p40, NMRN.

Chapter 19
1. Docs 11497, p105, IWM.
2. Ibid, p107.
3. RMSY2-2, diary 3 November 1014, CAC.

4. Ibid.
5. RMSY2-4, notes of wife, CAC.
6. Ibid.
7. Ibid.
8. RMSY2-5, diary 11 November 1918, CAC.
9. ADM 116/1623, 18 October 1918, NA.
10. *London Gazette*, 23 May 1919.
11. Docs 10964, IWM.
12. Docs 11497, p109, IWM.
13. *London Gazette*, 27 August 1918, quoting Keyes, official dispatch 24 July 1918.
14. ADM 196/1413/642, NA.

Chapter 20
1. Bacon, *The Dover Patrol*, vol 2, p598.
2. Kipling, *Sea Warfare (The Fringes of the Fleet)*, p89/90.
3. Docs 11440, p5, IWM.
4. Ibid, p5/6.
5. CHAR 13/62/15, CAC.
6. Docs 11440, p7, IWM.
7. Ibid, p8.
8. Ibid, p5.
9. Ibid, p8.
10. Ibid, p6.

Chapter 21
1. Jackstaff, *The Dover Patrol*, p180.
2. Ibid.
3. Docs 1497, p85, IWM.
4. Docs 11336 VJR/3, p92, IWM.
5. Maxwell, *The Motor Launch Patrol*, Ch4 ff.
6. Docs 7431, 28 April 1917, IWM.
7. Docs 10964, IWM.
8. 2008.7, p11, NMRN.
9. Docs 11493, IWM.
10. 2008.7, p13, NMRN.
11. Docs 10823, p1, IWM.
12. Ibid, p2.
13. Docs 11497, p86, IWM.
14. Cunningham, *A Sailor's Odyssey*, p90.
15. Docs 11440, p19, IWM.

16. Sproule, *Letters*, p20.
17. Ibid, p23.
18. www.naval-history.net/OWships-WW1-31-HMS_Lord_minto.htm
19. Coxon, *Dover in the Dark Days*, p137.

Chapter 22
1. Cunningham, *A Sailor's Odyssey*, p97.
2. Evans, *Keeping the Seas*, p35.
3. Coxon, *Dover During the Dark Days*, p58.
4. Bacon, *The Dover Patrol*, vol 2, p584.
5. Philpott, *Attrition*, p131.
6. Bacon, *The Dover Patrol*, vol 2, p591.
7. Ibid.
8. Ibid.
9. Ibid, p595.

Chapter 23
1. Bacon, *The Dover Patrol*, vol 2, p603.
2. McCartney, *Lost Patrols*, p141.
3. Bacon, *The Dover Patrol*, vol 1, p85.
4. Ibid, p83.
5. Ibid, p88.
6. Goldrick, *Before Jutland*, p137.
7. Wellington to Thomas Creevey after Waterloo, widely cited.
8. Docs 11440, p8, IWM.
9. Smith, *Yellow Admiral*, pp211–12.
10. Docs 10823, p3, IWM.
11. Ibid.
12. Marder, *FDTSF*, vol 5 (2014), p40.
13. Cunningham, *A Sailor's Odyssey*, p98.
14. Docs 11497, p158, IWM.
15, Ibid.
16. Roskill, *Earl Beatty*, p187.
17. *London Gazette*, 4 July 1916, Beatty Dispatch after Jutland.
18. HTN-101-129, diary 7 June 1916, NMM.
19. Callo and Wilson, *Who's Who in Naval History*, p176.

Chapter 24
1. Inscription in St Margaret's church.
2. *Hansard* 1923, vol 163, c2328.

Appendix 1
1. Based on http://www.naval-history.net/WW1NavyBritishShips-Locations2PL1411.htm (retrieved 22 Feb 2016).

Appendix 3
1. Bacon, *The Dover Patrol*, vol 1, p63.
2. Jackstaff, *The Dover Patrol*, p189.

Appendix 5
1. Based on http://www.naval-history.net/WW1NavyBritishShips-Locations2PL1411.htm (retrieved 22 Feb 2016).

Index